MILITARY HISTORY FROM PRIMARY SOURCES

THE FIRST OPIUM WAR

The Chinese Expedition 1840-1842

THE ILLUSTRATED EDITION

BY DUNCAN McPHERSON

EDITED BY
BOB CARRUTHERS

BOOKS LTD

This book is published in Great Britain in 2013 by

Coda Books Ltd,Office Suite 2, Shrieves Walk, Sheep Street, Stratford upon Avon, Warwickshire CV37 6GJ.

www.codabooks.com

ISBN 978-1-78158-360-9

A CIP catalogue record for this book is available from the British Library.

This book was first published by Saunders and Otley, London in 1843 as 'Two Years in China. Narrative of the Chinese Expedition from its formation in April, 1840, to the Treaty of Peace in August, 1842', and was written by D.McPherson, M.D.

CONTENTS

ABOUT THE AUTHOR

Surgeon General Duncan McPherson, MD (1812-1867), was an army surgeon and writer. He studied medicine at Edinburgh University, and after he qualified, he was appointed surgeon to the Army in Madras in 1836. During 1840-1842, he was sent with the 37th Grenadier Guards Regiment to China with whom he served during the First Opium War, after which he wrote this book. He returned to India and had a long and successful military career. The Army List states that McPherson:

> "Served in China 1841-42, present at the battle of Chuenpee, bombardment of Bocca Tigris, in investment of Hong Kong and battle of the heights of the City of Canton 1841-42. Wounded in the head and blown up by the explosion of a mine at Chuenpee, the hearing of the left ear partially impaired in consequence, served on three tours in H.H. Nizam's service in 1842-43-44. Medal for China. Served in the Crimea in 1855-56 as Inspector General of Hospitals to the Turkish Contingent amounting to 30,000 men."

After the Crimean War, he was promoted to Inspector General of the medical service of Madras, and his most notable achievement was the improvement of the sanitary conditions. In recognition of his valuable services, he was decorated by Queen Victoria with the insignia of the Imperial Order of the Medjidia, which was the highest order for officers of the Army of Madras, and he was the only medical officer of this Army so decorated.

Please note all original spellings and place names have been preserved.

Bob Carruthers

Daguerreotype of Field Marshal Hugh Gough, 1st Viscount Gough (1779-1869), c1850.

DEDICATION

To his excellency
Lieut.-General Sir Hugh Gough, K.C.B., G.C.B.,
Commander-in-Chief of Madras,
and of the land forces in China,
this volume is with every sentiment of respect and esteem, dedicated, by the author.

PREFACE

The following work was planned and executed during a passage of six weeks between the ports of Hong-Kong and Madras, in those hours which the author could snatch from his professional engagements, and at a period when he laboured under repeated and severe attacks of sickness.

His aim throughout has been to produce a simple and correct narrative of events, and in this he trusts that he has succeeded. The chief portion of the work has been compiled from notes taken by himself at the period of the occurrence of the scenes detailed.

Two papers published by the author, and now incorporated in this volume, have already appeared in the "Chinese Repository," an excellent periodical, published at Macao, to the editor of which, as also to all who have furnished him with material for his work, he begs now to offer his best thanks.

The author has to plead good intentions alone against the imperfect execution of the task.

May, 1842.

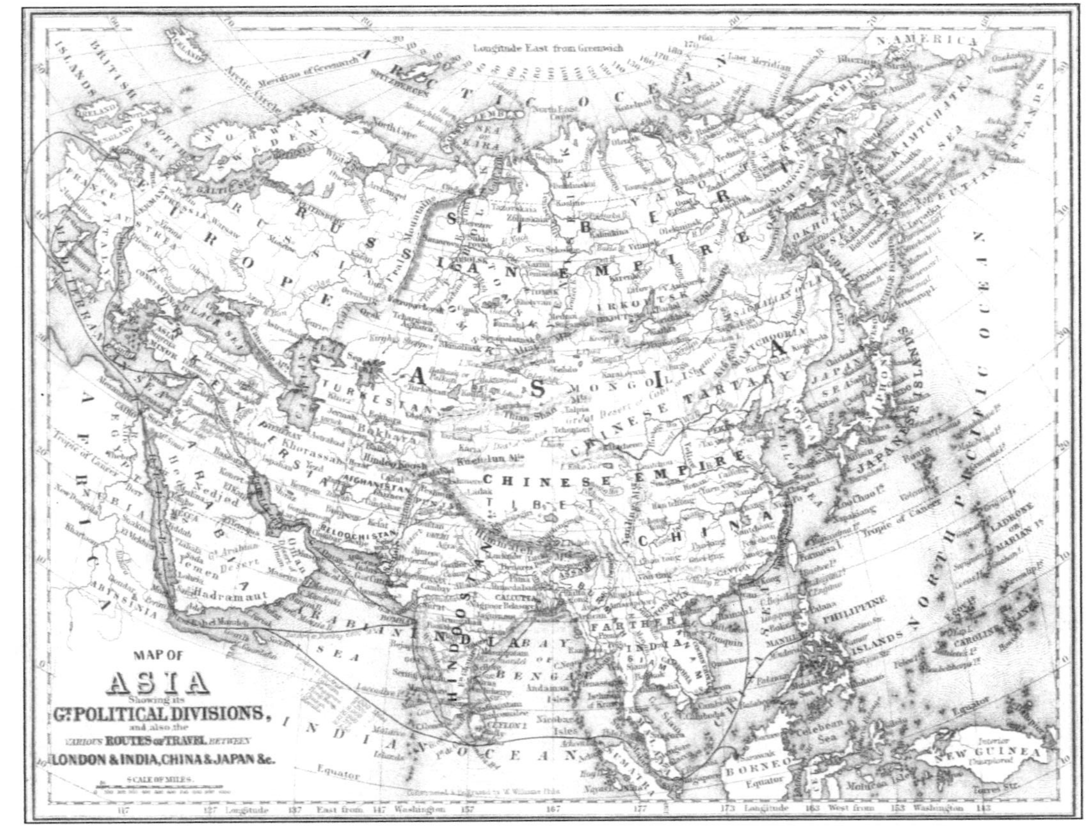

Samuel Augustus Mitchell's map of Asia, c1864, showing the various routes of travel between London, India, China and Japan.

CHAPTER I

A general view of the character of the Chinese—Their repeated insults to British subjects—Immediate cause of the present rupture.

It were no easy matter for a campaigner, or for one who comes on a mere casual visit to the outer regions of so vast an empire as China, to enter into anything like an acute analysis of the inhabitants of the land—that is, had he to depend solely upon his own chance resources and natural powers of discrimination. Much, it is true, may be acquired in the abstract; much political duplicity and craft may come to light from among the upper classes; and much low cunning, and treachery, and selfishness, may he found lurking beneath the garb of the lower order, even where little had been previously dreamt of; but the time has now come, when this extraordinary race are to be viewed no longer in this abstract form. A new era is breaking in the moral history of nations, and England, never-tiring England, has thrust her hand forward to raise the curtain from scenes hitherto secret and unknown to all save the actors themselves; while the other children of civilization sit watching, with intense anxiety, the result of her boldness. The audience will benefit; let them not then interfere. Few boys will venture into a haunted house, although it interfere materially with their comforts; but how many would congregate to see the one bold adventurer daring to enter its precincts, and endeavouring to dissolve the spell!

But, as we have said, it were no easy matter to start on a subject of the nature of that in which we are now engaged, solely on the strength of our own experience; we will therefore, without scruple, glance occasionally into the few works of well-versed travellers, and others, brought daily to our notice, to enable us to furnish a brief summary of such matters as will permit all lovers of light reading to take up the same position as ourselves, when first setting foot upon the Chinese soil.

The population of China Proper is estimated by Medhurst at 361,221,900, and that of Formosa as 1,000,000; yet one written character serves for the communication of thought throughout this vast empire, and the laws of the imperial council are as easily read by the poorest as by the richest in China.

A glance into the lesser traits of their character will, indeed, tend to convince one that they really have been cast in a different mould from all other nations. For instance: in matters of simple navigation the pilot tells us that his port lays west-north, and that the wind is east-south; and on explaining the use of the compass, he describes the needle as pointing south.

In the common routine of literature, the moonshee, or teacher, reads the date of publication of his book as the fifth year, the tenth month, and third day. He commences at what we consider the end of the book, and reads from the top downwards. The title is found on the edge of the leaves, and the marginal notes at the head of the page, and the volume has sometimes a heavy line in the middle of each leaf, which separates two works contained in it. When in the matter of simple social life, as on the death of a relative, they dress in white; and on a marriage, nothing is to be heard but sobbing and crying; and to crown the distinction between our own acknowledged axioms and theirs, the most learned men are of opinion that the seat of the human understanding is in the belly.

The motto selected for the title-page of this volume describes most correctly, in very few words, the true character of the Chinese, taken in a public point of view. Haughty, cruel, and hypocritical, they despise all other nations but their own; they regard themselves as faultless. Next to the son of heaven, a true Chinaman thinks himself the greatest man in the world, and China, beyond all comparison, to be the most civilized, the most learned, the most fruitful, the most ancient—in short, the only country in the world. They style all foreigners barbarians, and they tell them, "We can do without you, but you cannot do without us; if your country is so good, why do you come here for tea and rhubarb?" No argument will induce a Chinaman to adopt a different style of reasoning.

In private life they excel many other nations. Here, indeed, do we find a direct contrast to the character given of them by the world. There are no castes among them, consequently the great barrier between man and man, so generally subsisting among eastern nations, is altogether done away with, and the passing stranger is at all times welcome to partake of the poorest man's fare. Their food is plain and simple,—rice, fish, and vegetables are their stable articles; at a pinch, however, nothing comes amiss, for they have the most accommodating stomachs imaginable. In the animal kingdom, anything from the hide to the entrails, and in the vegetable, from the leaves to the roots, is made available for the support of life. Frogs are common food; young puppies are esteemed a delicacy, in the same way that lambs are in Europe; and the flesh of the kitten is an expensive luxury, and only seen on the tables of the opulent. Rats and mice are confined almost exclusively to the poorest people; the flesh of these animals is daily to be seen in the public market, skinned, and otherwise prepared, hung up by dozens in long rows, with a piece of wood passed across from one hind leg to the other.

The great majority of the population of China, obtain a livelihood by cultivating the soil, or by fishing. The Chinese seas are said to contain a far more abundant supply of fish, and superior in quality, to any found in the known world; and the land yields a vast return to the laborious cultivator.

In the useful arts, the Chinese ages ago excelled all other nations. The manufacture of paper and gunpowder, glass and porcelain ware, and the art of printing, were all known to them long before they came into use among us more civilized nations. Their paper is chiefly manufactured from the bark of trees and from cotton.

The Chinese respect their parents during life, and worship them after death. In fact, the worship of ancestors is the religion of the great majority; complete obedience to the father of a family is enforced in the most rigorous manner, the emperor being not only considered as the father of all his own subjects, but of the several sovereigns of Europe also; and both from them and their people implicit and unconditional obedience is claimed as a rightful due. All consult their joss, or god, before commencing any undertaking of importance. If they have any material event in view,—to marry, to go on a journey, to conclude a bargain, to change a situation, &c,—it becomes necessary first to consult the superintending deity. Many believe in the transfiguration of souls; a common belief is, that if proper funereal honours have been paid to the departed, the soul leaves the body, and in three days after death joins that of their deceased parents; whereas, if the body remains unburied, no change takes place; to use their own words, "then same like one dog."

As will be seen in the sequel, the Chinese are not a warlike race. Their industry and never-ending perseverance enable them to build extensive and powerful batteries; their guns are in many instances equal to any of European manufacture; but their gunners never calculated on the sharp practice employed so much to their cost during the past two years.

The community of China are divided into four grades. The cultivation of the mind is the first and most honourable; agriculture stands second on the list; mechanical labour, third; and trade or commerce, fourth, or lowest grade.. The peculiar views entertained by the Chinese of the inferiority of mercantile employment is, perhaps, some apology for the repeated insults so frequently cast on our British merchants, with whom they have hitherto disdained to treat on equal terms. Long before the lamented death of that esteemed nobleman, Lord Napier, and subsequent to his time, insults innumerable have been borne with impunity by the British nation. These are too well known to require detail here; suffice it to say, that the Chinese, emboldened by the pacific temperament of our government, proceeded at length to the utmost extent, and not satisfied with imprisoning and threatening the lives of the whole foreign community, laid also violent hands on the British representative himself, claiming, as the purchase of his freedom, the delivery of the whole of the opium then in the Chinese waters—property to the amount of upwards of two millions sterling. After a close imprisonment of two months' duration, during which period our countrymen were deprived of many of the necessaries of life, and exposed repeatedly, as in a pillory, to the gaze and abuse of the mob, no resource was left but to yield to the bold demands of the Chinese, relying with confidence on their nation for support and redress; nor did they rely in vain, for immediately the accounts of the aggression reached London, preparations commenced for the Chinese expedition, the chief objects of which are supposed to be,—To obtain redress for imprisoning and insulting her Majesty's Plenipotentiary and subjects in China; compensation for British property seized; and direct official intercourse with the emperor.

CHAPTER II

The formation of the Expedition—Its strength and constitution—Its departure from India, and arrival at Chusan.

It was supposed by Lord Palmerston and the other advisers of her Majesty that the mere presence of a force off the China coast would of itself be sufficient to awe the Chinese, and that they would at once submit to our demands without its becoming necessary to proceed to hostile measures. Contrary, therefore, to the advice of the greatest general of the age, an "army of demonstration" only was directed to proceed to China. This army was formed by her Majesty's 18th, 26th, and 49th regiments, Madras Artillery, and Sappers and Miners, and the Bengal Volunteer corps, in all about 3000 strong. The naval portion of the force consisted of three lines of battle ships, two frigates, carrying 44 guns, and fourteen other ships, carrying some 28 and some 18 guns. There were also four armed steamers attached to the expedition. With this small force Great Britain had the audacity to suppose she could bring under subjection a nation, an idea of the immense population of which will be gained by the reflection that its present generation (according to Gutzlaff) consists of nearly as many people as have lived in our small island since the creation of the world.

So far back as the reign of Queen Elizabeth, when England gained for herself a name never to be erased from history, the highest naval and military commanders concurred in the opinion that a conjoint expedition is rarely well-conducted; and I am confident that the heads of the present expedition will agree with me that this one has throughout been retarded by impediments which only can arise where two distinct authorities are employed to effect one end and purpose.

The force as detailed above rendezvoused at Singapore, in April, 1840; and on the 4th of July our troops were in possession of the island of Chusan, which they entered with little or no opposition. In passing by the mouth of the Canton river, her Majesty's Plenipotentiaries detailed certain ships of the squadron to blockade that port, taking the main body of the force with them as near the seat of government as possible, so as to excite terror in the capital, and to enable them to carry on negotiations with at least the semblance of power to enforce their demands. The authorities at Ningpo were thunderstruck by the occupation of Chusan. The news rapidly reached Pekin, new governors and generals were appointed to take command of the provincial cities, to the support of which large reinforcements of troops were directed to proceed.

Our troops were landed on the island of Chusan in high health and spirits, and burning for active employment; a natural distaste and disgust arose when the pacific nature of the expedition was discovered; so great was the dread of exciting a bad feeling and causing discontent among the natives, that our men were obliged to live in their tents when there were thousands of houses available for that purpose; and without regard to the health of the men, or consulting medical authorities on the subject, positions were laid out for the encampment of the troops. Parades and guard mountings in full dress, with a thermometer ranging from ninety to a hundred degrees, made the scene resemble the routine of garrison duty in India, and satisfied the heads of departments that they had there a body of hale and healthy men, who, at a moment's notice, were capable of performing any duty that fell to their lot. Alas! how soon had they cause to alter their opinion.

CHAPTER III

Her Majesty's Plenipotentiaries proceed to the Pieho — Affair at Amoy—Battle of the Barrier —Sickness at Chusan.

After the delay of several weeks, and the rejection of Lord Palmerston's letter by the provincial authorities, and when all due arrangements for the comfort of our men on shore, and the protection of the coast, had been completed to the satisfaction of the authorities, Admiral Elliot, and his relative Captain Elliot, R.N., Chief Superintendent of Trade in China, joint plenipotentiaries, proceeded with a small proportion of the squadron to the Pieho. The presence even of this force so near the capital caused no small alarm, and communications with the imperial government became at once respectful, courteous, and pacific. An imperial commission had been directed by the Emperor to proceed thither to meet them. True to his time, Keshen waited their arrival, and received the plenipotentiaries with all due pomp and ceremony. The repeatedly rejected letter was at once received, a long private interview was held, after which the company were regaled with bird's nest and shark's fin soup, truffles (manufactured probably from puppies and kittens), fruits, and in fact every delicacy that China can produce, a full description of which will be found in that interesting little work published by a noble lord, entitled "Six Months with the China Expedition." That the arguments used by Keshen were amicable as well as convincing was certain, for soon after the interview our ships weighed anchor and returned to Chusan.

Transports, laden with provisions and stores, were now daily arriving at Chusan. The merchants, availing themselves of the protection afforded by the presence of the force, sent their clippers with opium and British manufacture, both of which, in a short time, found a ready sale among the natives.

The inhabitants of the capital city of Tinghae, who, on our first taking possession of the island, had deserted, gradually regaining confidence, returned. The peculiar attractions of the *tolah* (dollar) and *loopea* (rupee) quite won over the hearts of many. Strangers were by common consent called *fokee*, the Chinese word for friend; but when there were no interpreters, considerable difficulty arose in explaining matters, as where bullocks, fowls,

&c, were required. This, however, gradually wore away; a language, "sui generis," was soon formed, the striking peculiarities of which consisted in imitating the sounds emitted by those animals.

About this time the Blonde frigate (44), in sailing up the coast, went into the harbour of Amoy to deliver a chop, or official despatch, to the authorities there. A boat, carrying a white flag, was sent on shore. Mr. Thom, the interpreter, landed to deliver the chop; the latter, however, they would not receive, and on returning to his boat he was fired at by some soldiers who were drawn up on the beach, and who evidently had been sent for on seeing the boat approach. Mr. Thom succeeded in reaching the boat, upon which a brisk fire was now directed. Fortunately, however, no serious injury was done. Guns from several batteries now opened upon the Blonde; she immediately weighed, stood in, and picked up her boat; then approaching as near the batteries as the depth of water would permit, skirting the edge of each, she gave the garrison repeated broadsides of canister, grape, and round shot, and then took her departure. Shortly after this, the Alligator, 28 guns, accompanied by the armed transport, Braemer, were sent from Chusan with directions to make another attempt to send the chop on shore. The same reception awaited them as the Blonde received. The Braemer, when the firing commenced, thinking discretion the better part of valour, and her native crew saying that they were not paid for fighting, declined to approach within gunshot of the forts, and the Alligator, already wounded, soon became convinced of the inability of her remaining alone in the position she had taken up, took to sea also. The Chinese now boasted that on two different occasions they had driven off the barbarian ships. The affair they exaggerated into a great battle. It was reported to the Emperor that, after many hours of hard fighting, in which more than ten ships of war, and several fire-ships (steamers), belonging to the barbarians, were sunk and destroyed, victory was at length decided in favour of the celestial troops, with very trifling loss. Honours, in the shape of peacocks' feathers, white, red, and blue buttons, were consequently showered down upon the victors.

While affairs were thus proceeding on the coast, matters began to assume an alarming aspect at Macao, whither all the British merchants had resorted for further security. Commissioner Lin, by whose instigation our countrymen had been imprisoned in 1839, and who, on a former occasion, by his threats, had so intimidated the Governor of Macao as to oblige him to expel all the English from that city, aware that his career was drawing to a close, and hating the very name of Englishman, determined, if possible, thoroughly to exterminate them. For this purpose, he had recourse to the usual artifice and cunning of his nation. Under the cloak of friendship, he now expressed sorrow for all the mischief he had done, and pretended to grant great favours.

The Thirteen Factories in Canton, by William Daniell (1769-1837)

'All this time he was collecting a large force in the proximity of Macao, of which he himself, it was generally believed, took the command.

The town of Macao, it is necessary here to remark, is built on the peninsula of an island granted to the Portuguese for certain favours rendered, on payment to the Chinese of a rent equal to £300 per annum. On an isthmus, which connects the main body of the island with that small portion inhabited by thePortuguese, a high wall has been built. This wall runs across the isthmus, and is styled the barrier-wall; on it several guns are mounted, and on the Chinese side of the wall are barracks for troops. It was here, then, that Lin concentrated his forces—he strengthened his position on every side by sand-bag batteries. He detached daily his satellites into Macao to mark out the residences of the English merchants. The day, it was said, was fixed for the massacre. The unusual appearance of so many soldiers in the immediate vicinity of Macao, and about the merchant's houses, naturally caused suspicion and alarm. Reports soon reached the ears of the senior naval officer, which convinced him that firm and decided measures must at once be taken to drive the Chinese from their position. With his usual promptitude, Captain Smith at once prepared to attack them. Taking with him, therefore, two companies of the Bengal Volunteer Corps, H.M.'s ships Hyacinth and Larne, both 18 guns, and the Enterprise steamer, he proceeded to the barrier. The volunteers, and as many jacks and marines as could be collected, were landed about a mile from, and on the Chinese side of, the barrier. The ships took up their positions, and at once opened their guns upon the batteries; our troops on shore, when the firing had in a measure subsided, advanced and cut off the flight of the cowardly enemy; some war-junks, on the opposite side of the isthmus to that held by us, cut their cables and put to sea—two of them, however, had been sunk by the shot from the Hyacinth. Lin, it was supposed, had early in the day taken flight in an open boat to Canton by the back passage. Such was the activity with which Captain Smith put his resolves into execution, that the enemy were quite taken by surprise; nor was it till after the firing had begun that the inhabitants of Macao became sensible of the presence of an armed force. That Captain Smith, by this gallant action, and the promptitude with which it was effected, was the means of saving the lives of the British community at Macao, there cannot be a doubt.

The month of October had now commenced, and each arrival from Chusan brought with it the most gloomy reports of the insalubrity of the island and the health of our men. This had long been foretold. It required no gifted soothsayer to prognosticate what the results would be, where men were placed in tents pitched on low paddy fields, surrounded by stagnant water, putrid and stinking from quantities of dead animal and vegetable matter. Under a sun hotter than that ever experienced in India, the men on duty were buckled up to the throat in their full dress coatees; and in consequence of there being so few camp followers, fatigue parties of Europeans were daily detailed to carry provisions and stores from the ships to the tents, and to perform all menial employments, which, experience has long taught us, they cannot stand in a tropical climate. The poor men, working like slaves, began to sink under the exposure and fatigue. Bad provisions, low spirits, and despondency drove them to drink. This increased their liability to disease, and in the month of November there were barely 500 effective men in the force. A sort of infatuation seemed to possess the minds of the authorities. Medical men, as is often the case, were put down as croakers, their recommendations were neither listened nor attended to. True, it was reported that the general was one day about to visit the hospitals, but when almost at the door of one, some pressing business called him away. Once, also, the Admiral and Captain Elliot were known to have walked through the hospital of H.M. 26th regiment. There were at that time upwards of 400 poor sick fellows on mats, stretched on the ground—many, alas! never to rise from it. This melancholy sight called forth expressions of pity and compassion. The surgeon was directed to spare no expense—to procure everything he considered necessary—to be unremitting in his exertions, and to make application to the admiral direct if aught was wanted. The surgeon recommended that a ship should be laid apart as an hospital ship, and that another should be given to take a portion of convalescents to sea, for change of air. Unfortunately however, there were no ships available at that time!

We will bring this melancholy picture to a close, and trust that soon a change for the better will take place—that a new order of things will be established.

Commissioner Lin Zexu (1785-1850) was a Chinese scholar and imperial commissioner of Guangdong province and was responsible for the destruction of the opium stores in 1839, one of the main triggers for the war. He famously wrote an open letter to Queen Victoria in 1839, although she never received it, stating: "We find that your country is sixty or seventy thousand li from China. Yet there are barbarian ships that strive to come here for trade for the purpose of making a great profit. The wealth of China is used to profit the barbarians. That is to say, the great profit made by barbarians is all taken from the rightful share of China. By what right do they then in return use the poisonous drug to injure the Chinese people? Even though the barbarians may not necessarily intend to do us harm, yet in coveting profit to an extreme, they have no regard for injuring others. Let us ask, where is your conscience?"[1]

1 China's Response to the West, Ssuyu Teng and John Fairbank, Harvard University Press, 1954

CHAPTER IV

Wreck of the Indian Oak and Kite Transports— Capture of Captain Anstruther.

The transport, Indian Oak, sailed from Chusan in August, with despatches for the Governor-General, and in October, a boat belonging to that ship reached the harbour of Chusan, bringing intelligence of her total loss on the coast of Lew Chew. The islanders treated the passengers and crew in the most friendly manner, fully bearing out the character given them by Basil Hall. On the ship going on the rocks, the inhabitants collected in great numbers on the shore, offering every assistance to save the ship-wrecked crew— not to imprison, starve, and torture, but to feed and clothe them. Wandering along the beach, they collected portions of the wreck, all of which they handed over to the owners. They immediately set to work to build a ship, to enable them to leave the island, and on the arrival of H.M. ships Nimrod and Cruizer, which the Commodore had dispatched for the relief of the crew, the little craft was ready for sea, and actually conveyed them from the island of Lew Chew to Chusan; nor would the hospitable islanders receive any reward for what they had done.

Contrast the description of the above wreck with that of the Kite, armed transport, which took place about the same time on the coast of China. This vessel struck on a quicksand, in which she immediately sunk, as far as the main top-mast. To this the survivors clung for life, with the exception of the captain's wife, Mrs. Noble, Lieutenant Douglas, R N., and two cabin-boys, who succeeded in getting into one of the ship's boats, but without sails and without food, and almost naked. After tossing about for a couple of days, the boat drifted on shore. Here Mrs. Noble was forcibly separated from her companions in misfortune: a heavy chain was put round her neck, and by this she was dragged, bare-footed and bare-headed, through rivers and over rocks, a distance of upwards of twenty miles. Hungry and tired, she leant on her keepers for support. In passing through cities, the inhabitants crowded around her, hooting and yelling frightfully; and when permitted to rest, the chain round her neck was fastened to a ring in the prison wall. The Chinese at Canton, at no time would permit an European woman to proceed up the river to the British factories; and even from those who were brought to Macao they exacted a large fine for presuming to come to their country.

The unfortunate Mrs Noble. Drawn by E.T. Wigan, c1844.

Here, therefore, where never European male nor female had ever trod, the appearance of Mrs. Noble caused the greatest excitement. Crowds from all parts flocked to see her. They examined her height, the size of her feet, the length of her hair, and, in short, scrutinized her most minutely. She, poor woman, suffering much both in body and in mind, for she had lost a husband and a child in the wreck, was obliged patiently to bear all! When all appeared satisfied, she was placed in a cage one yard high, three-quarters of a yard long, and half a yard broad. The chain round her neck was locked to the top, and heavy irons were placed on her hands and feet; a long bamboo was then passed through the middle of the cage, at either end of which a man was placed. For two days and nights was she carried about in this cage, nor was she permitted to get out on any account whatever. At length she reached Ningpo, where she had the satisfaction to meet with Lieutenant Douglas, and all those that survived of the crew of the Kite, the latter having been taken off by a native boat. They were now all placed in prison, heavily chained. How different is the treatment these unfortunate people received from that the crew of the Indian Oak met with in Lew Chew; and yet this latter island is tributary to China.

The dull monotony existing at Chusan from the difficulty of communication with the island during the prevailing N.E. monsoon, and the melancholy gloom cast over all in consequence of the continued great mortality among the troops, drove the officers to their shifts for means to pass the time. Some were satisfied with laying in bed all day; others, more active, formed shooting excursions; while others, anxious to acquire knowledge and to communicate it to the world, profiting by their education, commenced a survey of the island. Captain Anstruther, of the Madras Artillery, was one of the latter. On the morning of the 16th Sept. he had gone out as usual to survey, taking along with him his old Lascar. In the evening, at mess, he was nowhere to be found. Inquiry was immediately made, but to no purpose; an armed party scoured the island in search, but no trace of either he or his Lascar could be discovered. A general favourite with all, he was very much missed and regretted; the worst was dreaded, and the anxiety and fear of all were much increased by a circumstance, in itself trifling, which had happened the evening before he disappeared: an officer, in passing by Captain Anstruther's tent on the evening in question, was surprised to hear moaning and groaning within. Fearing some one was unwell, he immediately entered, and, to his surprise, perceived Anstruther on his bed, writhing as if from pain. On approaching he found him fast asleep; and on being awoke, he said that he had been dreaming that the Chinese had surrounded him while out surveying, that they were binding him hand and foot, and that he was struggling to extricate himself, when he was awakened. The dream was told as a good joke that night at mess, and nothing further was thought of it, until some one recalled it to the recollection of all on the following evening, when he was missing. As will afterwards be shewn, the chief features of Captain Anstruther's dream turned out true, which certainly goes to prove that the theory of dreams is not always fallacious.

CHAPTER V

Arrival of the 37th M.N.I. in China—A typhoon in the China seas—Her Majesty's plenipotentiaries return from Chusan, and proceed with the force to the Canton river—The admiral goes home.

In noticing the arrival of a native regiment in China, we would call the attention of our readers to the importance of our Indian settlements in carrying out a warfare with the celestial empire; not only do we find the Governor General of India made, as it were, the fountain head of the expedition, but it is from that vast country, over which he holds almost imperial sway, that we are enabled, from its proximity and natural qualifications, to derive our supplies, our transports and their crews, and even the greater portion of our army, whether European or native.

In a conversation with the Governor of Macao, this latter was heard to observe, that no other nation save England *could* at this moment engage in a war of this description. "For," said he, "you have the key to all difficulties in its operation—India, a country whence you may derive all the means of warfare;" and, in truth, his Excellency, whatever his real feelings towards the invaders may be, was right in this respect.

With regard to native corps proceeding on foreign service, there is a wide distinction between the Bengal, and what the Bengalees are pleased to term the 'minor' presidency—Madras. In the former, it is necessary to call for volunteers from the various regiments to form the number requisite, whereas, in the latter, any one regiment among the fifty-two ordered, has but to make its salaam for the honour, and obey. This is attributed by the Bengalees to superiority of caste, but we need not say which of the two is the most advantageous. The 37th regiment, N.I., sailed from Madras, in August, fully equipped for field service, and mustering about 1000 bayonets. The men marched to the beach for embarkation, the air ringing with their native "deen," or war-cry. The transport Golconda, with the head quarters, sailed first; the Minerva, Sophia, and Thetis, following her in a few days. In the China seas, we fell in with one of those fearful typhoons, so frequently met with here; and in lat. 16°, on the 22nd September, the very date and place in which Hapsburgh remarks, "A typhoon may here be expected," was the

Thetis dismasted and rendered helpless; the ship was permitted to drift with wind and tide, till, on the storm abating, jury masts were raised. On the 29th September she was close to the island of Tyloo, on a lee-shore, about forty miles from Macao, and in six fathom water. Here they cast anchor, which was hardly done when the ship was surrounded with hundreds of very suspicious-looking boats, evidently Ladrones. The presence of so many troops on board must, however, have terrified them, for they soon departed. A fisherman was enticed on board, and with the assistance of the carpenter, a Chinaman, it was explained to him that if he took a letter to Macao, leaving his family, who were in the boat, as hostages, on his return he would receive a reward of 300 dollars. The man agreed; his trust he executed faithfully; and on the third day after his departure, he made his appearance in the Enterprise steamer, to the joy of all. The Thetis was towed to Tonkoo Bay, where the protection afforded by the senior naval officer induced all the merchant ships to resort for the purpose of trade. After an ineffectual attempt to reach Chusan, the N.E. monsoon having set in, the Minerva and Sophia also returned to this anchorage. The men were encamped on the small island of Saw Chow opposite to this bay. Barren and uninhabitable, this island possessed not one solitary advantage. It consists of three conical-shaped hills; on the shoulder of the largest, and on a small intervening plain, the encampment was placed. Here were also 200 men of the Bengal Volunteer corps. Reports soon became current that a large body of troops was about to come from Canton to drive us off this island. We were, therefore, obliged to be on the *qui vive*, more especially as, shortly before our arrival, an attempt was made to set fire to the shipping by fire rafts. On the island of Lantow, distant about a couple of miles, was a Chinese camp. The soldiers were daily to be seen at drill, but they never molested us. The men, shortly after being landed, began to suffer much from sickness, attributable, in a great degree, to their exposed situation. It is but justice here to remark, that to the zeal and attention of Captain Smith, of the Druid, senior naval officer, were the officers and men on this island indebted for every comfort that could be procured.

On the 20th November, the admiral and Captain Elliot arrived from Chusan; it having been stipulated by Keshen, that in consideration that affairs would terminate peaceably, one-third of the force should be removed from Chusan, a general truce should be proclaimed, and negotiations should be carried on at Canton, to which city he himself should proceed for that purpose with all practicable despatch. Never did wily statesman so gull "John Bull" as on this occasion. Relying on the scrupulous good faith of the very eminent person with whom negotiations were pending, the plenipotentiaries at once agreed to the terms asked for. How foolish! and how often since that period has England had cause to regret placing the honour of the country in the hands of two such imbeciles. Had the force at first destroyed the forts on the Bocca Tigris, and afterwards the city of Canton, where the cause of the present quarrel originated, and then proceeded to the Pieho, there, removed only eighty miles from the capital of China, to insist on their demands, the best informed in Chinese matters are of opinion that they would never have had reason to enforce them.

The Admiral took with him the three line of battle ships, Wellesley, Melville, and Blenheim, the Queen steamer, and Volage, 26 guns, which, with the fleet at this anchorage, (consisting of the Druid, 44, Calliope, Samarang, and Herald, 28 guns; Larne, Hyacinth, Modeste, and Columbine, corvettes; and Sulphur, Starling, and Louisa, surveying ships,) formed a very powerful naval force. The troops, consisting of the 37th regiment, M.N.I., and a detachment of the Bengal Volunteers, a few days after the arrival of the Admiral, embarked on board their respective transports, and proceeded, in company with the fleet, to the mouth of the Canton river.

The head quarters of the 37th regiment, which had sailed from Madras in the Golconda, some days previous to the other portion of the corps, had not, unfortunately, yet arrived. Much anxiety was felt for their safety.

The Admiral, being seriously unwell, was, on the 4th December, obliged to throw up his command, and return home in the Volage. Captain Elliot was now sole plenipotentiary to H.M. in China.

CHAPTER VI

A visit to Macao—Camoeus' Cave—Small-feet women.

When weeks had passed in tiresome and unsatisfactory negotiations between the British and celestial powers, in company with several others, I availed myself of an opportunity which occurred to visit Macao. This city, as has already been remarked, is built on the peninsula of an island, called, by the Chinese, Gowman. The extreme breadth of the Portuguese settlement is about three quarters of a mile, and its length three miles. The chief beauty of the town consists in a long line of well built houses on the beach, with a broad walk in front called the Pria Grande. On the heights above the town, forts are built, which certainly have the appearance of strength from without, but a glance into the interior (which the Portuguese are not fond of granting) will at once convince the most superficial observer, that they would soon yield even to a small nine pounder battery. True, there are large guns in their forts, but like those of the Chinese, they have vent-holes large enough to allow the thumb to enter; and their gun carriages would certainly tumble to pieces in the first fire. The British merchants are the sole prop and support of the town; independent of the money circulated by them, two-thirds of the revenue is derived from a tax levied upon their goods and property.

The Chinese authorities exercise supreme sway over the city. In a few hours they have the power of stopping all supplies; not a house can be built, nay, even a door cannot be made to communicate between one house and another, without first obtaining the permission of the resident mandarin to do so. Robberies and assaults are of common occurrence in the city, but no redress can be obtained; the Portuguese hand the party over to the Chinese authorities, who, in return, refer them to the Portuguese. The majority of the Portuguese inhabitants are the most wretched miserable looking beings possible. From constant intermarriages with the Chinese, it is with difficulty that the natives of the two separate countries can be distinguished, and with the exception of the governor and his staff, there is not one family with whom the English associate.

There are about three hundred soldiers in the town, all of whom originally came from Goa and other Portuguese settlements in India. They are respectful and well-dressed. The pay their officers receive appears miserably small in our estimation, though they themselves live very comfortably on it. An ensign receives eight dollars, a lieutenant ten, and a captain twenty dollars a month, besides perquisites.

The greatest attraction in Macao is Mr. Beale's aviary, where the noble bird of paradise is seen. This bird has been in Mr. Beale's possession for upwards of twenty years. Another place worth visiting is Camoens' Cave. It is situated in the centre of a large garden, and is formed by several immense piles of granite rocks, thrown as if casually together, a large hollow space being left in the centre. It was here that Camoens composed the Lusiades. An inscription over his tomb denotes that he was born in 1524, and died in 1579.

The chief curiosity to be seen at Macao is an occasional small-foot woman. I was most anxious to see and examine one of them, but my repeated attempts to accomplish this proved abortive, till at length, through the kindness and influence of a friend, I succeeded. This is really a most extraordinary deformity. That the human foot was capable of being reduced by mere compression to the size of those model-shoes we have all seen at home, I never could bring myself to believe till now. The smaller the foot is, the more it is considered, by the Chinese, as a beauty. If the girl promise to be handsome, she is invariably crippled, so as to give the finishing touch to her beauty. In the interior of the country, the habit is universal among rich and poor; but here, only those who have some pretension to rank undergo the operation. The poor creatures with the "lily feet," as they term it, totter along, like one shuffling on their heels only, without putting the fore part of the foot to the ground. They stump about with great apparent ease, but I certainly cannot agree with those who say it adds gracefulness to their gait. They reminded me, when first I saw them, of a boy walking on stilts. The miserable creature destined to undergo this deformity, is, in infancy and before the bones are completely ossified, placed in the operator's hands. Shoes of pasteboard, or leather, and in obstinate cases, of wood or iron, are made to fit close to the foot: these are retained *in situ* by a tight bandage. If properly applied at first, it is not removed until the foot is considered to be formed. Less pressure is afterwards required, though a certain degree of this is necessary throughout life to cramp and impede the growth of the foot. The young lady now presented to the reader was about twenty-five years of age. For a Chinawoman she was tall and well made, plump, rosy features, chubby-cheeked, and delicately florid complexion. On being introduced, she bowed gracefully, and directed me to a seat. Having previously been prepared to receive me, little explanation was necessary. My friend, therefore, walked out, and left us alone. I must confess, I now felt exceedingly puzzled how to proceed. She understood only Chinese and a little Portuguese, neither of which languages was I versed in. We were not above a few minutes alone, when she burst into an immoderate fit of laughter. This gave me confidence; and, intent on my object, I pointed to her feet, and was advancing towards her, whereupon she immediately sprung from her seat and disappeared at a side door with a rapidity I never could have given her credit for. Annoyed at having been thus used, I returned to my friend, who was in an adjoining room, and requested his intercession. The young lady again appeared, but she would not permit me to touch the deformed limb till it was explained to her that I was a doctor, and merely wished to examine her foot to satisfy curiosity, and that I would not divulge what I had seen, (for they cannot bear its being afterwards repeated that their feet have been submitted to the gaze of any of the other sex, more especially to barbarians,) and till, what was perhaps the best placebo of all, I had slipped a few dollars into the pocket of her apron. When again left alone, she unfolded the bandage, on the removal of which, the state of filth the foot presented convinced me that the general opinion is correct—viz., that the limb is seldom exposed, even for the purpose of cleanliness. A cursory glance at the deformed limb would lead even a professional man to suppose that a partial amputation had been performed, wherein the metatarsal bones (those immediately articulating with the toes) had been removed. On a closer inspection, the great toe was found to end in a sharp rough point, having at its extremity what might either be construed into a shapeless nail, or a portion of bone protruding, from not having been properly protected by the flap after an amputation. On the upper surface of the foot there was no peculiar appearance, save that the smaller toes appeared to terminate in a knuckle-like point. On examining the sole of the foot, I was surprised to see the four small toes bent under and deeply imbedded in the soft substance of the foot, and in a wonderful degree capable of flexion and extension. In the foot itself there was no motion, the joint, I presume, having been anchylosed (or a bony union formed) by constant pressure. This, however, I afterwards found not to be the case, for on examining a skeleton foot I found the bones all separate, but displaced. The ankle was thickened, its capability of motion being in a great degree curtailed. The calf of the leg was round and well proportioned. The extreme length of the foot was three inches and a quarter; yet, when properly bandaged and shod, this young lady hobbled up and down her stair with apparent ease.

The pain and irritation excited by the horrid process of cramping the foot, as well as the want of exercise, must, it will be supposed, materially injure the general health. This, however, is not allowed to be the case. Subsequent to the above period, I met some children who were passing through the usual ordeal of perfecting beauty, whose pallid, sickly look contrasted greatly with the healthy, rude appearance of the poorer Chinese, who teach their children at a very early age to assist in all domestic employments.

It would be as difficult to account for the origin of this barbarous practice of the Chinese, as for that of squeezing the waists of English women out of all natural shape by stays, or flattening the heads amongst the natives on the Columbia.

CHAPTER VII

Letter from Captain Anstruther — Melancholy accounts from Chusan — The missing Golconda — The Nemesis Steamer.

When last we parted with Captain Anstruther, we left our readers in uncertainty as to the fate of that officer. Let them not, however, for a moment suppose that his brother officers remained inactive in the matter. Anstruther had frequently, on his return in the evening, amused his companions with the occurrences of the day,—how he had met with such assistance and extraordinary attention on the part of the Chinese—how they used to collect about him, examine every portion of his dress, his instruments, his sketches, &c.—and how, at length, they became so familiarized with each other, that while one sat for his likeness, others surrounded him, and, looking over his shoulder, admired the resemblances. He was repeatedly warned not to permit such familiarity, and that from the well-known character of the Chinese, he should treat them as rogues until they proved, themselves honest men. He was confident they meant him no harm. Their laughing, good-natured countenances so dispelled all alarm, that latterly he went out without his pistols, and sometimes alone. This was what the cunning scoundrels all along aimed at.

The direction he had taken on the day he disappeared was well known; thither, therefore, his friends, with an armed party, directed their steps, and seizing the head men of the villages, threatened them with death unless they immediately divulged all they knew on the subject. The cringing cowards at length confessed that he had been carried off to Ningpo by an armed party of soldiers, who, in disguise, had been watching him some days; and prostrating themselves to the earth, declared that they were in no way instrumental in capturing him. When it had been satisfactorily ascertained that this story was correct, application was made to the authorities to insist upon and enforce the release, not only of Captain Anstruther, but also of the whole of the other prisoners at Ningpo. This, however, they declined, although the whole of them had been seized after the truce agreed upon at the Pieho had been sealed. When all resorts to effect a communication privately with the captives by their friends at Chusan had failed, Anstruther himself, by his peculiarly fascinating and winning manners, met with better success. One evening, towards the beginning of the month of November, a man made his appearance in the artillery camp. He was the bearer of a private letter from Anstruther to Colonel Montgomerie, commanding his corps. From that day till the period of his release this man was true to his employer. Previous to this period, however, official intercourse was carried on with the mandarins at Ningpo, who made no objections to receive money, clothes, and provisions for the prisoners, all of which were scrupulously handed over to them.

The following extract of a letter, written by Captain Anstruther in prison, and forwarded to his friends, at Chusan, by his faithful Blondell, as he termed him, on account of his loyalty and honesty, I must here insert, as explaining fully and particularly the manner in which he was captured, and his treatment in prison:—

"On Wednesday, 16th September, 1840, I left camp at ten o'clock, a.m., and passed out from the northern gate of Tinghae, about 1000 or 1200 yards, where there are several houses and gardens, and from whence a road branches off to the westward. Proceeding along this road, I ascended the pass between the hills, and then, turning to the left, gained the top of a knoll, where I pitched a small flag, and took sundry bearings, in order to facilitate the survey in which I was engaged.

"From the knoll, I went to the westward of the pass, and in a very short time was sensible that I had gone too far. My path led by a joss-house on the right, which was so overhung with trees on each side, as to make it quite dark. I determined, so soon as I could get through this dark and dangerous-looking place, to return to camp; but on reaching the end of the grove, I found that I was followed by a crowd. I now turned to the left, meaning to ascend the hill again. I had hardly turned, when a Chinese soldier, rushing out from the crowd, struck furiously at my only attendant, an old Lascar, who, to avoid the blow, and in great alarm, ran up to me. Taking from him the iron spade which he had used to pitch the flag-staff, I met the soldier and drove him back, but a number of others, armed with double-pronged spears, renewed the charge. I now bade the Lascar to make the best of his way up the hill, thinking the Chinese would only follow me; but the faithful old man refused to leave me; moreover, the armed people collected on the hill-side, so as to cut off, if possible, all chance of escape in that direction; I therefore determined to attempt to force my way through the long valley.

"I am but a bad runner, and my poor old servant was worse; so I went slowly along the valley, turning round now and then to keep the Chinese at bay. Meantime the whole population of the valley gathered with loud shouts in our front, and it was evidently a hopeless job. I could not get my old man to leave me and try to escape unnoticed, so we went

The Nemesis and the boats of the Sulphur, Calliope, Larne and Starling destroying the Chinese war junks in Anson's Bay, January 7 1841. The Nemesis was the first ocean-going iron steam ship used by the British. Launched in 1839, she was particularly effective in this war because her shallow draught enabled her to travel up-river, and was instrumental in the capture of Canton.

on together. At a turn in the path, I was opposed by a few scoundrels with sticks and stones. I charged them, and they all got round me, and then my poor old man ran back about 80 yards, where he was struck down. I have an inexpressible reluctance to write what follows, but must. I attempted to force my way towards him, but could not; and I saw the inhuman villains pounding his head with large stones, as he lay with his face downward. I cannot doubt that he died.

"I now saw that attempt at flight was useless, and, expecting a fate similar to that of my Lascar, I set to work to make the rascals pay for it, and fought my best—numbers of course prevailed, and I was knocked down. Instead of dashing out my brains, they bound me hand and foot, and tied a large gag in my mouth. Then taking a large bamboo, they hammered my knees just over the knee-cap, to prevent any possibility of escape. I was then carried to a village about ten miles west of the camp. Here we waited till night-fall, my conductors comforting me by repeating the word Ningpo, and by drawing their hands across their throats. At midnight I was placed in a boat, and arrived at Ningpo in the afternoon of the following day. I was now sent to jail, and forced into a cage one yard long, one yard high, and two ,feet wide. In this cage, heavy irons were placed on my hands and feet, an iron ring attached to the roof of the cage was put round my neck, to which my handcuffs were also locked. At night, a chain was also locked to my leg-irons, and the jailer, with a light, slept close to me.

"These irons weighed, I suppose, about 18lbs., and were worn by me for four weeks. I was frequently taken before the magistrates, who at all times inquired particularly about our steamers. One day I offered to sketch one, which sketch so pleased their honours, that they gave me a good dinner, and some hot water to wash off the blood and dirt which had accumulated during the struggle. I found my head handsomely laid open to the bone—my legs and arms covered with bruises, but no wounds of any consequence.

"Some days after my capture, I was surprised to meet at the magistrate's, Mr. Noble, my friend Lieut. Douglas of the navy, and several Europeans, who informed me they had been wrecked on the coast, and had been carried prisoners into Ningpo."

From this period the prisoners met with better treatment, chiefly through the intercessions of Capt. Anstruther. The mandarins were very fond of having their portraits taken, and as Anstruther excelled in this art, he was, therefore, frequently brought before them. At first he was all submission; latterly, however, he claimed, as a reward for his labours, either better food or more extended liberty, until which was granted, he withheld the picture if taken, or refused altogether to sketch one.

There is an amusing anecdote told of him when in confinement, which is said to have come in a private letter from himself. One day a mandarin sent him a very savoury stew, garnished with sharks' fins and birds' nests, in compensation for a likeness which he had taken of the nodding gentleman. Anstruther having tasted the delicious contents, gave an inquisitive look at the attendant, and pointing to the stew, said—"Quack, quack, quack?" The servant shook his head, and replied, "Bow, wow, wow."

It has been well remarked—"That the most fatal and mischievous errors are constantly occurring from the want of some distinct and well-defined knowledge of military hygeiana, will be self-evident to all who study, with a sufficient degree of care and attention, the history of the Anglo-Indian army, from the earliest occupation of the country to the present day. The improper selection of encamping grounds, the malposition of barracks and lines, the undue exposure of the men to the noxious influence of the atmosphere, the misdirected zeal of many commanding officers in fixing upon injurious times for parades, punishments, &c, have furnished a frightful catalogue of mortality, far outnumbering the devastating destruction of the sword, or the deadly march of the most destructive pestilence. It is painful to contemplate the reckless waste of human life and large expenditure of treasure which have resulted from these and similar causes, completely within the control of man, and requiring the exercise of a very small amount of intellect and trouble on the part of those upon whose fiat the fate of thousands depend." As an illustration of the truth of these remarks, many instances are familiar to all, such as the Walcheren expedition, the destruction of the French army sent to re-conquer Saint Domingo, and our present occupation of Chusan. From this latter settlement the most heart-rending accounts continued to be received; the 26th Cameronians suffered most. This regiment, which sailed from Calcutta upwards of 900 strong—a pattern to all other corps for sobriety and good conduct, its average mortality during the previous ten years being barely twenty—was, in the short space of three months, reduced to 291. The entire amount of force on the island did not, on the 1st of January, 1841, exceed 1900 men. Many hundred coffins were found on first taking possession of Chusan, it being a common habit with the Chinese, when they become independent, to get a coffin made, and keep it by them till their death. These coffins were at first found useful for fire-wood, but as applications for them increased, this means of disposing of them was put a stop to. It was by no means an uncommon occurrence for an application to be made to the first adjutant, for nine, twelve, and upwards daily. At length deaths became so common, that neither coffins were required, nor were military honours paid the departed. Heaped one upon another, the corpses were consigned to the earth, and thought no more of. Several of the houses in the suburbs being still unoccupied by the Chinese, it was now agreed upon by all that our men should enter them, more especially as the cold weather, had set in. From this period dates the improvement in the health of the force. Encounters, some of an amusing nature, were of frequent occurrence about this time at Chusan. On one occasion, two middies—one fifteen, the other thirteen years old—went out on a foraging excursion for the benefit of their mess. They had taken the precaution to carry with them a double-barrelled gun, loaded with ball. Proceeding inland, they soon met a Fokee in charge of a flock of goats. The younger of the boys now tried to strike a bargain, and sporting his dollars rather too freely, advanced towards the latter, who, however, instead of receiving the dollars, caught the boy in his arms and was running away with him. His progress, however, was soon stopped; the elder boy having, on seeing his companion seized, advanced, and placing the muzzle of his piece to the Chinaman's ear, blew his brains out; whereupon some men who were looking on proceeded to seize the boys. The latter stood still till the foremost was within shot. The younger boy now snatching the gun out of his companion's hand, said it was his turn now to have a shot. He fired, and lodged the contents of the second barrel in the man's chest. The remainder of the Chinamen, not much liking the aspect of affairs, took to their heels.

All hope of the ill-fated "Golconda" was now at an. end. With reference to this subject it was remarked, in a Bengal journal—"The last account which we are ever likely to hear of the unfortunate Golconda is now given. She was seen in the China seas, all well, on the 18th September, 1840. Soon afterwards came on the terrific gale, in which she is supposed to have perished, with one half the officers and men of the 37th regiment Madras Native Infantry. This vessel was unseaworthy, and was known to be such before she was engaged. No conscientious man would have risked the lives of others in her." It will be recollected, that it was on the 22nd September that the Thetis was dismasted and so nearly lost. On that date, too, it is supposed the Golconda must have foundered. This is an awful warning of the results of engaging inferior class vessels for transport service. The mortality on this occasion far exceeded that which attended the ill-starred President.

Early in December, the Nemesis, steamer, direct from England, joined the fleet. She is a great acquisition to the force: being built entirely of iron, and drawing only four feet water, she is in every way well adapted for the creeks and shoal water in this neighbourhood, in which the war-junks take refuge on being hard pushed.

Captain Hall, R.N., her commander, is a bold and resolute officer, whose repeated acts of gallantry have already been rewarded by Her Majesty, and have called forth the admiration and praise of all who have been witness to them.

CHAPTER VIII

Treacherous conduct of the imperial commissioner—Massacre of six mandarins—Battles of Cheumpee and Tycoctow.

Keshen's first act on reaching Canton was to release the Rev. Mr. Stanton and other prisoners who had been seized at Macao shortly before his arrival. All gave him credit for acting with openness and honesty; an ample apology was made for an accidental shot that had been fired on a flag of truce in the Queen steamer, and which divided one of the iron bars of her paddle-wheel; and negotiations went on. Keshen gave out that the full power of settling all differences rested with him, that he held the imperial sign manual, and that he ardently desired to bring things to a favourable termination. Lin, who it was at one time supposed had been recalled, was still suspected to be at Canton, and by command of his sovereign directed to watch over Keshen's acts. At this time the reply of Captain Elliot always was, "Negotiations are proceeding satisfactorily, and in ten days or a fortnight all will be settled." Thus nearly two months passed over our heads, during which time workmen were seen employed, day and night, in strengthening and extending the batteries and defences on shore. At those of Cheumpee, removed about gun-shot range from the more advanced ships of the squadron, troops were daily collecting, and their out-posts becoming more numerous. Boats which supplied the ships with fresh meat and vegetables, and had accompanied them from Saw Chow, would not now leave the ships, to which they respectively attached themselves, and proceed on shore for supplies, giving as a reason that they were afraid of being seized by the mandarins. It was evident to all that a crisis was approaching. From Tonkoo Bay, and the neighbourhood of Lintin, where, as has been shewn, the whole of the merchant fleet lay, intelligence was received of that nature which convinced us all that Keshen was playing a double part. That crafty minister3 well knowing that the chief portion of our force was at anchor off Cheumpee, at which place he had collected a large land and sea force, sufficient in his opinion, if not for aggressive, at any rate for defensive purposes, resolved as a primary measure to destroy the merchant shipping. With that view he constructed fire rafts on a great scale, and directing his emissaries to superintend this work of destruction, he established, it was generally supposed, his own head quarters at the Bocca

The iron steam ship Nemesis destroying the Chinese war junks in Anson's Bay, January 7th 1841. Painting by Edward Duncan (1802-1882)

Tigris, which is distant about a league from the batteries of Cheumpee. Deep as his schemes were, they did not escape our notice; in fact, his own countrymen were the first to publish them. The mandarins who had been sent to Tonkoo Bay, six in number, were prowling about the villages situated in that neighbourhood, for the purpose, not only of collecting volunteers to their ranks, but also of taking down the names and description of those Chinamen who supported and frequented the shipping.

Here, however, they reckoned without their host; their purpose becoming suspected, the latter were forced to adopt measures of self-defence. Taking the party by surprise, a scuffle, in which several lives were lost, ensued, and the mandarins fell into the hands of the mob. The chief they boiled alive in oil, and the five others, bound hand and foot, were chained in a boat which had previously been filled with combustibles of every description, and drifting out to sea with the tide, suffered a fearful and awful death. Even the vacillating Elliot now began to suspect treachery, more especially as Keshen had refused to reply to, and latterly even did not acknowledge, any of his communications. An imperial edict was about this time received and widely circulated in Canton and other provincial cities, breathing forth everlasting extermination to the barbarians, and annulling the armistice announced in the month of November. Affairs were in this state, when, on the 6th of January, it was determined that if no communication was received from Keshen before the following morning, the forts and out-works of Cheumpee and Tycocktow should be stormed—the latter being on the western side of the channel, and built in shape like a horse-shoe, having a powerful battery of

25 guns fronting the water. This appears a favourite mode with the Chinese of constructing their forts, the side walls being intended not only .to check the approach of an enemy, but also for the purpose of preventing the escape of their own soldiers. Those of Cheumpee, for they consist of an extended line of batteries, are on the eastern side of their river, and separated from the forts of Anunghoi by Anson's Bay On the hill, immediately above the fort of Cheumpee, is a watch tower, around which a strong fortification had recently been built, and guns planted. In the valleys, between hills, and at every position at which an approach was likely to be made, temporary stockades had been erected, and to the south of the hill fort of Cheumpee, a high wall was built, which extended to the base of the hill, partially encircling it; it then stretched across a deep valley, and up the face of an adjoining hill. Along this wall was a deep dry fosse; on its summit were broken glass and sharp spikes, and pieces of Bamboo in shape of *chevaux de frieze*, and strongly palisaded at all points. None of those latter defences were in existence when the fleet originally arrived off Cheumpee.

The period allotted to receive a reply from Keshen having expired, on the morning of the 7th, the troops disembarked on the island of Cheumpee, at a small bay, removed from the enemy's position about three miles, and separated from it by rising ground and intervening valleys. The land force was commanded by Major Pratt, H.M. 26th regiment, and consisted of Royal Artillery, and marines, and seamen, 674; 37th regiment, M.N.I , 607; and Bengal Volunteers, 76. They were also joined by about 100 invalids who had about this time arrived from Chusan. The artillery, with one brass howitzer and two nine-pounders, took up a commanding position, about 300 yards from the hill fort. H.M. ships Calliope, Larne, and Hyacinth, under Captain Herbert, proceeded to bombard the lower fort, while the steamers, Nemesis and Queen, threw shells into the hill fort and entrenchments on the inner side—the Wellesley and other large ships moving up into mid-channel, in case they might be required. The enemy kept up an uninterrupted fire for about an hour, the balls passing over our heads. Had their guns been a little more depressed, much mischief would have been done. When their firing had slackened a little, the infantry advanced. Three companies of the 37th regiment were detached to intercept the enemy in their flight, the main body of the force advancing directly upon the wall, already mentioned as partially surrounding the base of the hill. On the wall were several small field pieces and ginjalls, and from behind it matchlock men were directing their fire upon our advance. Barbed rockets, arrows, &c, were also showered down upon us in great numbers. After a short struggle, we succeeded in clearing this wall; the column then divided, one portion ascending towards the hill fort, while the other proceeded round the base of the hill to the lower fort. The former was found deserted, but from the latter, and from a wooded hill near it, the enemy still kept up a brisk fire. A party of marines soon dislodged them from the wooded hill, and our well-directed fire upon the lower fort soon obliged the Chinese to evacuate it. The flying enemy were now mowed down in every direction. Finding escape no longer possible, they concealed themselves wherever opportunity offered, some in out-houses and behind walls, and thence, when not perceived, attacking their captors, which soon brought upon themselves indiscriminate slaughter; others, taking to the water, met with the same fate, and those who, from the distance they had gone from the fort, had flattered themselves that their escape was safe, were cut off by the detached companies of the 37th regiment. Several small mines had exploded during the day, without doing much injury. It was when all was over, and the troops were resting after the fatigues of the day, that a large mine exploded, in which, with several others, I happened to sustain some injury, having been not only exalted several feet, but also considerably scorched, and bruised by the fall of bricks and other missiles.

The Nemesis meantime was engaged in burning and destroying the war-junks in the neighbourhood. The first congreve rocket she fired passed through the magazine of the admiral's junk, and blew her up with a crew of 150 men. Thirteen junks, in all, were destroyed; the steamer followed them into the creeks, and with her grappling-irons dragged several out at a time, and afterwards set fire to them, the shot in their guns going off as they became heated. In the forts of Cheumpee there were 82 guns, and in the war-junks about the same number. The strength of the enemy in this position was about 2000, of whom, 600 must have been killed, and as many wounded. In the meantime the fort of Tycocktow was attacked and carried by the division under command of Captain Scott, consisting of the Druid, Samarang, Modeste, and Columbine. In half an hour from the commencement, a practicable breach was made in this fort. The crews landed, and, entering the breach, carried the place by storm. In doing this there was some hard fighting; the Chinese, displaying determination and strength, were soon, however, obliged to yield. At this fort there were about thirty dead bodies discovered, but many were found afterwards, on the sides of the hills above the fort, who had died of their wounds.

Thus, after an engagement of a few hours, fell Cheumpee and Tycocktow. The former (fortunately for its moral effect) was carried chiefly by the land forces. The Chinese allow us to be superior to them at sea, but on shore, hand to hand, they fancy themselves far superior. "Let the barbarians," remarked General Loo, in a memorial to the emperor, "but meet the imperial troops on shore, and though there be ten of them against one son of heaven, the celestial forces must conquer—nay, even the very rocks must melt before the terrific splendour of our arms, and at the dreadful thunder of our artillery."

CHAPTER IX

The day after the battle—Flag of truce and treaty of peace-Columbine sails for Chusan.

On the morning after the events detailed in the last chapter, the steamers were again busily employed in taking in troops, and distributing them to the several small ships of war, for the purpose of facilitating their landing; the squadron had all weighed, and were proceeding to take up their several positions opposite the North Wang-Tong and Anunghoi forts, and the steamer, Nemesis, had commenced her work of destruction, by throwing shell and rockets, with beautiful precision, among a large body of the enemy, who were drawn up on the Anunghoi island to oppose our landing.

Suddenly the eyes of all were directed towards the Wellesley, from which ship a gun was fired, and a white flag raised at the main.

The appearance of this flag of truce was very disheartening to all who, flushed with the success of yesterday, and not yet satisfied with the quantity of human bloodshed, were eager to dip their hands yet more deeply into it.

How little does a victorious army think, when reckoning on the numbers of the dead and wounded enemy, that these, too, had friends who deplore their loss and weep for their fate. To survey a battle-field after an engagement, and to behold the ground covered with the corpses of those who, but a few hours before, were in the full enjoyment of that health which our Creator has given us, but who now lie dead and cold, their bodies mangled and torn to pieces by shot and by shell, and the green grass dyed with their life's blood, would, it will naturally be supposed, excite feelings of compassion or remorse, more especially to those who have not been hardened and rendered callous by such sights, and have ever been accustomed to regard the dead body with fear and with awe; but with few only, I suspect, are such feelings present. At no time does man so nearly resemble the brute animal as in the field of battle, when two parties meet, each striving to obtain the mastery at the expense of life; then do all the finer feelings vanish, and the conqueror surveys his victim with a proud satisfaction, and he points to him afterwards as a fine specimen of one of God's created beings. Such are the effects of war, and such were the callous feelings of the majority who proceeded to survey the battle-field of Cheumpee, when disappointed in prosecuting the work of destruction.

The true cause of the sudden appearance of the white flag was soon known.

The commandant of the fort had sent to request of Captain Elliot a truce for three days, to enable him to communicate with Keshen, who, he stated, was at Canton. The truce was readily granted. Working parties were, therefore, in the meantime busily employed in destroying the forts and batteries which yesterday fell into our hands; in rendering the guns unserviceable, and in burying the dead; while the more compassionate among the surgeons were attending the wounded, and alleviating their sufferings.

The slaughter on the Cheumpee side was dreadful; independent of those bodies on shore, the sea was quite blackened with floating corpses, and the beach for miles around was strewed with them. On shore, the dead, in many places, lay heaped one upon another; at one place, where resistance had been greatest, the dead lay piled several feet high. It was here that the *heètac*, or brigadier, was found; he was a tall and powerful man, and was killed by a musket bullet through his chest. His son, who was observed to fight most manfully by his side, on finding that his father was dead, leaped into the water, and there perished. Many bodies were dreadfully scorched and disfigured, from the burning of their garments padded with cotton, which were set on fire by their lighted matches as they fell, wounded, upon them. Some, indeed had been literally blown up from the explosion of their cartridge boxes, which are always worn around their waists. The appearance inside the fort was horrifying in the extreme. There the round shot and shell had done fearful execution. The walls, in many places, were bespattered with brains; and it was difficult to discover whether the mangled remains before you ever possessed the human shape. Close to the site of the explosion of the mine, many of the enemy must have secreted themselves; but now a blent, blackened, smouldering, stinking mass was all that remained to point out their mortal remains. About 200 bodies were thrown into a deep pit immediately under the hill fort, and about half that number in an adjoining one. Some careless, thoughtless Jacks employed in this operation, raised a board over the former, with the inscription—"This is the road to *gloary*," printed upon it.

The poorer Chinese shewed no appearance of fear at our having taken Cheumpee. Many of them, a few days after the engagement, came to recover the dead bodies of the slain, which they exhumed; and, although in a state of decomposition, they carried them away in coffins, hundreds of which had been brought from Canton for the purpose. One old small-foot woman, who made herself conspicuous on the 7th, running about wildly, crying aloud, "You have killed my two sons; you have burned my house, and stolen my property—kill me too!"—appears now to have domesticated herself with our men, and assists in cooking their food. Poor wretch, she, like many others, lost that day all she held dear! Alas! what a cruel monster is man, thus to destroy the only bonds which, even in the most savage country, bind us to each other, and make life a comfort and a pleasure.

The forts, on both sides the channel, were in a few days dismantled; the guns spiked, their trunnions knocked off, and cold shot rammed home into them; and the rough gun-carriages burned or otherwise destroyed, so that they could not possibly again be rendered efficient. The bum-boats, compradors, and fishermen, gaining confidence by our boldness, continued to frequent the fleet in great numbers; they expressed great dread of falling into the hands of the mandarins. There are hundreds who would be glad to join us if they had encouragement. Never was there so despotic a government as the Chinese; yet there is no struggle for freedom, for power appals them.

The third day had passed, and the period of truce was at an end, yet there were no signs of a renewal of hostilities; and Captain Elliot, by public proclamation, on the fourth day, announced a cessation of hostilities, and a conclusion of preliminary arrangements between the imperial high commissioner and himself, involving certain conditions,—of which the chief were—1st, The cession of the island of Hong-Kong to the British Crown; 2nd, An indemnity of six million of dollars to the British government; 3rd, Direct official intercourse between the two countries, upon equal footing; and, 4th, The re-opening of the trade at Canton.. On its being intimated to the Chinese, that we laid claim to the island of Cheumpee by right of conquest, Keshen replied, "How can you ask to have a place where you have killed so many men? their spirits would haunt you for ever." The intention of retaining this position was afterwards abandoned. On the part of Great Britain, it was agreed that her troops were to evacuate Chusan without further delay; and although the Chinese government gave no security for the due performance of the treaty, the fast-sailing corvette, Columbine, was despatched to the north with the announcement to the authorities there, and to order the immediate evacuation by H.M. forces of that island.

On the 21st February, the fleet sailed from the Bocca Tigris, under a salute from the Chinese forts, the garrison of which were, no doubt, laughing in their sleeves at having again so effectually gulled the bristle-headed barbarians.

CHAPTER X

A description of the harbour and island of Hong-Kong— Interview between Captain Elliot and Keshen—Perfidy, and interruption of negotiations.

On the morning of the 26th February, we anchored in the magnificent bay of Hong-Kong, and on the evening of that day the island was taken possession of in Her Majesty's name, under a royal salute from all the ships of the squadron.

Hong-Kong forms the most northerly of the group of islands, at the mouth of the estuary that leads to Canton. It is in lat. 22° 17' N., and long. 114° 12' E. It is distant from Macao forty miles, and from Canton about a hundred.

The island is about eight miles in length, and two and a half in its greatest breadth. The strait which separates it from the main land is, in some places, barely a mile in breadth, while at others it is five and six miles broad. The bay of Hong-Kong cannot probably be surpassed by any in the world, not only by reason of the infinite number of ships which it can accommodate, but also of its safe anchorage from typhoons, compared with any other harbour in China, and the depth of water close to the land, which along the greater part of the bay is sufficient for a seventy-four to float at a distance of a cable's length from shore. From this circumstance alone, the island must prove a possession of enormous value as a commercial acquisition. Magnificent granite quarries are found all over the island, so that warehouses on any scale can be built close to the water's edge, and wharfs with ease thrown out, which will enable ships to approach for the purpose of loading and unloading. There is at all seasons an abundant supply of fresh water procurable on the island.

In other respects this new colony possesses but few advantages. Its northern side is formed by a connected ridge of mountains, the highest of which is about 2000 feet above the level of the sea. Except in a few spots, these mountains are barren and uncultivated; formed by black projecting masses of granite, the intervals giving shelter to herbage and brush-wood. There are no trees of any size; and unlike the generality of mountainous districts, it possesses but a few valleys, and these not of any extent. The mountains, for the most part, fall perpendicularly into the sea, thus leaving but little space for building at their base. The interior and south side is chiefly formed by level and undulating land, and appears to be far better adapted for private residences than on the north side. Here, too, there are some very fine bays, the chief of which are Ty-tan and Chuck-pie-wan. At the former place a military post has been established. The latter place, which is removed about five miles from Ty-tan, forms a very convenient and well-sheltered site for building dock-yards, &c. Partridge, quail, and snipe, have been found on the island; and in the jungle, pheasants and deer have been seen. The population, oh our first taking possession, was barely 1000, but it is now daily increasing, and already numbers upwards of 10,000. Opposite to the northeastern extremity of Hong-Kong, and across the bay, is the town of Cowloon, a small fortified Chinese position, from which the fleet derive supplies in abundance. A peninsula of considerable size, with only a few Chinese hamlets upon it, extends from the town of Cowloon in a southeasterly direction. This mostly consists of rich level ground, and would prove of inestimable value to us, were it to become an appendage to our present possessions. The appearance of Hong-Kong is anything but prepossessing; and to those who have hitherto resided upon it, the climate has proved far from salubrious. There is a good deal of rank vegetation on the face of the hill, the ground on which, after a heavy fall of rain, becomes elastic and boggy. On the Cowloon side of the bay the atmosphere is at all times more pure, and the changes of temperature less sudden; indeed, altogether it appears a far more likely and preferable spot to form a settlement than on the Hong-Kong side. At present it has been decided that this peninsula is to be considered as neutral ground.

In order to facilitate the permanent adjustment of affairs, it was agreed, on the part of our Plenipotentiary and the Imperial Commissioner, that a meeting should be held, at which both parties should come attended by their respective guards of honour. The 27th of January was the day fixed for the interview, on which day Captain Elliot proceeded in the Nemesis steamer, attended by sixty picked men of the Royal Marines, and a number of officers of the army and navy. On the bank of the river, near the second bar, Keshen received and regaled our Plenipotentiary and suite at a splendid banquet prepared for the occasion, at which, in addition to the usual luxuries of the Chinese on such occasions, the tables groaned with a profusion of Highland mutton, venison, grouse, and other European delicacies, among which hock, champagne, and cherry brandy formed no small part. This cunning statesman appears to have discovered the right road to an Englishman's heart; and as will be supposed, after a feast of this description, little business was transacted. Keshen requested of Captain Elliot to put his party through some of their movements, which the latter performed with such dexterity and execution as to surprise every mandarin present, and to call from them loud expressions of wonder and astonishment. From the portly make of some of the men, he suspected they were padded, nor would he be convinced to the contrary, until he had stripped and examined them. Captain Elliot, in his turn, examined the celestial bodyguard. They were all dressed alike—viz., large loose white pantaloons and a crimson jacket, having a white star over the chest, and a corresponding one on the back. On the former, the words "Indomitable Courage" was marked, and on the latter, the name, battalion, and general number of the owner. Many mutual compliments passed, until the day being so far spent, it was agreed, that Keshen should have ten days more to consider matters, before placing the final seal upon the treaty. At the appointed time H.M. Plenipotentiary held another interview with Keshen, after which an official circular was issued, informing the British subjects that negotiations were proceeding satisfactorily. Trade, however, was not yet opened, although the day agreed on in the treaty had gone by. It was well known, too, that soldiers were collecting at Canton and at the Bocca Tigris in great numbers, and that the latter place was daily becoming stronger and more formidable.

About this time an edict was published, and widely circulated in Canton and elsewhere, offering large rewards for British ships and subjects. This document at once exhibits the characteristic duplicity of the Chinese government, and, if possible, indelibly fixes a more foul stain upon their character. Resolved upon and made known, whilst ostensibly amicable negotiations were going on with those who were to be its victims, the document set forth by pardoning all native traitors who repent of their crimes and quit the service of the English. Rewards were then offered for ships according to their size; 100,000 dollars for a 74; 50,000 dollars for a steamer; and 30,000 for smaller ships;—50,000 dollars were offered for the Commodore, Captain Elliot, or the interpreter, Mr. Morrison, dead or alive, and smaller rewards for all other officers according to their rank: a Sepoy, or Lascar, was valued at fifty dollars. Pensions were awarded to the families of those Chinese who lost their lives in the execution of this duty. So much "for the scrupulous good faith of the very eminent person with whom negotiations are still pending." Keshen is of opinion that foreigners are altogether in the power of the Chinese, and that after they shall have been excluded for some time, and after their stocks of rhubarb and of tea, of which he supposes them to keep stores sufficient for ten or twenty years' consumption, shall have been exhausted, they will beg for permission to trade again, in the most abject language, and then they will have to pay gold and silver in exchange for tea and rhubarb, instead of, as now, deluging the land with opium, and taking away in return Sycee silver. The foreigners, says Keshen, "subsist day by day upon beef and mutton, and every day, after meals, they take this divine medicine (i.e., tea and rhubarb) in order to ensure the proper action of their bowels." It seems, in fact, to be Keshen's opinion, that without those two articles, foreigners must die of constipation, and his plan is humanely to extirpate them by denying them this medicine. The Viceroy of Pechelee, therefore, recommended that an imperial proclamation be published, prohibiting all intercourse with foreigners, thus "defeating their schemes, and, having done this, you (the Emperor) have merely to bend down their back, and pin them by the collar."

CHAPTER XI

Recommencement of hostilities, and bombardment of forts at the Bocca Tigris.

It will at once become evident to all those who have perused the preceding document, that matters could not long remain in their present state. Henceforth, no one can say, that specific measures have not been sufficiently tried. Even the sanguine Elliot appeared now convinced that the Chinese entered into the above treaty merely to gain time. As a final measure, however, he despatched the Nemesis steamer to the Bocca Tigris, and had yet some hopes that she would bring back the treaty, ratified. The steamer returned to Macao on the 19th February, and it soon became known that every effort on her part to communicate with the Bogue forts proved abortive, and that a boat, which was being sent on shore for that purpose, had been fired at, and nearly sunk by the guns from North Wang-Tong. The following proclamation was,, soon after the return of the steamer, issued to the British community at Macao:—"Circumstances have induced the Commander-in-chief to announce to H.M.'s Plenipotentiary his intention to move the forces towards the Bocca Tigris." All naval and military officers on leave were also directed to join their respective ships without delay. When this intelligence was brought to me, Cumchung, a wealthy and respectable Chinese merchant, happened to be present. I remarked to him, that we were about to proceed to the Bocca Tigris immediately, to knock down the forts there. With a smile of scorn and derison, and pointing upwards towards the heavens, the old man replied, "Same time you Englesman take that fort, same time that sky make fall down." Such was his opinion, and such was the general opinion of his countrymen, with regard to the impregnable nature of the forts in this position; and, indeed, on our arrival there a few days afterwards, the batteries presented a most formidable appearance, and if held by an European power, would have cost a severe struggle and great loss of life to take them.

During the brief period that had elapsed since our departure from Cheumpee, the forts and batteries we were now about to attack had spread rapidly; so thick was the island studded with workmen and soldiers, that at a distance it resembled an ant-hill. The utmost breadth of the river at this point is two miles; the island of North Wang-Tong being situated nearly in the centre of the channel. The island is about a mile in circumference;

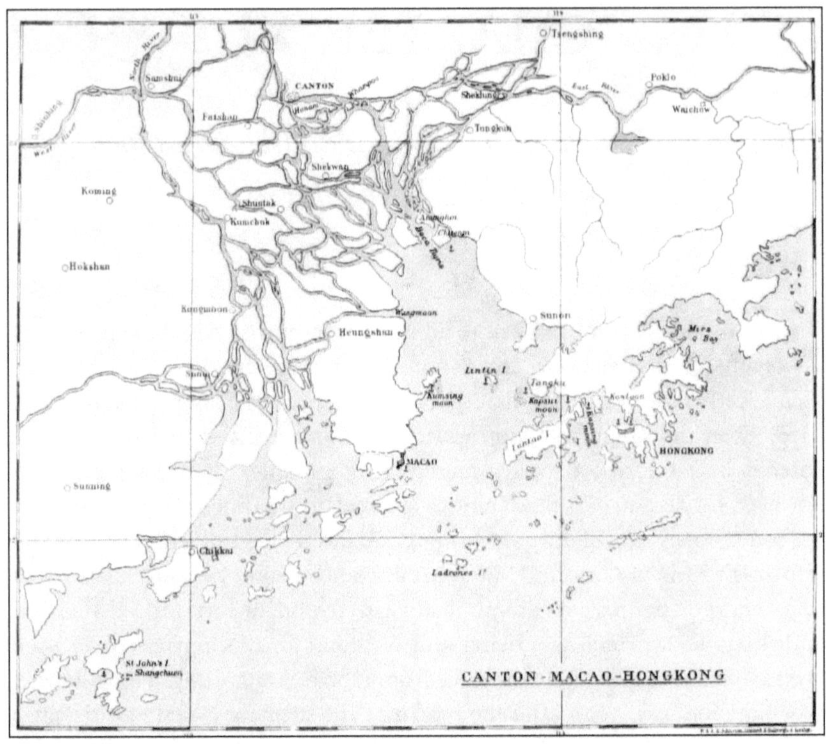

Map of the Canton Estuary, showing the Bocca Tigris (literally 'Tiger Gate'), a narrow strait in the Pearl River delta.

point is two miles; the island of North Wang-Tong being situated nearly in the centre of the channel. The island is about a mile in circumference; on its eastern side was a double fortification, the lower of which was an enormous, strong battery, built of solid granite, and mounting 42 guns, some of very large calibre. On the western side was an exactly similar battery, with the same number of guns. To the inside of those were barracks for the troops, and along the shore, a strong breast-work, communicating with these batteries, had been lately thrown up, mounting an innumerable number of small guns, wall pieces, ginjalls, &c. On a rising ground is the hill fort, or citadel, the guns from which have a commanding range on every side; and in the centre of the island was an extensive encampment.

On the eastern side of the river, and opposite the islands of North and South Wang-Tong, are the great and little forts of Anunghoi. They are of enormous strength, constructed solely of large blocks of granite. On the summit of these, a peculiarly firm cement, made from chunam and gravel, was placed several feet thick, so as to prevent the stone from splintering. On this side of the river the same activity prevailed as on the island in the centre;

alert. From the south Anunghoi fort, a chain, several inches in thickness, ran across the river to South Wang-Tong island, on the surface of which, at short intervals, rafts were attached; a second chain was also run across from the island of North Wang-Tong to the corresponding forts on the Anunghoi side, but the tides had been so strong at our present visit, that it had been carried away. This was the only channel through which ships passed up to Canton, which was at once effected by slackening the chain, and permitting it to sink to a certain extent.

On the western side of the river was also a fort, and, as on the Anunghoi side, the commanding positions on the heights had also been fortified, the brow of the hill being one continued line of encampment. Through this channel no ships were permitted to pass. In fact, it was never supposed that there was water sufficient for the purpose. Nor was it until after repeated surveys, untiring exertions, and great risks, on the part of Captain Kellett, R.N., that it was discovered that in this passage alone a two-decker could pass up. It is singular, that with all the care the Chinese seem to have bestowed in protecting and fortifying the several positions in this narrow channel, they should have neglected every means of defence on the island of South Wang-Tong, removed from the other island of the same name a few yards. On this island it was soon discovered that a landing could be effected without being exposed to the fire from the surrounding batteries. This was a fatal mistake on the part of the Chinese, for it afforded us a stronghold which commanded their forts on every side.

The morning of the 25th of February saw the whole of the force collected off the Bogue forts. The enemy, evidently, were not long in discovering the object of our visit, for the Wellesley had hardly cast anchor, when a boat from the shore with a flag of truce approached her. This boat conveyed a requisition from the General commanding on shore, requesting "that more three days would be allowed," after which they should be prepared to receive us; and so averse was Captain Elliot to resume hostilities, that he was about to grant the cool request, when the commodore insisted, that now affairs were placed in his hands they must proceed. Hostilities had already commenced on the 24th of February, when a masked battery at the back of Anunghoi island was destroyed, and eighty guns of various calibre rendered unserviceable.

On the evening of the 25th, three howitzers were landed on the island of South Wang-Tong, by the Nemesis, under the superintendence of Sir Le Fleming Senhouse; a party of Royal and Madras Artillery, commanded by Major Knowles, and Lieutenant Cadell, and 150 men of the 37th regiment, M.N.I., under Captain Wardroper, were also landed on the same occasion. A fire was opened by the enemy upon this party during the landing, which was kept up at intervals the whole night, without, however, doing any injury.

By daylight on the following morning, the 26th, a battery, sufficient to protect the artillerymen while working their guns, having been raised, operations commenced, by throwing a few rockets into a large pile of building, the hoppoés, or custom-house, situated at the entrance of the North Wang-Tong fort; and such was the precision with which these were directed, that the place was soon in a blaze of fire, which rapidly communicated with the encampment, and presented an animating and inciting appearance. From this battery, shells and shot were also fired with splendid effect; and although the concentrated fire of the whole of the Chinese forts was directed against it, not one accident happened.

It was originally intended that a combined and simultaneous attack should be made on all the Bogue forts; but owing to the calmness of the weather, and a strong ebb tide, this was found impracticable. It was, therefore, necessary to postpone operations, and wait for the flood-tide to serve. About 11 o'clock, a.m., the Blenheim, 74 guns, was under weigh. Her intrepid commander, ever foremost in difficulties and dangers, having command of the wing of the squadron appointed to bombard the great and formidable Anunghoi forts, becoming impatient, could not wait for the change of the tide. She was accompanied by three rocket boats, and the Queen steamer. The Melville, 74 guns, soon afterwards got under weigh, and followed her. The flagship, Wellesley, and other ships about to attack Wang-Tong, were also on the move. They had been at anchor about a mile and a half from the forts, and in consequence of the slack tide and dead calm, the ships dropped down very slowly. An occasional shot was still fired from the forts, and from our battery on South Wang-Tong; beyond this, not a sound broke the ominous stillness that reigned around. The troops had embarked in the steamers, and were following in the wake of the shipping towards Wang-Tong.

The Blenheim was hardly yet within range when the forts of Anunghoi opened their fire upon her. With breathless interest all watched her coolly gliding to her work of destruction without returning a shot to the brisk fire that was now directed against her. The Queen and the rocket-boats had already commenced the action, and the Blenheim, when about 500 yards from the fort, brought to, clewed all up, and then opened her broadside. The Melville, Captain the Hon. — Dundas, followed about ten minutes later, and took up an admirable position, in the same cool, gallant style, about 400 yards from the fort, a little way a-head of the Blenheim, and close to the chain-raft. Like the latter ship she did not fire a shot till she had brought to, when she gave her starboard broadsides in quick succession. Operations had hardly yet begun on the opposite side of the channel, consequently the interest excited by the opposing parties at Anunghoi was intense beyond expression. The Queen steamer, though at good shell distance from shore, was too far removed to suffer much injury from the Chinese guns. The entire force of these enormous batteries, mounting upwards of 200 guns, was, therefore, concentrated against the two line-of-battle ships. At times, columns of smoke and dust concealed everything from our view; and now that the action was fairly begun at Wang-Tong, the continual roar was terrific, and was echoed back from the surrounding hills. The blaze of fire through the smoke resembled bright flashes of sheet lightning, obscured by dark clouds.

From the Anunghoi forts, where the contest had now lasted nearly two hours, the fire began to flag—the repeated broadsides having evidently taken effect. On the smoke clearing away, the enemy were seen leaving the forts in hundreds, and running off in every direction; an occasional shell from the Queen would burst over their heads, and the canister and grape now fired from the seventy-fours mowed them down by scores. The villages and encampments around had long since been set fire to by the rockets. During the heat of the engagement, a boat drifted from the Melville, close under the guns of the fort. It was recovered in fearless style, and without loss.

Against the batteries of North Wang-Tong, the Wellesley, Druid, and Modeste, Calliope, Samarang, Herald, and Alligator, had long since opened their fire. The starboard guns from the three former were chiefly directed against the western defences, while the larboard ones kept up a perpetual fire upon the forts and batteries on the opposite side of the channel. The fire from the other four ships was brought to bear upon the northern and eastern portions of the island. Thus an enfilading fire, most harassing to the garrison, was kept up, and continued without a moment's intermission, for upwards of an hour. Shortly after the engagement had begun on this side, four boats filled with men were observed to leave the island, and to the surprise of all, the Chinese opened a fire upon them. It was afterwards ascertained that these boats contained the general commanding, and all the chief mandarins, who fled panic-struck, taking with them the only boats on the island, having previously taken the base and cowardly precaution of barring the gates to prevent the garrison from molesting them in their flight. Thus deprived of their leaders, the fire soon slackened; and on the troops landing, the little opposition offered was chiefly of a passive nature. Here and there, however, a body of determined fellows driven at bay, resisted to the last, preferring to be shot down or bayoneted to yielding themselves prisoners. The loss on this island, on the part of the Chinese, was 250 killed and 150 wounded. Here also many were drowned in attempting to escape. About 1400 prisoners were taken, all of whom, with the exception of a working party to clear the fort and bury the dead, were landed on the western side of the river, and set at liberty. Over the Anunghoi forts the union-jack was proudly waving. The veteran, Sir Fleming, at the head of his blue jackets and marines, 300 in number, had landed; a chance shot had torn the door of the fort off its hinges—the party, therefore, at once entered. The ramparts were all deserted, but in the centre of the fort an armed party, in strength equal to their own, were drawn up in good order. At the head of this party was a venerable-looking old man, with a blue button and peacock's feather in his cap, evidently a mandarin of distinction. At first, it was expected they were going to surrender. A shower of arrows and some matchlock bullets soon convinced our men to the contrary. The old chief himself, advancing and brandishing his double-handed sword, seemed to court death. A musket bullet through the chest closed his career, immediately on which the party surrendered. It was now discovered that the chief above alluded to was Admiral Kwan, he who had two years before engaged H.M. ship Volage, at Cowloon Bay, and on a later occasion, with his fleet, attacked the Volage, Hyacinth, and Larne, off Lantao. He was buried with military honours, Sir Fleming firing from the Blenheim minute guns, corresponding ia number to the old man's probable age. Another mandarin of high rank was also killed in this fort.

About four p.m., the Nemesis steamer, with a party of marines, proceeded to occupy the fort on the western shore under the Tanan Hills. This fort had been previously silenced by the admirable firing of the Wellesley and Druid, but the enemy still retained a position in an entrenched camp on the face of the hill, from which they occasionally fired upon the shipping. The force landed, and soon dispersed the Chinese, and set fire to their encampment. It burned in a circle of nearly two miles; the fire continued long after dark, casting a bright light over the waters of the Bogue, forming, as it were, a vast illumination in commemoration of our triumph, and a grand closing spectacle to this eventful day's work. The blaze must have been seen for miles around, and told the sad tale to the Chinese of the fall of the Bocca Tigris, the Gibraltar of the East.

CHAPTER XII

Advance upon Canton—Arrival of Sir Hugh Gough, and the Chusan force—Release of the Ningpo prisoners—Armistice and arrangements for trade agreed on.

Notwithstanding the enormous expenditure of powder and shot by the two contending parties during the engagement just detailed, still, surprising to say, on the side of the British, not one man was killed, and a few only were slightly wounded. The casualties on the part of the enemy must have exceeded 600. About 500 pieces of cannon were taken. Among these were four large brass 72 pounders, of Spanish manufacture, which were put on board the Blenheim. There were also several English and Portuguese guns, all of which were spiked, and rendered unserviceable. As a proof of the ingenuity of the Chinese, it may here be mentioned, that some guns which had been spiked and deprived of their trunnions at Cheumpee, were here recognised, mounted on carriages, having had a vent-hole boared on the opposite side, and a strong iron hoop, with trunnions attached, placed on the centre of the piece. The spars, rigging, and hulls of our shipping had been considerably cut up, more especially that of the two line-of-battle ships engaged at Anunghoi.

The day after the destruction of the Bogue forts, a garrison of 200 men of the 37th regiment having been left on North Wang-Tong, the plenipotentiary and commodore proceeded towards Canton, with the steamers and ships of light draught. The fort on Tiger Island, about two miles above the Bogue, was found deserted. At the first bar, however, which is situated about half way between Whampoo and the Bocca Tigris, was a Chinese force of upwards of 2,000 elite, strongly entrenched on the left bank of the river, and defended by upwards of 100 pieces of artillery; and the late British ship Cambridge, of 1400 tons burden, recently purchased by the Chinese, was moored close to a raft which stretched across the river to the west of the encampment. The advance squadron, consisting of the Calliope, Herald, Alligator, Sulphur, Modeste, and steamers Nemesis and Madagascar, opened their fire upon the enemy at this position on the afternoon of the 27th. Here the Chinese fought manfully; nor was it until after a hard struggle of a couple of hours' duration that they yielded. This force had but recently arrived from the district of Hoonan, and consisted of tried old soldiers and "water braves," (marines,) who had been specially selected for the purpose of expelling the English, having repeatedly, on former occasions, signalized themselves by acts of bravery. Upwards of 200 dead bodies were here found, among whom was the chief officer in command, and several others of inferior ranks. The wounded had been carried away by their comrades. On our side, there was one man killed, and several severely wounded. The shipping, also, sustained considerable damage, and the Nemesis received a shot in her steam condenser. The ship Cambridge was blown up, the encampment and ammunition destroyed, and the guns rendered unserviceable.

On the 2nd of March, Sir Hugh Gough arrived in H.M. brig Cruizer, and assumed the command of the land forces.

A masked battery on the island of Whampoo had, on the morning of this day, fired upon a division of boats engaged in towing the Sulphur, surveying ship. The tow-line was immediately cut, the boats proceeded on shore, their crews advanced, and gallantly carried the position, killing twenty men, and destroying twenty-three guns. On the following day the kwanchowfoo, or lord mayor of Canton, had an interview with Captain Elliot, the result of which was a truce.

During this week the Chusan portion of the force arrived, and the island which had become the grave of so many British troops was again in undisputed possession of the Chinese. The Columbine had gone up in fourteen days, arriving a few hours after the overland dispatch. Such was the belief of Captain Elliot in the good faith of the Chinese respecting the treaty of Cheumpee, that the regiment of Bengal Volunteers had been ordered to proceed direct to Calcutta, thus depriving the force of the services of upwards of 500 effective soldiers. One of the articles stipulated in the treaty was the return of prisoners; and, much to the gratification of all, they had been released, and had come down with the fleet. The suspicious Chinese would not, however, give them up until the whole force had left Chusan, and were under weigh.

On the 6th of March, the truce expired, and from this date Captain Elliot's acts became daily more clouded and veiled in obscurity. In private conversation he changed his opinion every few minutes; and as for his public acts, his proclamations will at once shew the vacillating nature of his temperament. His sole object seems to have been to re-establish trade; whether on terms honourable or otherwise to Great Britain, it did not appear to matter much to him. On the same day that the truce expired, he intimated to H.M.'s subjects that the works in immediate advance of Howqua's Fort were occupied, and he issued a proclamation to the inhabitants of Canton,

Dutch Folly Fort c1832. Watercolour by George Chinnery (1774-1852)

stating, to allay their fears, that "their city was spared because the gracious Sovereign of Great Britain had commanded the high English officers to remember, that the good and peaceable people must be tenderly considered." What was the inference drawn by the Chinese on perusing this document? Simply, that we were afraid to take possession of the city; and what certainly gave this construction of our acts some appearance of truth, was, the arrival of Aug-fang, a generalissimo, in the neighbourhood of Canton, with 30,000 men.

Subsequent to the above proclamation, Captain Elliot issued several circulars, in one of which he states that the forts in the Macao passage, near Canton, which are strengthened by flanking field-works, were carried on the 13th. On the same day the Nemesis, with a division of boats, proceeded from Macao towards Canton by the inner passage. In her progress she destroyed seven small works or batteries, nine sail of men-of-war junks, and 105 pieces of cannon. This extraordinary little vessel, through the coolness of her intrepid commodore, "was moved onwards for some succeeding miles in her own depth of water, and with the breadth of the river so near her own length, that it became necessary, on several occasions, to force her bow into the bank and bushes on one side to clear the heel of the dry ground on the opposite." The whole of the river, and its branches, as high up as Howqua's Fort, was now in our possession. A flag of truce proceeding to Canton on the 16th, with a chop for the authorities there, was fired at. H.M.'s forces, therefore, moved up, and on the 18th all the works in immediate advance and before the city, including the Dutch Folly, were taken, and the whole of the enemy's flotilla sunk or destroyed. Canton was now under the guns of the squadron; all approaches to the city were completely commanded, and Captain Elliot held possession of the British factory. Here he was soon waited upon by a deputation of the Hong merchants, who besought him to suspend hostilities for the present; they guaranteed that trade should be immediately opened, and benefits innumerable be showered down upon the English. The plenipotentiary's compassion was moved, and hostilities ceased. A few days hereafter, he issued a circular, intimating that "a suspension of hostilities was agreed upon between the imperial commissioner Yang and himself, and that the trade of the port of Canton was opened to British and other foreign merchants, who may see fit to proceed thither for the purpose of lawful commerce."

It is worthy of remark that, during the successive engagements above enumerated, in which the Chinese lost about 2000 men, reckoning from the 7th of January, there was killed on the side of the English, by the Chinese shot, only one man.

With the exception of a few of the smaller ships of war, and a party of marines left to protect the factory, and a wing of the 37th regiment to garrison the island of North Wang-Tong, (the other forts in this position having been destroyed,) the remainder of the force returned to Hong-Kong.

In Wang-Tong an hospital for the wounded Chinese had been established; here military-surgery, in all its varieties, was to be seen, and capital operations were of daily occurrence. These the Chinese at all times submitted to with stoical indifference. At first they supposed the operations were performed for the purpose of torture, and on the wounded limb being removed, the sound one was held forth to be operated on also; nor could they, to the last, understand or appreciate the purpose of our daily visits to dress the wounds. On one occasion, after removing an arm, several of the instruments used during the operation were missed; these, after minute search, and some trouble, were found, some in the possession of the man operated on, and others on a prisoner attending upon the sick.

The force now present consisted of the skeletons of three Queen's corps, and the 37th regiment, M.N.I.; detachment of Madras Artillery; and Sappers and Miners, and Bengal Volunteers—amounting, in all, to about 2300 men;—a body of marines, also about 500 strong. The naval force consisted of three line-of-battle ships; five ships carrying 28 guns; and ten, 18 guns, and downwards; one bomb-ship, and five armed steamers.

CHAPTER XIII

Commodore proceeds to Calcutta—Keshen recalled—Three new commissioners arrive at Canton—They act with duplicity.

The movements of the naval and military commanders had been hitherto so curtailed and thwarted by Captain Elliot, the British flag so repeatedly slighted and insulted, and operations checked just at the time when they were about to become creditable to Great Britain, and to produce a permanent and salutary effect on the Chinese government, that the commodore resolved at once to proceed to Calcutta for the purpose of representing to the governor-general the peculiar position in which affairs were placed, and at the same time to solicit reinforcements previous to a renewal of hostilities. For this purpose he departed in the Queen steamer on the 31st of March. The steamers Enterprise and Madagascar, standing in need of repair, returned also to Calcutta about this time. On the departure of the commodore, the direction of the naval portion of the expedition devolved on Sir H. Le Fleming Senhouse.

The Emperor's entire disapproval of the treaty entered into by Keshen at Cheumpee had been for some time known, and that officer was threatened with disgrace. As a proof that this treaty never was granted with sincerity, the imperial commissioner, in his report to the Emperor on the subject, makes use of the following words:— "As a temporary expediency, I pretended to grant what was requested."

On the 3rd of April, the reply to Keshen's report concerning the loss of the Bogue forts was received. That minister was now ordered to be degraded, to be deprived of rank and command, and directed to be sent in chains to the capital, there to be delivered over to the board of punishment. Among the several articles of accusation against him, the most important are—his having held interviews and exchanged documents with Captain Elliot on equal terms—his having entertained Captain Elliot at the second bar—and his having fixed his seal to a document ceding the island of Hong-Kong. The emperor evinced the greatest indignation at the rebellious conduct of the barbarians, and swore "that both powers shall not stand—that one or other must perish." Yihshan, the emperor's nephew, was invested with the office of "general pacificator of the rebellions," and Lungaran and Yangfang with that of assistant ministers. Extensive levies of troops were made from all the surrounding districts, and directed to proceed to Canton, "so that, with great celerity, the work of attack and extermination may be carried out." Yangfang reached Canton on the same day the British troops took possession of the factories there. He had left his army encamped some miles from the city, but instead of proceeding at once to the work of extermination, he proclaimed, on the walls of the city, the re-opening of trade, with protection for the lives and property of all foreigners, as has already been shewn in the extract of Captain Elliot's circular, at the conclusion of the last chapter.

How surprising it is that H.M. Plenipotentiary, who has, during a residence of six years, been brought so repeatedly into communication with the Chinese, both officially and otherwise, should yet remain in ignorance of their true character, and continue to place confidence in their faithless promises. True, in this instance, Yihshan, on his arrival at Canton, appeared to give a tacit consent to his joint-minister's terms of truce—and why? Because the Canton treasury had been emptied in preparing and perfecting the defences on the course of the river, and paying the workmen and garrison. Moreover, the large army assembling in the neighbourhood of the city required that no time should be lost in replenishing it. They naturally concluded that the foreign merchants, so long shut out from trade, would avail themselves of the first opportunity of its being opened, and eagerly come forward. Nor were they disappointed in their expectations. Trade was resumed, and continued to be actively carried on, although prices had been considerably raised, and in very few instances did the Chinese dealers receive manufactures or other imports in barter for teas, &c, insisting, for the most part, in being paid in hard cash. Thus their sanguine hopes were being realized, and their treasury being filled.

The courtesy and attention of the newly-arrived ministers to our plenipotentiary became quite marked; messages daily passed between them; and from time to time Captain Elliot issued circulars, stating that satisfactory declarations continued to be received from the commissioners "declaratory of their good and faithful intentions." A proclamation was also issued by him "to the quiet and industrious people of Canton," directing them not to be alarmed at the constant rumours of warlike preparations against their town and province upon the side of the British forces; and he clearly declares to all the people that these reports are "false and mischievous;" then follows a long eulogium on Yang and the other high functionaries of the province. How little did he suspect that, during the time professions of friendship were thus lavishly expended, they were all false and treacherous, and that preparations on an extensive scale were concerting at once to attack the British forces at all points, and murder or make prisoners the foreign merchants in Canton. To prove to the Chinese the confidence H.M. Plenipotentiary felt in their pacific intentions, the guard of marines, hitherto stationed at the British Hong, had been withdrawn, and the ships of war removed from opposite the city.

About this time, two officers of the Blenheim, in company with another Englishman, were proceeding from Macao to their ships, anchored in these roads. They never reached the vessel; and the body of one of them, washed up on shore some days afterwards, bore marks of violence, which tells but too truly the fate of his companions. Captain Stead, the master of a transport ship, which had arrived at Chusan a few days after the island was evacuated by our troops, and who had gone on shore to make some inquiry on the subject, was immediately attacked, and carried off wounded to China, where, it was afterwards discovered, he was tortured to death.

These, and many other like incidents, will at once point out to the reader the feeling the Chinese entertain against the English.

Meantime trade continued, or rather was tolerated, at Canton. The dealers, becoming distrustful in consequence of the large bodies of troops daily pouring into the city, and other hostile preparations in progress, became more chary, and dreaded introducing goods to any amount; moreover, the system of squeezing was at this time carried on to such an extent, that the merchant derived little or no profit upon his property; he had not, therefore, much encouragement in disposing of it.

Edicts against the English continued to arrive from Pekin: "Exterminate the rebels at all points," was the Emperor's reiterated orders. At this period it was said that he would listen to no proposals for an amicable arrangement, and he threatened with death those who talked of making peace with the English. Other documents, purporting also to be imperial edicts, were about this time freely circulated at Canton and Macao, recommending peace and quietness, &c.

These were afterwards discovered to be pseudo documents, apparently got up by the Canton authorities, in order to blind the plenipotentiary and put him off his guard. The continued warlike preparations of the Chinese, the enormous number of soldiers collected in and about the city, calculated at upwards of 50,000 men, and the departure of the Hong and other wealthy merchants, with their families and valuables, induced Captain Elliot, as a measure of precaution, to move the ships of war nearer to Canton, and in front of the factories.

On the 20th of May, Yihshan and his colleagues issued a proclamation, which was carefully put into the hands of the foreign merchants, and pasted upon the factories and in the streets, telling the "people of Canton, and all foreign merchants who are respectfully obedient, not to tremble with alarm and be frightened out of their wits at the military hosts that are gathering around, there being no probability of hostilities." On the succeeding day, Captain Elliot issued, at Canton, the following circular:—

> "In the present situation of circumstances, her Britannic Majesty's Plenipotentiary feels it his duty to recommend that the British, and other foreigners now remaining in the factories, should retire from Canton before sunset."

Such was the critical appearance affairs at Canton now suddenly presented.

CHAPTER XIV

Hostilities are resumed—Third advance up the river—Battle of the heights above Canton.

When, on the 18th of March, it was stipulated that Canton should be spared without ransom on condition that no military preparations were to be made by the Chinese, and that the trade of the port was to continue as usual, it was well known that the objects of the expedition would now be directed northward. The Chinese flattered themselves that, on the departure of the main body of the British force, there would then be little difficulty in seizing and destroying that portion which still remained in these waters. While promising faithfully to abstain from hostilities, the authorities were employed in erecting new batteries, and re-arming old ones; in assembling a large army, and in collecting immense flotillas of war-junks and fire-rafts. As the advantages were to be great, no expense was spared; complete success in their deceitful purposes was to be the sure and triumphant result. The better to carry out their plans, as the reader has already seen, both the foreign community at Canton, and the native inhabitants, were assured, by repeated proclamations from the imperial commissioner, that their property and persons were in perfect safety, while at the very time these proclamations were published, soldiers and arms were being privately brought into the warehouses of the Hong merchants, not far from the factories where foreigners were weighing teas. These solemn assurances were repeated until the very day on which their combined attacks were to be made. These, however, appeared to have been accelerated by the discovery that their base designs had been detected.

By sunset on the day on which Captain Elliot issued his last circular, no British merchants remained in the factories. The bustle of the day closing as evening approached, no signs of immediate hostilities were visible. The second watch of the night had not, however, passed, ere Yihshan's operations commenced. With the ebb-tide, boats filled with combustibles of every description, chained together, two and two, and well manned with "water braves," bore down in disguise upon the English shipping. When within a few yards of the advanced ship, the Modeste, from the forecastle of which the sentry hailed, these boats were simultaneously set on fire, and became almost instantly wrapped in flames; their crews were so near the shipping when they took to their small boats, that they were shot down in numbers by our musketry. The fire-rafts were promptly, but with considerable risk, warded off, and the ships sustained no material damage thereby.

In concert with the movements of the fire-vessels, guns from masked batteries, which were, till now, never known to exist, opened their fire upon the shipping; gun-boats, or floating batteries, approaching close to the ships, kept up a perpetual fire during the whole of the night. At Howqua's fort (three miles), at Whampoa (twelve miles), and at North Wang-Tong, thirty miles below the city, similar efforts were made to destroy the shipping at those stations, but in every instance without effect. At daylight the following morning, the ships moved into positions which commanded the batteries that had proved so troublesome during the night; and the Nemesis, hastily getting up her steam, dashed into the midst of the flotilla of boats, numbering more than 200, one-half of which, in the course of three hours, she destroyed, the remainder having been either abandoned, run on shore, or driven into some of the shallow creeks. The Goddess of Revenge, though in the midst of repeated explosions while performing this gallant feat, from being entirely constructed of iron, returned unscathed, decked with Chinese flags and banners, and her crew habited in mandarins' coats and caps. Her rockets and the Chinese fire-rafts (which latter she, with the assistance of her grappling-irons, towed to the mouths of some of the numerous creeks and canals in this direction, from whence they floated up with the tide) had already set fire to the suburbs in many places.

In the course of the morning, a body of soldiers, joined by the mob, entered the factories, the whole of which were ransacked, and everything in them destroyed or carried away. Some American merchants who still remained in the factory were wounded, and sent into the city in chains, where they were insulted and imprisoned, until it was satisfactorily ascertained that they were not British subjects.

While this part of the scene was being enacted opposite the factories, the British force, which on the 18th of May got under weigh at Hong-Kong, was hourly approaching the city. H.M. Plenipotentiary had intimated to the naval and military commanders, some days previously, that the contemplated expedition to Amoy must of necessity, for the present, be postponed, as he suspected that the local government were meditating evil, and a speedy rupture was to all appearance inevitable. Operations were, therefore, planned accordingly; and it was decided that an advance upon Canton should he forthwith made, and that, if possible, this should be effected before the enemy had matured their plans. In this, however, the Chinese had anticipated vis; nor was it until the morning of the 24th that our right column, consisting of the 26th Cameronians, and a portion of the Madras Artillery and Sappers,

British sailors towing warships toward Canton on 24th May 1841. Watercolour by Dr Edward Cree, a Royal Navy surgeon present during the First Opium War.

took possession of the factories, for the purpose of drawing the attention of the enemy to that quarter, and at the same time to co-operate with the naval force appointed to attack the river defences. The Chinese, who had kept up a fire upon the ships at intervals since the morning of the 22nd, now again, on the appearance of our troops, recommenced, with greater avidity, to fire from the tops of houses and from numerous new works lately thrown up opposite to the factories and in front of the city. These in the course of the day had been silenced; in one of the batteries, four guns, 10 1/2-inch bore, and weighing about 50 cwt, were taken and destroyed.

Her Majesty's ship Blenheim took up her position within six miles of Canton, in the Macao passage, on the 21st, but in consequence of light and variable winds, the whole of the force was not assembled till the 23rd. Nothing of importance occurred during the passage up the river, save a ship occasionally running over a sunken junk, which, however, caused no further annoyance than the delay until a breach had been formed in the side of the rotten junk, or the flood-tide had floated the ship off.

It was an extraordinary sight to see the Blenheim in tow of a steamer proceeding leisurely up the back channel, a passage through which nothing but Chinese junks were previously known to pass, and which since this period has been denominated Blenheim Channel. In fact, the Chinese never would permit foreign ships to enter this passage, which, indeed, from its being at all times blocked up with fishing-stakes, offered but little temptation to its being preferred to the old and better known one by Whampoa. Through this latter, a line of battle-ship could not approach nearer the city than twelve miles,

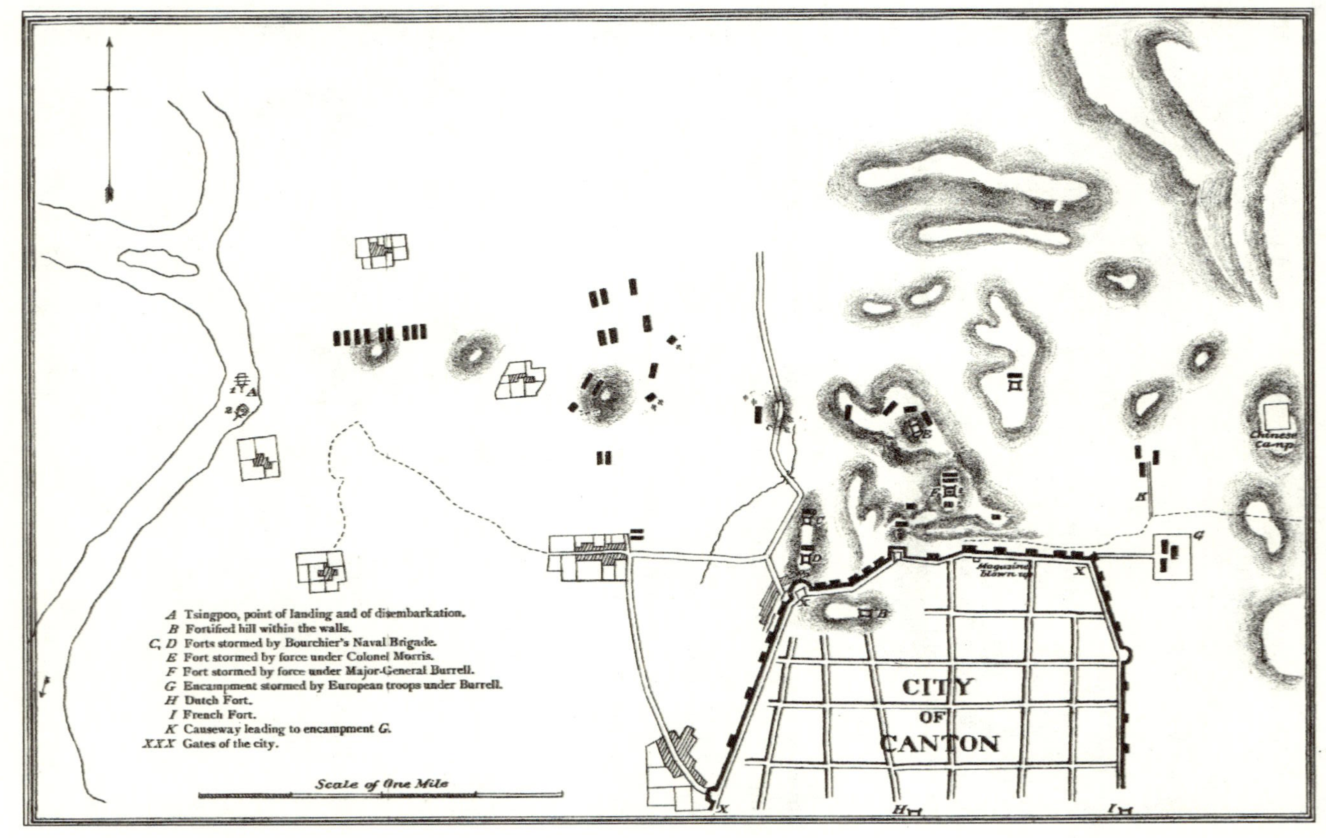

The assault on Canton, 25th May 1841.

whereas in the former, Captain Belcher, R. N., (whose zeal and ability in forwarding the interests of the public service are too well known to require comment here,) discovered, after careful surveys, that a seventy-four could proceed to, and float with ease, at low water, six miles distant from the city. This, of course, proved a most valuable discovery, affording as it did every facility in conveying our men, stores, and heavy ordnance, so much nearer the point of attack than would have been the case otherwise.

The principal point of debarkation selected by Sir Hugh Gough was at a village about five miles by the river line above the factories; but there were few sources from which information could be obtained as to the feasibility of effecting a landing at this point; the country to be passed over, the amount of the enemy's force, or any other difficulties which might present themselves, were also totally unknown. A spirited reconnoitre, made by Captain Belcher, of H.M.S. Sulphur, established the practicability of accomplishing the former.

At noon of the 24th, a royal salute was fired from all the ships, in commemoration of the birth of our sovereign, soon after which the troops were placed in various craft, procured by the great exertions of the Royal Navy. Each of these boats were capable of accommodating from 50 to 200 men, and were admirably adapted for protecting them from the sun. This fleet of boats, conveying upwards of 2700 men, besides quantities of ordnance and commissariat stores, was taken in tow by the Nemesis, and reached the village of Tsinghae, the point of debarkation, about seven o'clock, p.m., without one accident happening. Had the enemy been on the alert, they might here have committed dreadful havoc amongst us. The 49th regiment landed immediately. With this corps the general made a reconnoissance a short distance, and drove back some straggling parties of the enemy. After the picquets had been placed, the 49th returned to the village to cover the landing of the guns, which was effected during the night by the arduous exertions of the artillery. A false alarm roused us about midnight; it was caused by the fall of a pile of arms in one of the boats.

At daylight, on the morning of the 25th, the 37th regiment, M.N.I., and detachment of Bengal Volunteers, proceeded as an escort with the general in a westerly direction to a rising ground about a mile from the landing-place. From hence a good view was obtained of the line of country we were to pass over. The enemy's picquets were seen at their posts for miles on every side. They were all armed with a matchlock, spear, and shield. They beckoned us to advance, but as we neared them they retired. A portion of the escort ordered forward to reconnoitre was attacked by a large party of soldiers, who advanced from the suburbs of the city. These were permitted to come within good musket range, when a volley from our party soon checked their impetuosity; they speedily retired to a more respectful distance, and again faced round, but satisfied themselves this time with brandishing their swords and spears, and going through every gesture of defiance. They appeared to have the will to exterminate our small party, but they wanted the courage to do so.

A good view of the position we were about to attack was obtained from the rising ground we now occupied. The heights to the north of Canton, covered by four strong forts, and the city walls, which run over the southern extremity of these heights, appeared to be about four miles distant; the intervening ground undulated much, and was intersected by flats, under wet paddy cultivation, and extensive burying-grounds.

The general having ascertained all he wished, his escort was directed to join the main body. By this time the left column had debarked. This column (the right having been stationed at the factories) was divided into four brigades; the first—reserve or right brigade, under Major General Bunnell—consisted of the Royal Marines, and 18th Royal Irish, under Captain Ellis and Colonel Adams; the second brigade was divided into two battalions, one commanded by Captain Maitland, of the Wellesley, and the other by Captain Barlow, of the Nimrod; the third brigade, under Captain Knowles, R.A., was formed by the Royal and Madras Artillery, the former commanded by the Hon. Lieutenant Spencer, and the latter by Captain Anstruther; and the fourth, or left brigade, consisted of H.M.'s 49th, and 37th M.N.I. and Bengal Volunteers, which corps were commanded respectively by Major Stevens and Captains Duff and Mee. These now received orders to advance. We had not gone many yards when the headless trunk of a camp-follower was discovered; his body was untouched, but his murderer had, no doubt, carried away the head of his victim, to enable him to claim the promised reward.

Owing to the rugged nature of the ground, there was considerable difficulty and delay in bringing up the rocket-battery and artillery; and long before they could be brought to bear upon the forts, the enemy had opened a brisk fire upon our advance. About nine a.m. our guns were in position, and a well-directed fire was opened on the two western forts, which had much annoyed us all the morning by a heavy fire.

Accounts were about this time received of an attack that was made on H.M.S. Sulphur and Nemesis steamer, and an attempt to destroy the boats at the village of Tsinghae. This was bravely repulsed by the crews of these ships and a detachment of the 37th regiment left at the village. It was here that Captain Hall, of the Nemesis, finding that a rocket which he was about to fire became obstructed in the tube, thrust his hand in and pulled it out. In doing this his hand was much injured, but he was the means of saving the lives of many by his boldness.

When the firing from our guns had lasted for about a couple of hours, every shot having taken effect, the enemy were seen to collect in great numbers at the entrance into their forts, evidently deliberating on the safest direction for flight.

The fourth brigade was, about 11 a.m., directed to carry a hill to the left of the nearest eastern fort, and the first brigade one immediately in front of it. Simultaneous with these attacks, the brigade of seamen was directed to carry the two western forts; the advance of both to be covered by the concentrated fire of the whole of the guns and rockets. While these movements were in progress, large bodies of the enemy debouched from the surrounding suburbs, threatening our right and rear, and it ultimately became necessary to detach the marines to cover these and support the seamen's brigade.

On the advance being sounded, all parties appeared to vie with one another to reach their respective posts. In the greater part of the advance, the troops had either to wade through recently ploughed fields covered with water, or proceed by single files over a narrow path between two paddy fields. The Chinese were strongly drawn up on the face of the hill, from which missiles of every description were hurled down upon us. From the walls of the city, and from the forts also, volley after volley of round shot and grape were showered forth. Nothing, however, could for a moment withstand the determination of our men. The ascent to the forts was in some places steep and rugged, but they soon gained the summit, by which time the enemy had evacuated them, and were running down the opposite side of the hill, letting off myriads of barbed rockets, which, however, did no further injury than most effectually to prevent the course of their flight being seen. In one of the forts to the west, however, the sailors had hard work of it, the enemy not leaving their stronghold till by means of escalading ladders the British tars had effected an entrance, and then, hand to hand, cut them to pieces.

The result of these combined attacks was, that the whole line of forts was, in the course of one short hour after the order to advance was given, in the possession of the British, whose standard proudly waved over their highest battlements, and whose troops looked down on the immense city of Canton, from the walls of which they were barely one hundred paces distant.

To the north-east of the city, and removed about half a mile from the two eastern forts, was a strongly entrenched camp of considerable extent; here the enemy appeared to have rallied, and soon became reinforced by bodies of troops from the city. From this encampment parties frequently sallied forth to attack our men, and although as frequently driven off, it exposed us to an annoying fire from the city walls. In the course of the afternoon, they were evidently joined by some officers of distinction from the city, who, riding at the head of their men, selected a large detachment from the encampment, and proceeded to take possession of a village close to our left. These the 49th soon dislodged. This corps was afterwards reinforced by the 18th, and a company of marines, who also received orders to take and destroy the encampment. Finding that the 49th had already effected their purpose, the 18th, headed by Colonel Adams, proceeded direct to the camp, which, independent of its own defences, was also well covered by the guns from the city wall. Well and gallantly did the Royal Irish do their duty that day; regardless both of the shot from the walls, and the showers of grape from the entrenched camp, they advanced all the way at the double, and in a short time everything was in their possession. The enemy were defeated at all points, and fled across the country; the encampment was burnt, and the magazines blown up; after which the force returned to the heights. In this advance there were four officers and several men severely wounded.

Our total casualties on this day amounted to about seventy. On the side of the enemy the actual loss was never ascertained, but it must have been very great. As on all like occasions, many hair-breadth escapes occurred, but none had so narrow a one as the general, having been at one time completely covered with dust and mud, from a shot that struck the ground close to his feet. One chain-shot fired from the city, at the western or Jack's fort, did fearful execution, having shattered the legs of Lieutenants Fox and Kendall of the Nimrod, besides wounding two seamen.

The general decided upon taking by assault, and before the panic ceased, a strong and extensive fortified height within the city wall; but from the great difficulty in transporting ordnance and ammunition, a few only of the lighter field-pieces had arrived, and the day being so far spent, it was found necessary to postpone further operations till the following day. The few troops, therefore, off duty, bivouacked as best they could during this night.

CHAPTER XV

The seven days bivouac on the heights.

The morning of the 26th had yet hardly dawned when our chief was on the move. All was now still and quiet. The enemy who, till midnight had kept up an uninterrupted fire upon our positions, disconcerted and fatigued at their vain efforts to dislodge us, appeared to have retired to repose. From the ramparts, which poured forth such volleys yesterday, not a soul was to be seen. From the heights we could perceive the inhabitants deserting the city in great numbers. Crowds, bearing their property on their shoulders, thronged the streets, and were hurrying with all speed towards the gates furthest removed from the forts in our possession; from whence, if the eye followed them, myriads of living masses were seen to pour out and disperse throughout the surrounding country. From the city, a constant and unceasing hum went forth. Horses, bullocks, chairs, and every available means of carriage, appeared eagerly sought after; women and children were heedlessly trampled down by the unthinking multitude, who, urged on by the great ruling passion in the human breast, thought of nought else than self-preservation.

The city of Canton—that proud city, which had so often defied us and insulted our flag, whose population alone was nearly one million, and whose boasted army numbered 50,000, was now humbled before one barely a twentieth part of its strength. The flag of truce, that badge of peace, respected all over the world, but by the Chinese so frequently treated with contempt, was now seen to wave from the most conspicuous parts of the ramparts; at the same time, a blue-buttoned mandarin, advancing to one of the embrasures nearest to our position, and waving a white flag, seemed to implore an interview. On this being granted, the Chinese officer stated that he had come to offer certain terms to spare the city. It was explained to him, that the general commanding the British could treat only with the general commanding the Chinese troops, and that if the latter wished for an interview with our general, it could not take place from the city walls, but that tents should be pitched halfway between our position and the city, and that then our general and commodore should meet only those of like rank from the enemy. This arrangement was at once agreed to; a cessation of hostilities took place for two hours, on the expiration of which the white flag was to be struck, unless the interview proved satisfactory. Hour after hour passed,

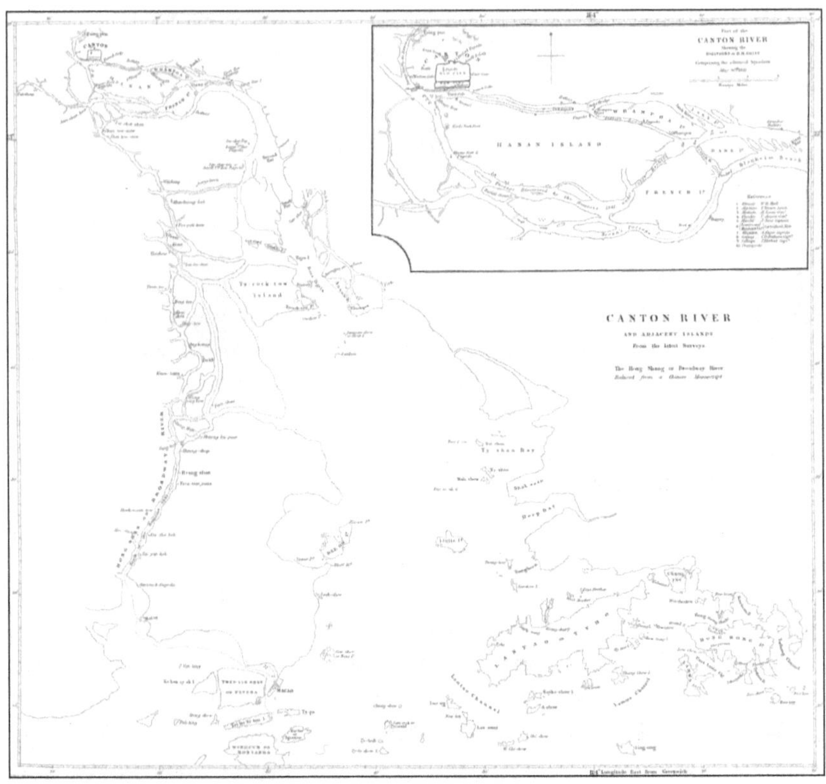

Map of the Canton River and adjacent islands. A larger image of the inset map is opposite.

but no deputation from the city made its appearance; at the appointed time, therefore, the white flag was hauled down. The Chinese, however, did not follow our example. This enabled the engineers and artillery to bring their guns into position, and to discover those places where the defences were weakest, without being exposed to the enemy's fire.

The rain, during the whole afternoon, fell in torrents, and not only prevented the resumption of hostilities, but thoroughly soaked the ground, which formed alike the bed for the general and common soldier. Yet no complaint was heard; and the troops, in their wet clothes, with little food and less drink, went to the respective duties allotted to them for the night without a murmur.

During this night the artillery and sappers were hard at work. Guns, mortars, rocket-tubes, with their formidable appendages, were all placed in position. Orders had been given for the batteries to open at seven a.m., and for the assault an hour afterwards. The assault was directed to be made in four columns, each of which was to be covered by a sharp fire of musketry to prevent the enemy working their guns.

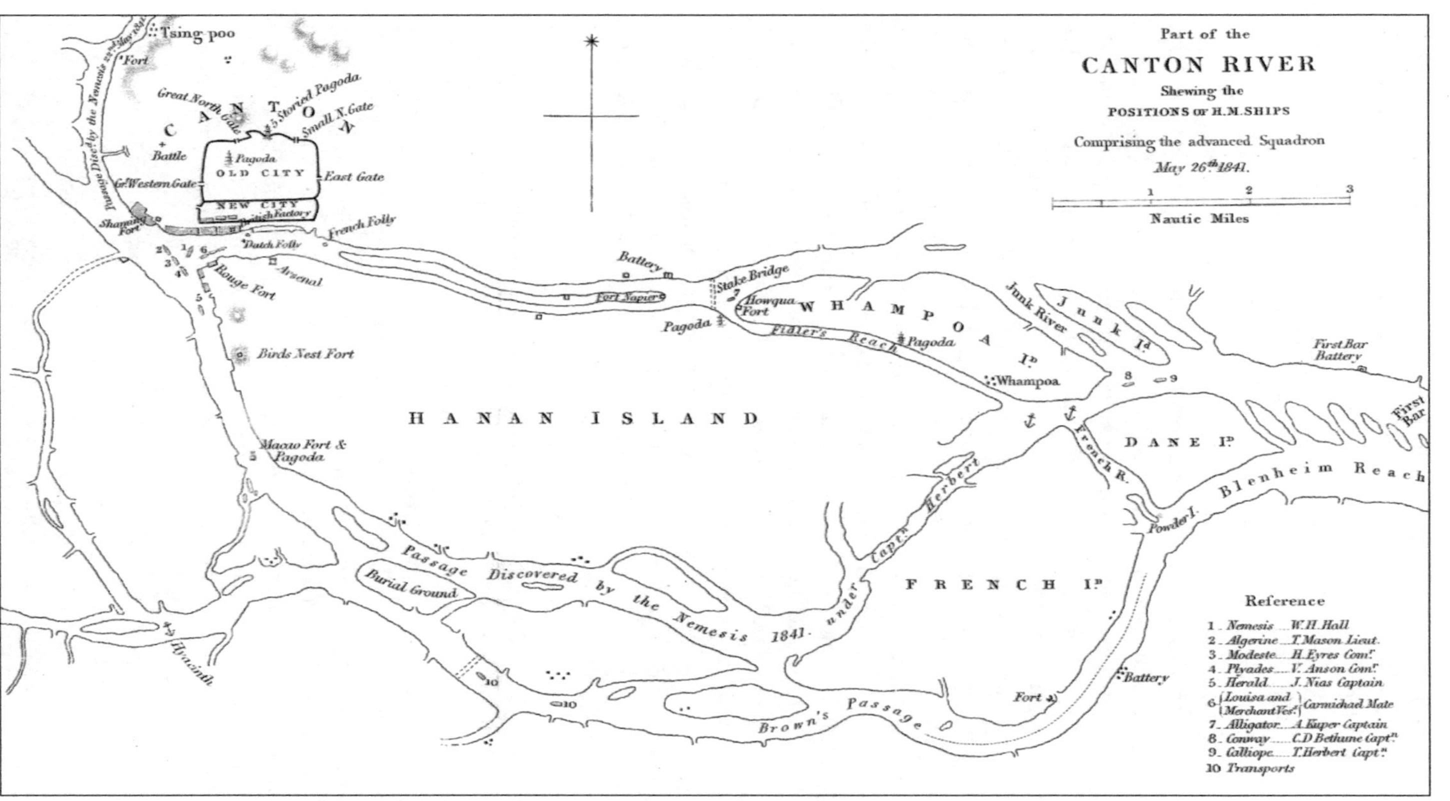

Part of the Canton River showing the position of the British ships comprising the advanced squadron on 26 May 1841.

An entrance into the city was to be effected either by escalade, or, if practicable, by blowing the gates open with powder-bags. Each column, on effecting a lodgment, was directed to communicate with, and support that on its inner flank, and when united, to take possession of the fortified hill within the walls. The walls of the city were in some places thirty feet high, but it was expected that the concentrated fire from our artillery would form a breach, or reduce the height considerably, so as to facilitate the escalading.

Long before daylight on the 27th, our troops were in their ranks; not a man was absent. Their several duties had been assigned them. The guns were loaded and primed, the port-fires were lit, and the general and commodore were taking a last look previous to giving the signal to commence firing. The enemy, too, now seemed on the alert. They evidently expected an attack, and numbers were seen running backwards and forwards on the ramparts, and taking up their positions at their guns. A few minutes more and the work would have begun; but suddenly, an unlooked-for obstacle occurred; a messenger arrived with dispatches from the plenipotentiary to the general and commodore. How anxiously did we all watch the features of those brave and determined men as they each perused their documents. Sir Fleming was the first to speak, and those nearest heard him say, "I protest against the terms of the treaty in toto." The news soon spread; Captain Elliot, as usual, acting on the spur of the moment, had, without even paying those who were so far superior to him in every way, even the compliment of asking their advice, concluded a peace with the Chinese, and ransomed the city of Canton for six millions of dollars. I leave the reader to judge of the disappointment felt by the troops on hearing this intelligence.

The peace was concluded chiefly on the following terms:—1st, That the three imperial commissioners and all the troops not of the province of Canton, proceed sixty miles from the city within six days; 2nd, That six millions of dollars be paid within one week from this date as ransom for the city, for the use of the crown of England; and, 3rd, That until those terms are fulfilled, the British troops remain in their actual positions. Here again the advantages gained by British valour were recklessly thrown away. "Whatever might be my sentiments," remarks Sir H. Gough in his despatch to Lord Auckland, "my duty was to acquiesce; of the policy of the measures, I do not consider myself a competent judge." And Sir Fleming Senhouse, on the same subject, observes—"The terms were in opposition to the opinions of the Major-General (Sir Hugh Gough) and myself, as they left the troops in a precarious position for some days, when the conduct of the Chinese hitherto was considered, with whom delay has always been used to strengthen their defences, the result of which has always been a breach of faith. It gave another fair opening for Chinese treachery to work, and it took away the apparent symbol of capture, which would have been prevented by seeing the British banners floating within the city walls, and those walls lying crumbling before it. The fortified heights in the city once gained, the Chinese troops might have marched out and laid down their arms, and not a British soldier had any occasion to enter the populous part of the town." Doubts have frequently been expressed as to H.M. Plenipotentiary's power to frame the 3rd article of this treaty, more especially without taking the advice of the general commanding as to the practicability of carrying it into execution. Here was our small army to remain for a certain number of days, barely 100 paces removed from the city walls, surrounded by many thousands of an enemy of whose faith in adhering to their treaties we have already had several proofs, and who, if they felt inclined, could at once cut off all communication with our shipping; and in this peculiar position we were directed to remain by a post captain in the Royal Navy.

As the force was to remain in *status quo* until the money was paid, the most comfortable quarters that could be procured were given to the troops. The suburbs of the city, and the villages around, were completely deserted, except by a few old and diseased of both sexes, who were unable to move.

On the 28th, we entered our new quarters. Hitherto, whether from a burning hot sun, or from torrents of rain, the broad canopy of heaven was our only covering, and the grass our only bed; but up to this date, with the exception of the wounded, there was not a sick man in the force. When we left our ships, it was never contemplated that our residence on the heights would have exceeded a day or two at most, consequently the force had come very ill prepared for so long a sojourn. We were solely dependent on our transports for supplies, but these were removed about ten miles from our present position; besides, in transporting them, there was considerable risk and danger of being attacked by armed parties, who scoured the country for plunder. Fortunately, however, a quantity of rice was found in the enemy's forts, and our foraging parties occasionally returned well laden. Generally the most successful in those expeditions were the Madras Artillery and Sappers and Miners, the profusion and liberality of whose mess was, at all times, certain to attract numerous guests. The great advantage of our Madras servants, who do "yeverry thing for master," over those of Bengal, whose caste does not permit them to do more than one description of work, was here very evident.

It was most gratifying to see the unanimity and good feeling that existed between the European and native soldiers, when employed together. All caste seemed for the time thrown aside. On our advance up the fortified heights, on the 25th, some convalescents of the 49th regiment, who fell in the rear, were glad to avail themselves of the support willingly offered to them by some men of the 37th regiment, and on gaining the summit, mutual interchanges of the contents of their havresacks were made.

Occasionally laughable incidents happened to amuse and enliven us; on one occasion a foraging party which had travelled far, returned laden with every variety of stock. Fatigued by their day's exertion, they proceeded to a tank in the neighbourhood to wash and refresh themselves; some of them remarked, on getting into the water, that there were nettles close to the side, at the same time recommending their comrades to get in a little higher up. The nettles were found here also; and after paddling about in the water for some time, they returned on shore, when, to their astonishment, instead of having been stung by nettles, their bodies were covered with leeches. Two jolly tars were one day seen approaching the lines, driving before them a couple of pigs; as they neared the lines, the animals came to a sudden halt, nor would threats or blows have any effect upon them. If they moved at all, it was in the wrong direction. The sailors, after persevering for some time, could stand this no longer; each, therefore, seizing his pig, and, to use their own words, "with the cutlass cut their gullets," shouldered them, and proceeded quietly home. On the evening of the 28th, a party, which had been a few miles from camp, reported, on their return, that they had discovered, in a village, between sixty and seventy dead and dying Tartars. These evidently were carried there to give us a false idea of the number killed. The Chinese will brave any danger to carry off from the field a disabled or dead comrade. This, of itself, is a great redeeming trait in their character.

On the 29th, officers and men were to be seen in every direction walking through the deserted suburbs and villages round Canton. Over a large portion of the western suburbs are some extraordinary tombs and magnificent joss-houses, or places of worship; one very extensive line of building, close under the city walls, appears solely devoted to the reception of the dead. These are placed in vaults, in strong, substantial, japanned coffins, elevated on pillars, having painted screens in front, perfumed incense-sticks burning at the head and feet, and variegated lamps hung from the ceiling. These coffins are of enormous thickness and strength; they were, for the most part, placed two in one vault, and, with the exception of a close damp smell, there was no unpleasant sensation perceptible. Outside of these vaults evergreens and creepers were tastefully arranged, and over the doors of many, bee-hives were fixed. In some, the beautiful warbling of the lark and canary at once attracted attention. The poor little birds, neglected for so many days, now welcomed the sounds of approaching footsteps, little fancying that they, too, were to become lawful hat. The contents of a few of the coffins that were opened presented an appearance almost natural. The bodies were all embalmed. They were dressed in a long loose upper garment of silk or

Chinese soldiers armed with gingals, engraving c1843

crape, which crumbled into powder on being touched; tight breeches of the same material, and embroidered shoes. All those examined were males. In the right hand of each was a fan, and in the left a piece of paper, having Chinese characters written thereon. In the corners, and other empty spaces in the coffins, were small bags containing a strong and very peculiar smelling aromatic powder. To an antiquarian, there were many things in this village to excite interest.

The Tartar troops, 10,000 in number, this afternoon evacuated the city. They were permitted to carry away their arms and baggage; but no banner was to be displayed, nor music sounded. They passed out at the north-east gate of the city, and through the village occupied by the 37th regiment, M.N.I. Yang-fang, their general, a fine-looking old man, was carried in a chair at the head, and his officers rode on ponies by the side of the men. They presented by no means a very martial appearance, and our Sepoys were delighted at the opportunity of laughing at them. Since the arrival of our forces opposite to the wall of Canton, the Tartar and Chinese troops had been carrying on a civil war within the city, the loss on both sides being very great; moreover, the shipping and land force had so effectually blockaded and besieged the city, that few or no supplies could enter. It was even declared, by some very credible witnesses, that the Tartar troops ate the flesh of the Chinese that were slain. The authorities, in fact, were driven to that state, that they would have agreed to any terms we chose to dictate, and have granted a much larger ransom had it been demanded. How unfortunate that Captain Elliot's temperament should be so conciliating! As it is, however, both the navy and army will be well rewarded for the toils and troubles they have endured. This ransom money being quite unconnected with the original claims on the Chinese, it would be rather hard that those who succeeded in procuring it should not benefit therefrom. Besides, we know of no case in the annals of history wherein this practice was deviated from.

On the morning of the 30th, two-thirds of the ransom money was paid, and shipped on board the Modeste; another million was in course of payment, and as security was to be taken for the remainder, we expected to return to our ships the following day. Everything now looked pacific. There were certainly some rumours that reinforcements were expected for the protection of the city, and that this delay on the part of the authorities to pay up the balance of the money, was merely an excuse to gain time to enable those troops to arrive. But as the plenipotentiary gave no credence to these reports, of course no one else did.

We had not, however, yet finished that most agreeable of all medicines, in almost universal use among those whose fate it is to be resident for any period in a tropical climate,—namely, a cheroot after breakfast—when the bugle, sounding the alarm, was heard. The sound proceeded from the direction of the general's quarters. It was taken up on all sides. Major Beecher, the quarter-master-general, now made his appearance in the village occupied by the 37th regiment; to the officer commanding which corps, he said, "The enemy are advancing upon us, fall in your men, and proceed to support the Cameronians." The regiment was soon under arms and in position.

A large body of Chinese was here observed in front, drawn out in line, and certainly presenting a most formidable appearance. They covered a space of ground about a mile in length, and were removed from the heights about three miles. The 37th regiment was directed to proceed towards the left, the 26th to the right, and the marines, who had just come up, advanced in the centre. The day was one of the hottest the oldest Indian present had ever experienced, and the ground over which the troops had to pass was either paddy fields or thick jungle. However, where no paths were found, new ones were formed. The 37th had not proceeded far, when they surprised a large body of the enemy's advance. These were quietly sitting under the shade of some trees, drinking tea, nor were they aware of our approach until a few well directed musket bullets, from our light company, whizzed in amongst them, upon which they all took to their heels, leaving their spears, their cups, and their buckets of tea for their pursuers. We advanced upon the main body. These were soon in full flight. They did not at all appear to relish our steady advance, nor that of the Royal Marines and the Cameronians. We now fell back, and were shortly joined by the General and his staff, and H.M. 49th regiment; this regiment, with the Royal Marines, were now directed to return to their quarters; the General himself remaining, with the wing of the 26th and 37th regiments, to watch the movements of the Chinese, who had retreated to a range of heights in front. These were here joined by large reinforcements, and numbered certainly upwards of 10,000. They came down to the plain, and, shouting, beating their gongs, and waving their banners, continued steadily and boldly to advance. Captain Knowles, who had at this time arrived with some rockets, plowed line after line through their ranks; still they did not appear intimidated. The rain unfortunately began to threaten—a storm was evidently approaching. At this moment the heat was most oppressive, and both officers and men were greatly exhausted. The atmosphere was close and dense—the roll of distant thunder was heard, and the rays of the sun had so heated the air, that on its being inhaled, a sensation was left in the lungs similar to that felt when the vapour bath has been raised to too high a temperature. It was about this time that Major Beecher, deputy quarter-master-general, dropped down dead from a *coup de soleil.*

It was evident the enemy must be driven back and dispersed, otherwise they might advance upon our camp during the night. The threatening aspect of the weather rendered it necessary to effect this without delay. About two p.m. the General directed Major Pratt to proceed and disperse a large body that occupied an extensive line of paddy-field on his left, and to clear the hills to his front. The 37th regiment was at the same time ordered to dislodge a similar body to the right, and then push forward to clear the hills to their front. The latter corps was supported by the Bengal Volunteers. A company of the 37th regiment was directed to proceed to the left, to keep up a communication with the Cameronians.

As usual, the nearer we approached the Chinese, the further they retired. We pursued the enemy for upwards of four miles, when it was judged prudent to retire.

The thunder-storm was now awful, the rain fell in torrents, and prevented our seeing an object even removed a few yards distant. Many of our firelocks had got wet; at one time the 26th had been unable to fire a single musket, and many of them were surrounded by the Chinese, who, on seeing us retire, again collected on our flanks and rear. The want of a few light cavalry was here much felt.

It would be difficult to give a description of this retrograde movement. The rain had completely obliterated every trace of a foot-path. All before us was one sea of water. At times the leading files would suddenly disappear in some deep pit or ditch, which it was impossible to guard against. The thunder and lightning were perfectly terrific. The Chinese, no doubt, looked upon the storm as a judgment inflicted by their gods on the barbarians. About five p.m. the 37th had arrived at the position they originally started from. Here Sir Hugh Gough still stood, and how gratified must every man present have been to see him so satisfied with what had been done. He shook hands with and thanked the native officers for their exertions. The 26th were seen approaching; and as the detached company of the 37th was supposed to be in its rear, we were ordered to return to our barracks. We had not, however, gone far, when it was discovered that the detached company had never joined the 26th. An express was immediately dispatched for two companies of the Royal Marines, armed with percussion muskets. The portion of the force that had been employed all day were fatigued, and the rain had rendered their firelocks unserviceable, so that it would have been useless to have sent them in search of the missing men.

The rear of the 26th, while returning, had been much annoyed by the enemy, who, taking advantage of the almost helpless state of the men, whose bayonets were all but useless weapons when opposed to the enemy's long spears, could offer but little resistance beyond self-protection.

With an instrument resembling a shepherd's crook attached to a long bamboo, the Chinese contrived to pull over some of the rear-rank men, and afterwards rush on the unfortunate victims with their swords. Major Pratt, in saving the life of one, was pulled over with one of those weapons, but sustained no other injury than having his jacket torn from the collar to the cuff. The 26th lost in this affair three men, and had one officer and ten men wounded.

Great anxiety was entertained for the fate of the missing company. It was natural to suppose that, by this time, the men would be considerably fatigued. Their food had just been cooked, when the order arrived to fall in; and so anxious were they to close with the "soors" (pigs) who had been the means of bringing them from their own country, (an expression which the Sepoys were often heard to make use of) that they preferred leaving their meal untouched, saying that they would have a better appetite for it on their return; consequently none of them had tasted food since the previous day at noon. They were, moreover, exposed the whole of this day to most harassing duty; at one time, under a broiling sun, and at another, under drenching rain. In a small force like ours—at least, small compared to the numbers opposed to us, the loss of even one company of sixty men would be severely felt; but Providence had destined it otherwise. An occasional musket shot was heard by the marines in search, and on advancing towards the spot from whence it proceeded, a distinct "hurrah" was heard to follow each report. The marines also fired a few shots, and returned the "hurrah ;" and before they were aware of it, (for at this time it was quite dark, and continued to rain,) came suddenly upon a large body of Chinese, who scampered off so soon as they saw the reinforcement approaching, and exposed to view the lost party, drawn up in form of a square.

"It gives me no ordinary gratification," remarks the general in his dispatch to the Governor-General of India, "to say that a little after dark they found

Lieutenant Hadfield, with his gallant company in square, surrounded by some thousand Chinese, who, as the 37th's fire-locks would not go off, had approached close to them. The Sepoys, I am proud to say, in this critical situation, nobly upheld the high character of the native army by unshrinking discipline and cheerful obedience; and I feel that the expression of my best thanks is due to Lieutenant Hadfield, and to Lieutenant Devereux and Ensign Berkeley, who zealously supported him during this trying scene." A few well-directed volleys, fired by the marines in the direction of the cowardly enemy, instantly dispersed them with great loss, after which the whole party returned homewards, the marines carrying such as were wounded. It was about nine, p.m., when they reached the lines, where many hearty congratulations passed on all sides. Lieutenant Whiting commanded the detachment of marines which was thus the means of preserving the forlorn company of the 37th regiment. It now appeared that this company commenced returning about the same time as the rest of the force composing the advance; they had not, however, proceeded far when they perceived indistinctly through the rain a body of men, whom they supposed to be the 26th, advancing towards them. These soon approached sufficiently close to convince the party that their situation now was a most critical one, and that it was the enemy who were collecting again in great force. They attempted to retire, but were soon surrounded by about 3000 men, who, yelling like fiends, and considering the party their prey, were fast closing on them. A few well-directed shots from the muskets that were still serviceable told well in the crowd; among those first knocked over, was their chief and their standard-bearer. The former was immediately picked up, and was being carried to the rear on the shoulders of one of his men, when another shot from the square brought both to the ground. The rain, having now ceased, the party was enabled to fire a few volleys, which for a time dispersed the enemy, and allowed them to proceed a considerable way home, the Chinese, however, keeping at some distance in the rear. On the rain again coming on, they closed, and a second time surrounded our party, which had here the mortification to see, in the distance, the rest of the force proceeding on to camp. At this time not a musket would go off, and, as we have already said, little resistance could be offered with the bayonet against the enemy's long spears. The company remained in this position upwards of an hour, the enemy removed only from fifteen to thirty paces; had they possessed the slightest determination, they might have at once annihilated our small party, but the steady front of bayonets frightened them. The rain ceasing to fall for a time, enabled the party to discharge a few of their muskets, and every bullet told, as a matter of course. The men, who had been throughout as steady in their ranks as they could possibly be on parade, now commenced extracting the wet cartridges, and baling water into the barrels of their pieces, and with the lining of their turbans (the only dry thing about them) washed and dried them.. This was done, too, with the enemy removed but a few paces from them. The party was thus enabled to fire several volleys in succession, which forced the enemy to retire, and again our men proceeded a considerable way homewards, followed, however, though at a respectful distance, by the enemy. The rain again returning, encouraged the Chinese to advance; nothing, therefore, was left for our men but again to form square, in which position they made up their minds to remain till morning. It was here that one of the enemy, armed with a musket belonging to a sepoy who had been killed, retired behind a bank, distant from the square about twenty paces, and deliberately resting the piece on the bank, applied his slow match to the powder in the pan, and lodged the ball in Lieutenant Berkeley's arm. The party had been in this position for about two hours when they first became aware that assistance was approaching.

During the whole of the period this small party was so much harassed, no body of men could possibly have been steadier, or behaved with greater coolness and bravery. The eagerness with which they obeyed the orders of their officers, their agility in warding off every blow, and resisting the sudden rushes on the square, their determination in saving the lives of their comrades, who more than once fell into the hands of the enemy, and their steady conduct throughout, reflect not only credit on themselves, but also on the army they belong to,.and deserve to be recorded in the annals of British India as a proof of what can be effected by discipline and bravery.

The loss this company sustained was, two privates killed, one officer and thirteen men severely wounded. The party had hardly quitted their last position, when the enemy opened a fire upon them from a small gun which they had mounted on a neighbouring rising ground, but the shot fell short. There can be little doubt that the salvation of this company was mainly owing to its having its full complement of European officers present with it.

On the 31st, 8000 Tartar troops left the city, and the remainder were prepared to follow when carriage was provided. Doubts were entertained whether treachery was not contemplated, more especially as a large body of men was again assembling on the scene of yesterday's contest. Information was now communicated to the authorities in the city, that if there was again any demonstration of hostilities, the white flag should be hauled down, and the city immediately stormed. They declared that this hostile movement was without their knowledge, and against their consent; that they were villagers and militia, who, calling themselves "Soldiers of Righteousness," had assembled to protect the villages in the plain. A mandarin was sent from the city to communicate with them, upon which the whole body instantly retreated and dispersed. The troops, who had been again ordered out on the re-appearance of this force, now returned to their lines.

Five millions of dollars having been received, and satisfactory security procured for the remainder, the force left the heights above Canton on the morning of the 1st of June, the Chinese having furnished 800 coolies to convey guns, stores, &c, to the village of Tsinghae, from whence we were again taken in tow of the Nemesis, and reached our respective ships that evening, having left the great city of Canton a second time "a record of British magnanimity and forbearance."

CHAPTER XVI

Death of Sir Humphrey Le Fleming Senhouse—Return of Commodore Sir Gordon Bremer—Sickness at Hong-Kong—Typhoons of 21st and 26th July.

On the departure of Sir Le Fleming Senhouse from England, it was intended that he should have been second in command of the naval portion of the expedition. But from a succession of untoward circumstances, the intention could not be carried into effect. This, at the time, was very tantalizing, and it became the more so when, in November, 1840, on Admiral Elliot's proceeding home, the supreme command of the fleet devolved upon the officer who, by the merest chance, had superseded him, and who was his senior in rank by a few days only. Nor was it until the month of March, 1841, on the departure of Sir Gordon Bremer to Calcutta, that Sir Fleming became senior officer of the fleet.

As has been seen, it was during the brief reign of this gallant veteran that the most brilliant occurrences of the expedition have taken place.

In his own service, Sir Fleming was beloved and respected, except by those few whose zeal did not form a prominent part of their character.

With the army he was an universal favourite. From him they at all times derived every possible assistance; to co-operate with them seemed to afford him pleasure. Situated as that branch of the service is on this, and, indeed, on all joint expeditions, and dependent so frequently on the navy for many of their comforts, they have had every reason to feel grateful to Sir Fleming for his assiduous attentions, and his anxiety at all times to meet their wishes.

During the operations above Canton, he exerted himself in an extraordinary degree—at one time present with the fleet in the river, and at another with the general in the field. Like many others, however, excitement and hard work seemed to steel him against disease, though inhaling the poisonous miasma exhaled from the swamps and paddy which surrounded our position. It was on the passage down the river that sickness made its appearance in the force, and Sir Fleming was destined to be the first to sink under it.

On the morning of the 13th of June, when it was announced to him that all hopes of saving his life was at an end, he immediately directed that the signal be made for all captains of H.M.'s ships to repair on board; but ere the first had arrived, our gallant commodore was a corpse.

He carried with him to the grave the regret of all. "He participated in all the privations that the troops underwent on the heights above Canton, and has fallen a victim to the zeal that marked his character." He was buried at Macao, and a monument was erected over his remains by a joint subscription of the officers of the army and navy.

On the 22nd of June, Commodore Sir Gordon Bremer returned from Calcutta, invested with authority by her Majesty to co-operate with Captain Elliot as joint plenipotentiary.

Sickness had, in the meantime, prostrated many in the force and fleet. Death had numbered some of our best men among its victims. In a few weeks, however, a rapid improvement took place among those who had not been removed from their transports, or who, on the continued increase of disease, had returned to them. The troops who were obliged to remain on shore continued to suffer much. Two-thirds of the latter were, during the months of June, July, and August, quite unfit for duty. Nor was there a solitary European at this time resident on the island who escaped the prevailing fever, the recovery from which was frequently uncertain, or the convalescence tardy and unsatisfactory.

Malaria, always present in marshy and certain jungly districts, caused by the decomposition of vegetable and animal substances, is on the island of Hong-Kong to be found, where no vegetable is to be seen, and where no marsh exists. Fevers appear an endemic disease on the coast of China, to guard against which, even the poorest peasant spares no expense or trouble to make his dwelling comfortable, and thus protect him from those frequent and sudden transitions from heat to cold so frequent in this climate. Moreover, the natives so regulate their dress, that at one period of the day they may be seen in the thinnest and coolest habiliments, and in another, clad in furs and woollens; or what is a more general habit, they put on a succession of garments as the cold increases, and again throw them aside as it becomes warm.

The climate of Hong-Kong at this period was most variable, the thermometer ranging frequently 10°, 15°, and at times 20°, in the twenty-four hours. The troops were cantoned on the brow of a high hill, from whence cold blasts of wind and heavy falls of rain were in quick succession followed by a burning hot sun; and the barracks provided for them were wretchedly ill adapted for so changeable a climate. Is it a wonder, then, that disease increased? In the 37th regiment, 600 strong, barely 100 men were effective; two of the officers had died, and of the sixteen remaining, one only was fit for duty. In our crowded hospitals, sores of a frightful character made their appearance; these terminated in hospital gangrene. The slightest abraded surface speedily degenerated into a foul, malignant ulcer; wounds received in action at Cheumpee and elsewhere, but which had been cicatrized for days and days, now again broke out. Many poor fellows, proud of their wounds, and rendered thereby disqualified for further effective service, looked forward with pleasure and anxiety to the period of return to their native homes, where they would be enabled to spend the rest of their days in ease and comfort with their families, on the bountiful provision of their honourable masters, were now cut off.

The corps was exactly in this state, with an hospital crowded to overflowing, when the typhoon of the 21st of July came on. It had commenced about midnight, and continued steadily increasing in violence, and at six a.m. it blew a hurricane from the N.W. The hospital of the 37th, which fronted in this direction, was a continued line of building, constructed of bamboo and palmyra leaf, 200 feet long by 18 broad, into which upwards of 300 men were stowed—an additional hundred having a few days previously been placed on board ship.

I had about half finished my visit in the morning of this day, when I observed the side of the building facing the gale evidently yield to the force of the tempest. I immediately directed those of the sick who could move to leave the building forthwith, and was hastening to do so myself also, when suddenly I heard a tremendous crash, and ere I was able to reach the door, with many others, was thrown on my face, and crushed under the wreck of the building. The shrieks and groans of the miserable bed-ridden patients, the howling of the wind, and the crackling of the beams, sounded to me, when I had recovered consciousness, something more than horrifying, more especially as I was myself deprived, by an intolerable dead weight upon my shoulders and back, which pressed my chest to the ground, from taking part in it. The ground on which I had fallen was fortunately much softened with the rain, the building having been thrown several feet beyond its original foundation. I was thus enabled, after extricating my arms, and assisted by a sepoy, who was equally anxious with myself to become free, to scrape, or rather burrow, my way out, and tottering to my brother officers' quarters, apprised them of their danger, and announced to them what had already happened.

By dint of very great exertions on the part of the officers and the few men who could be procured, the sick were extricated from the wreck of the hospital, and placed in one of the other barracks—alas! merely to have the same scene acted over again. Barrack after barrack was levelled with the ground. The officers' houses followed; their kit was flying about in all directions. The force of the wind tore the very flooring from the sleepers. It was now *sauve qui pent,* for there was danger in remaining in the vicinity of the lines.

The sea, at all other times in this harbour so still and smooth, was now fiercely agitated, and had already encroached upon the island far beyond its natural bounds. Ships drifting from their anchorages were seen rapidly nearing the shore, while their crews were labouring hard to cut away the masts, their only chance of preservation. Occasionally, as the atmosphere cleared across the bay, several ships could be seen clustered in one spot, giving one another a friendly embrace. Ships of seven and eight hundred tons were on shore, in water which, on ordinary occasions, is barely knee-deep. Innumerable boats were scattered in fragments on the beach, while underneath and around them were many mangled and lacerated corpses of Chinese.

At three p.m. the typhoon was at its height; the wind and drenching rain continued unabated, and torrents, in form of cascades, poured down the hills, sweeping everything before them. The houses had all been destroyed, and no covering remained to protect from the raging elements. The natives were running wildly about, vainly beseeching succour from their gods. At times masses of loose stone would become separated from the mountains, and roll down the hill like a huge avalanche, threatening destruction to all below. The last days of Hong-Kong seemed approaching. It was a grand but truly awful sight.

It will be easier to conceive than to describe the helpless and wretched condition in which the inhabitants of this newly-colonized island spent this night.

On the evening of the 25th, and the greater part of the 26th of July, the island was again visited by a typhoon, which, though not so violent as that now described, swept away all that escaped the gale of the 21st. It destroyed the temporary buildings thrown up, and exposed the wretched inmates a second time to the fury of a dreadful tempest of wind and rain. The losses sustained, both in life and property, by these typhoons, have been fearfully disastrous. The closeness and oppressive nature of the atmosphere some hours previous to their coming on, evidently indicated the approach of a storm; and the native population, who are generally pretty correct in their indications of the weather, foretold, as did also the barometer, on both occasions, that a typhoon might be expected.

Connected with this subject, I shall devote the following chapter to a graphic and interesting account of the loss of one of H.M.'s cutters, (communicated by Lieutenant Morgan, R.N., to that admirable periodical, *The Chinese Repository*,) having on board the two plenipotentiaries, who fell into the hands of the Chinese, and who very narrowly escaped a trip to Pekin.

CHAPTER XVII

Narrative of the loss of H.B.M.'s cutter Louisa, in the typhoon of the 21st of July, 1841.

July 20th.—Went on board the Louisa, with the commodore and Captain Elliot, for the purpose of proceeding to Hong-Kong to rejoin the Wellesley. The wind being light, and the ebb-tide making strong, we were compelled to anchor about two o'clock, p.m., to wait for the flood, which made about five; and a good breeze then springing up, we stood along through the Lantao passage, though rather too far to the southward, having been drifted down by the tide. The wind gradually freshened to about a double-reefed topsail breeze, and at ten o'clock, finding we were going to leeward, we anchored close under the island of Laff-sam-ee; wind north.

July 21st.—At about half-past twelve o'clock at night weighed again, and endeavoured to weather the Island of Ichow, but could not; and the cutter being close to the shore, and having missed stays twice, we were compelled to go to leeward of it. Wind north, a little westerly: course to Hong-Kong, north-east. Attempted to work to windward, but could do nothing; cutter again missed stays, and in wearing, when the mainsail was jibbed, the main-boom snapped in halves. We double reefed the sail, got a sheet aft, and tried her under that sail, with the mizzen, fore-staysail, and jib, but she was lagging away to leeward so fast, that, the wind too having increased considerably, we were forced to anchor about half-way between Ichow and Chichow, with a reef of rocks astern of us; as we anchored, the mizzen bumkin went before the sail could be taken in.

As day broke, the prospect was anything but cheering; it was blowing a gale from N.W. to N.N.W., and evidently increasing in violence every moment: a heavy sea was running, which the little cutter rode out beautifully, only now and then shipping a sea; every hatch was now battened down, and the increasing sea frequently broke over us; our anchors and cables being good, we held on well. About eight o'clock, a.m., it was manifest that we must slip, but it was determined to hold on until we could do so no longer; about nine o'clock, a.m., the heavy pitching carried away the jib-boom; and the gaff-topsail being still aloft, after much difficulty it was got down, and the head of the topmast twisted off, but the spar could not be got on deck; it was accordingly lashed, and we stood by to slip. About a quarter past ten o'clock the land was seen through the haze, close under our lee, and the cutter was driving down upon it: we immediately slipped, cut away the mizzen-mast, and put the vessel before it, shipping some very heavy seas in the attempt. The fore-staysail was hoisted, but instantly blown out of the bolt-rope; the peak of the mainsail was then ordered to be swayed up above the gunwale, in order that we might have her under command;—the men clapped on the throat-halyards, and the peak fell down and was jammed in the larboard gangway abaft; we were by this time within sixty yards of the shore, upon which the surf was breaking terrifically. Mr. Owen, the second master, incautiously went before the gangway, and attempted to lift the peak out clear, the men swaying on the halyards at the same time; it suddenly flew out, and jerked Mr. Owen into the sea, swung round, and was brought up by the fore rigging; the gaff went in two, and the sail, with part of the gaff, went forward, and was jammed before the rigging,—the foot of the sail towing overboard, thus leaving us an excellent little sail to scud under; it was instantly lashed and made secure. A tumbling sea, which broke over us, washed everything off the deck that was not lashed, and amongst other things a hen-coop, which poor Owen got hold of, after having taken off his pea-jacket in the water. Another heavy sea broke on board, washed away the man at the tiller, and unshipped it; we were within twenty yards of the surf, and our situation truly awful. Owen's fate now seemed but the precursor of ours, and our moments, we thought, were numbered; but the hand of Providence was stretched forth to save us. Lord Amelius Beauclerk caught hold of the tiller, and endeavoured to ship it, but a heavy lurch sent him to leeward; I picked it up, and, with the assistance of the men, it was shipped, put hard a-port, and we passed clear of the end of the island, with the surf nearly breaking on board of us.

We could do nothing but run before the gale, keeping a good look-out a-head, and thus we passed about an hour of anxiety and uncertainty, lest there should be other land to leeward. Our doubts on this matter were soon over, for the cry of "breakers right a-head" seemed again to warn us that our lives were but of short duration; the land appeared towering many hundred feet above us, and the roar of the breakers, as they dashed against a precipitous wall of granite, was heard above the fearful violence of the tempest. "Hard a-port!"—and—"hard a-starboard!"— were shouted out in quick succession by Captain Elliot, who was standing forward, holding on by the fore rigging; as the little vessel obeyed her helm, a blast, which seemed a concentration of all the winds, threw her nearly on her broadside, but she gallantly stood up again under it, and we passed within a few yards of a smooth granite precipice, on which the sea first broke, and to have touched which would have shivered the cutter into a thousand fragments. We ran along this frightful coast, the wind nearly a-beam, for not less than 300 yards, expecting every moment to be our last; but God, in his infinite mercy, was pleased to have us in his special keeping, and we rounded the end of this land, with the feelings of men who had been delivered from a frightful, and, as we deemed, an inevitable death, with not a chance (from the nature of the coast) of one of our lives being saved.

We now had evidently (from the long following seas) got out of the immediate vicinity of the islands, and the wind abated a little; the sail was scarcely sufficient to steady the vessel, and to keep her before the seas, which frequently broke over us. We passed through a space of about two and a half or three miles, which was covered with floating fragments of wrecks of Chinese and foreign vessels, affording a melancholy proof of what devastation of property and loss of life must have been caused, and that, our lives being spared, we had much to be thankful for.

It was now about three o'clock, p.m., and the wind had gradually veered round to E. and S.E., and continued shifting between those points, so that our course was from W. to N.W., but nearer the former than the latter. We concluded that we had passed to the southward of the Ladrones, and if so, that we must, by steering that course, be running directly for the shore about Montanha. The water now became very much discoloured, so much so as to leave a sediment on the decks and on our clothes as the sea broke over us: two hand leads were lashed together, and we got soundings in seven fathoms. The gale was blowing with redoubled fury, and it was plain that, this time, as we were running on towards the main, (or rather, the western inlands,) there was only one chance of safety for us, and that was, to get into one of the many creeks or channels for boats which are rather numerous about that part of the coast; and, failing this, to run her into shoaler water, let go the anchor, and put our trust in that all-seeing Providence who had already twice preserved us. "High land right a-head!" again put to flight all our speculations; and we were once more to find ourselves saved from imminent peril. The wind literally howled and screamed through the rigging, and our little sail began to shew symptoms of being no longer able to withstand the fearful conflict. Again the land towered above us, and a surf broke close on our larboard beam, about 150 yards from the shore; we cleared this danger, and ran along the land. Suddenly, through the mist, a gap was seen in the outline, and high land trending away beyond on both sides, which Captain Elliot instantly declared to be a creek: our hopes were fixed on rounding the point, where we should be, comparatively speaking, in shelter; but the thing seemed impossible. The wind and waves, as if determined not to be again robbed of their prey, raged with inconceivable fury; and the serf, breaking to a height of 150 feet, gave us too sure intimation of what would be our fate should we but touch the iron-bound coast. We steered as high for clearing the point as possible; we gradually neared it; each surf broke closer,—we could only hold our course; we seemed bearing down upon the breakers: it was an awful moment!—we were looking for and expecting the shock, beyond which all would be oblivion; a surf broke almost on board, and the cutter was hid in the spray—a terrific blast split our sail to shreds; "hard a-port!"—a moment of breathless suspense,—and, thanks be to Almighty God, we passed clear. We felt directly that we were partially sheltered, and stood by the anchor, for we were drifting right upon the shore; it was accordingly let go, and held, checking her way for a moment, and nearly taking her under water. A heavy sea broke over us, and I fancied we were lifted over a rock, for I was quite sensible of a shock, which a person who has once been aground cannot easily mistake; the cable flew out of the hawse, and the anchor again brought us on our beam-ends; the water was up to the combings of the hatchways, but she rose very slowly; we were within thirty yards of the rocks, and embayed; the cable had checked her considerably, and we slowly drifted toward the shore, Captain Elliot conning her. The cable running out, she struck about fifteen or twenty yards from the precipitous coast, the next sea lifted her so that she bilged, and filled instantly, with her starboard bow touching a detached rock, and receding with the sea. Several people jumped overboard, others got on the rocks on the starboard bow, and threw themselves down to prevent being washed off by the surf, which now swept the vessel, and threatened her with almost instant annihilation. Great danger was apprehended from the fall of the mast, which would have come upon those who were on the rock. One of the boys swam over, and a rope being thrown him, he made it fast to the shore, and it was passed round a portion of our rock of refuge, by which means all hands got safely on shore. Captain Elliot and two of the men were washed off the rock, but fortunately succeeded in reaching the land, though much exhausted.

There we stood,—out of all danger from the violence of the tempest,—and saw the gradual destruction of the gallant little vessel which had borne us along so well, through a storm hardly to be surpassed in violence, and through perils which men doubtless sometimes witness, but seldom live to recount; and I do not believe there was a man amongst our number, twenty-three in all, who (thoughtless though sailors be) did not offer up a fervent prayer of thanksgiving to God, who had so signally vouchsafed to stretch forth his hand and save us.

Two or three of the men now went up the hill to look at the surrounding country, but nothing was seen of any human habitation; they returned and reported accordingly. About half-past five the tide had fallen so that we went down to the wreck to endeavour to save a small quantity of provisions,

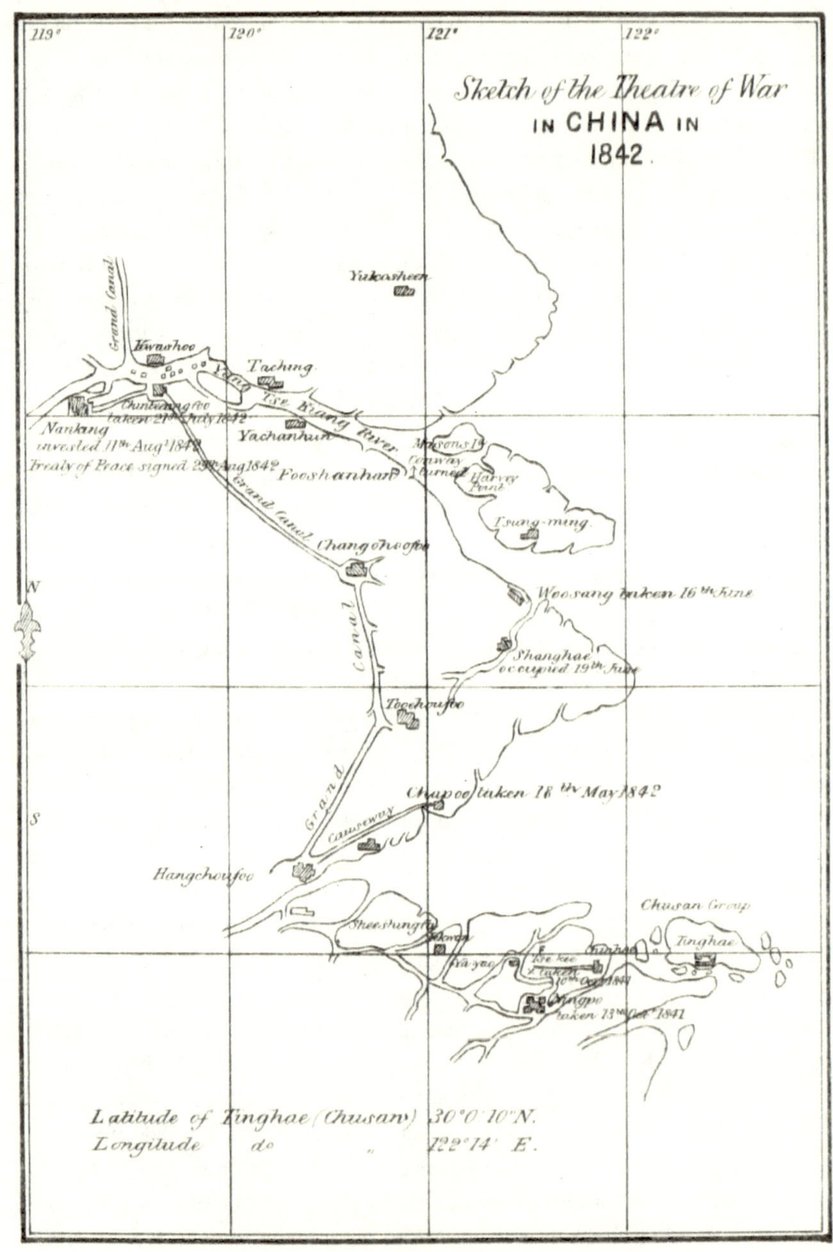

Sketch of the Theatre of War in China, 1842.

and to get some blankets and cloth clothing to shelter ourselves against the inclemency of the weather. We succeeded in procuring both, but not in such quantities as we could have wished; and as the vessel was going to pieces, it was not safe to make a very long stay on board. We got, besides a sail, or part of one, a tarpaulin, and eight bottles of gin, a small portion of which was instantly served out to all hands, upon which, with a small piece of raw beef or pork, we made our first meal after nearly twenty-four hours' fasting.

As many as could get them, put on cloth under thin trowsers, and those who had flannel waistcoats were fortunate. We then began to make arrangements for passing the night. Having found a fissure in the side of a precipice, open at the top with a small space outside, we placed stones so as to cover a small mountain stream that ran through the centre of our comfortless abode, and strapped the tarpaulin up across the entrance, where it was exposed to the unabated fury of the typhoon. Having taken off our clothes and wrung them, and put them on again, the Commodore, Captain Elliott, Lord A. Beauclerk, myself, the Commodore and Captain Elliot's servants, and a little Portuguese boy, sat down in a circle, with our backs to the sides of the cavern and the tarpaulin, and had a large blanket thrown over all. As there was no room for more inside, a wet sail was spread outside over the rocks. Mr. Fowler and Lena (second mate), and the men, rolled themselves up in blankets, and laid down exposed to the wind and rain. The latter descended in torrents all night, pouring down upon us in little cascades from all parts of the rock above, making a channel amongst the people on the sail; in fact, it was very like lying down to sleep in a running stream. Of course, few were fortunate enough to close their eyes in slumber, and the gradual breaking up of the little cutter continually called forth an exclamation from some of us, as crash after crash was heard above the noise of the wind and breakers. We who were within the cleft remained in a sitting posture all night, for there was no room to recline.

At length, morning of the 22nd dawned, and we saw all that held together of the Louisa; her taffrail jammed between two rocks, and a few of the deck planks adhering, but all the rest was scattered along the coast in fragments. We stripped, wrung our clothes, and put them on again, and having served out a small quantity of spirits, several exploring parties went out to endeavour to find some Chinese.

We were not very far from a sandy bay, on which were cast up many articles of wreck; along this bay a party was sent, whilst others went up the hills; some descended to our own wreck, and a few remained in or near the cavern. We had not been down long before we discovered under planks and timbers the bodies of three Chinese frightfully lacerated by the rocks; their vessel must have been driven on shore during the night. Suddenly, I heard myself hailed, and looking up, saw two Chinese, each of them appropriating a blanket. All hands were instantly recalled, and we began to talk to them; one of them had a most benevolent countenance, and to him was the conversation principally addressed. This man gave Captain Elliot a paper, which was folded and quite saturated with water, but after some time we got two of the folds clear, and were delighted to see Captain Elliot's signature, and some of the cutter's men said they recognised our friend as one of the boat people at Macao. He was instantly offered 1000 dollars if he would give us a fishing boat to take us thither; this he undertook to do very readily, and beckoned us to follow him, which we did, having first shouldered the beef and pork and gin, and put as many clothes on as we could get. On the top of the hill we were joined by the party which went round the sandy bay; they said they had found the bodies of eleven Chinese, and the wreck of a large junk, and one of them had picked up the box containing the commodore's decorations, which we distributed amongst ourselves, and put in our pockets. We were very badly off for shoes; I had only one, and the consequence was, my feet were much cut; we walked along over two hills in single file, and as we topped the third, saw an extensive valley with a long sandy beach, on which the sea was breaking heavily. A creek ran up on the left side by a considerable village or hamlet, and the place seemed full of people. Scarcely had we appeared over the hill, when we were seen by the Chinese; the women and children ran away, screaming Fanqui! Fanqui! and the men, armed with bill-hooks, rushed up the path in hundreds, railing at and menacing us. However, our benevolent guide explained matters to them, and about sixty passed us to go and plunder the wreck. At length one of them stopped Captain Elliot, and commenced rifling his pockets; I was walking behind Captain Elliot, and the same fellow thrust his hand into my pockets, in which was the star of the Hanoverian Guelphic order; I squeezed my arm to my side to prevent his taking it, when he shook his bill-hook in my face, and another fellow jumped upon a large stone, and flourished his weapon over my head; still I held on, when the first man struck me a severe blow on the arm with the back of the billhook. Captain Elliot looked round just then, and said it was no use resisting, and that I had better give up everything to them, they being twenty to one, and we wholly unarmed and in their power. I accordingly resisted no longer, and repeated Captain Elliot's advice to those behind me. Having taken the contents of our pockets, and eased the bearers of the beef, pork, and gin, of their loads, they returned and stripped us of clothing, just allowing a regard to common decency, after which they molested us no further. The only two amongst us who were struck were the commodore (who was knocked down) and myself.

On our arrival before a little shed, one of the outermost houses of the village, our friend commenced preparing it for our reception—a proceeding we did not by any means admire, as we had understood that a boat would at once take us to Macao; but he said the wind was too high, which in truth it was, and we were therefore compelled to enter and wait the result. Our man, who was named Mingfong, made a fire, and gave us a breakfast of rice and salt fish, which we were too happy to get; having satisfied our appetites, we endeavoured to dry our clothes, and make ourselves as comfortable as men in our situation could do. We presently ascertained, with great satisfaction, that there were no officers in the place, so that if we could manage properly, there was every probability of our escaping a trip to Pekin. Captain Elliot increased the sum originally offered to 2000 dollars, if they would take us to Macao as soon as the wind moderated, and after some difficulty it was agreed to.

We had the satisfaction of seeing the people passing and repassing with different articles of our property in their possession, many of which they brought to us to inquire the uses of. The bodies of three Chinese had been discovered almost on the spot where the Louisa was wrecked; and as they bore some frightful marks, caused by dashing against the rocks, it was supposed we had murdered them. This was a very awkward affair; but we could only deny it strenuously, with every expression of horror that such a crime should be imputed to us, who had so providentially been saved from the same fate as these poor men. However, they would not be persuaded to the contrary, or they did not understand our explanation, until Lena, by gestures, shewed them that in all probability the junk people had lashed themselves to spars, and in endeavouring to reach the land on them, had been dashed against the rocks, which accounted for their lacerated appearance, and the ropes found round their bodies. They went away apparently satisfied, but occasionally two or three would return and revive the matter, making demonstration of sharpening knives and cutting throats. When they found the cutter's arms, they were also very angry, and stormed and railed against us most violently.

All the women and children in the place crowded round to look at us (particularly when eating), and many were the inquiries made as to the sex of old Joe, the commodore's black Gentoo servant, who wearing earrings, and having his hair turned back and twisted in a knot behind, did bear some resemblance to a female; but on closer inspection, his thick beard, whiskers, and mustachios, might have satisfied the most sceptical amongst them. They had, however, taken away his earrings, and one savage attempted to cut off his ear.

We had another mess of rice towards evening, and that night slept around the fire, though not very soundly, for we were apprehensive the Chinese had some design upon us, but I believe no harm was intended. People were walking about all night, which kept us on the *qui vive.* The wind having moderated very considerably, Captain Elliot proposed to them to go that night; but they were afraid of the Ladrones, and though tempted by an additional 1000 dollars, they refused; their wives appeared to object to the proceeding, or I think they would have been induced to go. During the night, Captain Elliot made a final arrangement, by which we were to start at daylight on the morning of the 23rd, in two boats; in each boat there were to be but two people, the remainder to be sent for on our arrival at Macao, for which service they were to receive 3000 dollars, and 100 dollars for each of the boats.

At daylight on the 23rd we were prepared to start, but the Chinese tantalized us by making thole-pins, mending sails, &c.; at last, we had the satisfaction of seeing two boats come down the creek, and anchor abreast of our dwelling. The people to whom the boats belonged now refused to let them go unless 150 dollars were given for each, and this after some demur was agreed to, as every moment's delay increased the probability of our falling into the hands of the officers; but no sooner had the blackguards been promised the 150 dollars than they increased their demand to 200. Here our friend Mingfong took our part and abused his countrymen for their rapacity, and declared we should not be so imposed upon: he would sooner take but one boat. All was at length settled. We had chowchow (amongst which they gave us part of our own pork), and, having bid good bye to those who were to remain behind, at about eight a.m. the Commodore and Captain Elliot got into one boat, and myself and Captain Elliot's servant (who was sick) went in the other; they made us lay on our backs at the bottom of the boat, and covered us with mats. We got through the surf and out to sea without any mishap, as the weather was fine; further than that I knew nothing until about two p.m., when they uncovered us and gave us some rice. We had just finished our light repast, when the man sitting above hit me a pretty hard blow on the head, and made signs for me to lie down again; this I did, and was covered with the mat; a few minutes after, I heard a rush, as if some large boat were passing us, which was the case. They said nothing to us, but the other boat was hailed, and asked what was the news, and whether many vessels had been wrecked on their part of the coast; to which suitable replies were given and we passed on. This was a mandarin boat! They little thought what a prize was within their grasp — the two plenipotentiaries. Doubtless, we were throughout these three days of adventure and peril in the special keeping of Providence. In about two hours, I again ventured to look up, and to my great joy discovered two ships anchored at a considerable distance. I could not recognise the land, and was quite mystified as to our situation; at last, I determined that it must be the Typa, and I was right: we passed to the left of Monkey island, and Macao opened to our view; glad, indeed, were we, and thankful for our deliverance. We saw a vessel not far behind working up for Macao, which Captain Elliot made out to be a lorcha, and we could no longer remain under cover, but throwing off the mats, stood upon the thwarts and waved our hats to attract their attention, at the same time telling the Chinese to give way, which they did most lustily. My boat was a faster one than the other, and consequently got alongside first, when I met with an unexpected reception: all the Portuguese and Lascars were drawn up with swords, muskets, and pistols, so that I had nearly been shot at the moment of deliverance. However, Captain Elliot's servant explained who were in the other boat, and we went alongside instantly. They had mistaken us for Ladrones, hence the muskets, swords, and pistols. The Commodore and Captain Elliot were on board within a few minutes after us, and we were regaled with soft tack and pineapple by the people on board, who seemed overjoyed at seeing us.

We soon came to in the Inner Harbour, and were all landed safely at the Bar fort. The commodore was in a blue worsted sailor's frock, a light pair of trowsers of four days wear, shoes, and a low crowned hat; Captain Elliot, in a Manila hat, a jacket, no shirt, a pair of striped trowsers and shoes; I had shirt and trowsers, no hat, and a pair of red slippers, borrowed of a Parsee on board the lorcha. The commandant of the fort was most amiable, and particularly anxious to turn out the guard for the commodore, who certainly did not look in a fit mood to appreciate such a mark of respect, his appearance bearing a close resemblance to a highly respectable quartermaster who had been dissipating; consequently, the turning out of the guard was strongly deprecated, and the idea abandoned by the gallant Portuguese. Steps were instantly taken to procure the liberation of those still left in the hands of the Chinese. A boat was dispatched to the island, accompanied by Mr. Thorn, and all the crew brought to Macao on the 25th instant.

I hardly need add, that on our arrival at our quarters we instantly cleaned ourselves, and fully enjoyed the comforts of a good meal and an uninterrupted night's rest, after what had been our lot to undergo, and which, with God's help, we had so fortunately escaped—peril by water, peril by land, and peril of a captivity in the hands of the Chinese.

CHAPTER XVIII

Arrival of Sir H. Pottinger and Sir W. Parker— Departure of Captain Elliot and Sir Gordon Bremer — Second expedition to the north—Fall of Amoy.

The steamers sent in search of the little Louisa cutter, had returned without seeing any trace of her; she and all on board were supposed to have perished in the typhoon, until, on the return of the Commodore and Captain Elliot to Macao, their miraculous escape became known.

The May overland mail had arrived during their absence, bringing intelligence of the appointment of a new admiral and plenipotentiary; and in a few days afterwards, the steamer Sesostris joined the fleet, having on board Sir Henry Pottinger, sole plenipotentiary, and Sir William Parker, naval commander-in-chief. Immediately thereafter, preparations commenced for prosecuting the expedition northward before the change of monsoon, and by the 21st of August the fleet were again under weigh, and steering for Amoy in the following order:—

<table>
<tr><th colspan="5">Bentinck Surveying Ship</th></tr>
<tr><td colspan="2">Queen, Steamer</td><td>Wellesley, 74</td><td colspan="2">Sesostris, Str.</td></tr>
<tr><td colspan="2">Phlegethon, Str.</td><td>Blenheim, 74</td><td colspan="2">Nemesis, Str.</td></tr>
<tr><td>Columbine, 16</td><td rowspan="2">7 Transports</td><td>Marion (Staff-ship)</td><td>Modeste, 16</td><td rowspan="2">Blonde, 44 Wing-ship</td></tr>
<tr><td>Druid, 44 Wing-ship</td><td>6 Transports</td><td>8 Transports</td></tr>
<tr><td colspan="2">Pylades, 18</td><td>Cruiser, 18</td><td colspan="2">Algerine, 10.</td></tr>
</table>

About the same date, Captain Elliot and the Commodore took their departure for England. The health of the latter had been much broken by his recent disaster, and it was that alone obliged him to leave his post when the fleet was proceeding on active service. Captain Elliot certainly had a few friends who regretted his departure, but the majority of the foreign residents in China were delighted to get rid of him. In private life he was much esteemed, and even in public, except when employed diplomatically, he evinced talent of no ordinary description; all gave him credit for zeal and activity, but he wanted the decision and dignity of the diplomatist. The fleet rendezvoused off the harbour of Amoy on the 25th. In passing by a chain of islands which form the mouth of the anchorage, a few shot were fired by the Chinese from fortified positions on those islands. On the following day the plenipotentiary, Sir Hugh Gough, and Sir W. Parker, proceeded to reconnoitre the defences in the Phlegethon. These appeared to be of vast extent and great strength: every spot from whence guns could bear upon the harbour was occupied and strongly armed. From the point of entrance into the inner harbour, the great sea line of defence extended in one continued battery of granite upwards of a mile. This battery was faced with turf and mud several feet in thickness, so that at a distance no appearance of a fortification could be traced. The embrasures were roofed, and the slabs thickly covered with turf, so as to protect the men while working their guns. This work mounted about 100 guns, and it terminated in a high wall, which was connected with a range of rocky heights which run parallel to the beach. The entrance into the harbour is by a channel 600 yards across, between the island of Koolangsoo and Amoy. On each side of this passage there were also strong fortifications. As the Wellesley (flag ship) entered the Inner Harbour, a boat approached her from shore, with a white flag—an officer of low rank was the bearer of a chop from the authorities in the city, demanding to know what our ships wanted—directing us "to make sail for the outer waters ere the celestial wrath should be kindled against us, and the guns from the batteries annihilate us." He was answered by a summons, requiring the surrender of the town and island of Amoy to her Majesty's forces. About one o'clock a simultaneous attack was made upon these prominent defences. The line-of-battle ships and large steamers attacking the great sea batteries, the two frigates the island of Koolangsoo, while the smaller vessels engaged the several flanking works.

The capture of Amoy was chiefly a naval operation; and for four hours did the ships pepper at those enormous batteries without a moment's cessation. The cannonade was certainly a splendid sight. The stream of fire and smoke from the sides of the liners was terrific. It never for a moment appeared to slacken. The Wellesley and Blenheim alone each fired upwards of 12,000 rounds, to say nothing of the frigates, steamers, and small craft; yet the works were as perfect when they left off as when they began, the utmost penetration of the shot being sixteen inches. From twenty to thirty people were all that were killed by this enormous expenditure of powder and shot.

It was late before the first division of the troops landed. These immediately escaladed the wall which flanked the main line of batteries, covered by the

Queen and Phlegethon steamers. The flank companies of the 18th were the first to get over the wall, driving the enemy before them. They opened a gate through which the rest of our men entered, and advancing along the battery, quickly cleared it, killing more men in ten minutes than the ships of war did the whole day. The enemy fled on all sides so soon as the troops landed. An officer of rank cut his throat in the long battery, just as our men were coming up to him; another walked into the sea, and drowned himself, in the coolest manner possible. The island of Koolangsoo was about the same time taken possession of by the troops with little opposition. During the whole day, the heights above the city for miles round were densely crowded with people who had proceeded thither for safety.

On the following day, the city was entered. The inhabitants appeared to have early deserted the place, leaving it in possession of the mob, who had already plundered to a great extent. Much treasure had been carried away—the boxes which contained it were laying in every direction. Even after our troops were in possession of the city, many stratagems were resorted to, to conceal and carry off valuable goods and treasure, such as placing it in hollow blocks of wood, coffers, &c.; but these were soon detected, and put a stop to.

Amoy is a principal third class city of China; it has an excellent harbour, and from its central situation is well adapted for commerce. It is a great emporium of trade, and has constant communication not only with the neighbouring states, but also with Singapore and other settlements in the straits. The city is about eight miles in circumference; it is surrounded in part by a wall, and nearly its whole length by the inner harbour. Its population is fluctuating, from the major portion being so frequently absent on mercantile pursuits. It is at all times much infested by native robbers, who come in boats, and attack the inhabitants at night. These daring marauders paid repeated visits to the city, even while it was in possession of our troops, and gutted the temples and public establishments of much valuable property. The citadel is about a mile in circumference. It entirely commands the suburbs and inner town, and is surrounded by a wall which is occasionally turretted, and varies in height from twenty to thirty-six feet. In this citadel were several extensive granaries well filled, arsenals containing enormous quantities of gingalls, wall-pieces, matchlocks, military clothing, shields, bows and arrows, spears, and swords of all descriptions, besides extensive magazines of powder, and material for constructing it. There was also a foundry, with moulds for casting guns. But few war-junks were seen, the Chinese admiral having shortly before our visit proceeded on a cruise with the fleet. Very large quantities of timber and naval stores were found, and there were several war-junks on the stocks—one two-decker, moulded after the fashion of ours, and carrying

The 18th (Royal Irish) Regiment of Foot at the storming of the forts of Amoy, 26th August 1841. By Michael Hayes and James Lynch.

thirty guns, was ready for sea.

Among the anomalies to be met with at Amoy, is a foundling-house. The natives are said to be much given to the horrible crime of killing their female offspring, to prevent the incumbrance of their education, and the difficulty of providing a future husband for them. And, indeed, there appears to be some truth in the accusation, for not far from this foundling-house, in a tank covered with duckweed, a number of new-born babes were found sewed up in mats; these, apparently, had been drowned.

Several of the merchants never left their shops: these shewed far greater acquaintance with European customs and manners than is ever to be found at Canton. They could enumerate the productions and describe the government of many places in the Indian archipelago. But the name of Singapore was familiar to all, and produced many remarks in favour of the British nation. There, they said, property is always safe, no duty is paid, and there are no mandarins to squeeze.

The country in the immediate vicinity of Amoy is miserably barren—hence the means of subsistence are scanty and expensive. A few miles distant, however, the soil is rich, and affords abundant supplies. Green peas, potatoes, and other European vegetables were brought to market in great abundance when the general panic had ceased.

The batteries of Amoy having, on two former occasions, driven off the barbarian ships, they were, by the Chinese, considered impregnable. The capture of them, therefore, must have been a sad blow to their pride. Their magazines were blown up, their arsenals and their contents utterly destroyed, their best war-junks and dockyards .were burnt, upwards of 500 guns of various calibre rendered unserviceable, and their fortifications experienced much the same fate as did those of the Bocca Tigris, after which the fleet and force, on the 5th of September, took their departure, leaving a garrison of 550 men on the island of Koolangsoo, which completely commands the entrance into the harbour. H.M.'s ships, Druid, Pylades, and Algerine, were also left here to afford additional protection to the garrison and Island.

CHAPTER XIX

Recapture of Chusan, and battle of Chinhae.

In consequence of the north-east monsoon having set in with considerable violence, and the thick hazy weather, the ships were soon dispersed, and the passage towards Chusan became tedious and unpleasant. It was only by considerable perseverance, and taking advantage of the tides in shore, that the fleet were enabled to reach the Chusan group of islands. On the 25th of September they rendezvoused at "Just-in-the-way," a small island at the mouth of the Ningpo passage. In their progress up the coast, the Nemesis steamer, Captain Hall, running short of fuel, put into the harbour of Sheipo to procure a supply; she was fired at from a couple of batteries at the entrance of the harbour, both of which she attacked and carried, destroying their guns, and setting fire to their barracks. The Phlegethon steamer, Captain McCleverty, also exercised signal vengeance upon the village at which Captain Head was seized and murdered last year, and which, on a more recent occasion had decoyed on shore the crew of a boat belonging to the British ship "Lyra," under the pretext of selling them stock, and basely murdered the chief officer and two seamen.

It had originally been intended to take possession of Chinhae first, and afterwards proceed to Chusan; but the weather was now too boisterous to permit of this being accomplished. It was therefore determined immediately to re-occupy the island of Chusan. With this view, on the 26th, a reconnoissance was made in the two iron steamers, when it was found that the defences had been increased to an almost inconceivable extent since the British forces were withdrawn in February last. The fortifications had been built on the same principles and in the same manner as those of Amoy, that being now taken as the best pattern. The enemy were at their post, for they kept up a dropping fire on the steamers as they occasionally neared the beach. There was now a continual line of strong battery on the sea face, extending from outside Guards' Island, to almost half-a-mile beyond Joss-house, or Pagoda Hill, which has also been much strengthened. This battery was chiefly constructed of mud, and had 267 embrasures; though the majority were not yet supplied with guns. Independent of this formidable breastwork, others were placed on the several heights and valleys which commanded an approach to the harbour from the sea; many were in course of building, and some were finished, but had not yet their guns mounted. It was proposed to disembark the troops near Guard's Island, but here a stone battery with eight embrasures had been constructed, though as yet not armed; to prevent this being effected, the Nemesis, Modeste, and Columbine, proceeded to guard the position, and, at the same time to keep up a fire upon a strongly defended entrenched camp, situated about 1200 yards above it on a steep hill.

Pagoda Hill, which we had begun last year to fortify, had now been made a very strong position by the Chinese, who followed out our plan in constructing the battery. A breastwork was thrown up by us on Trunball Island, which is opposite to, and removed about 1000 yards from, this hill. This service was, with much labour, accomplished by Lieut. Birdwood, Madras Engineers, without accident, under a heavy fire from the enemy's batteries. One 68, and two 24 pounder howitzers were placed here, and threw shell with admirable effect into the Joss-hill battery. The extraordinary currents, and the continuance of north-east gales with incessant rain, rendered it impracticable to move the whole of the ships to Chusan till the 30th.

On the morning of the 1st of October, the attack commenced. The men-of-war proceeded to the several positions allotted them, and the landing took place in two columns at the point above mentioned. The first column, which Sir Hugh Gough accompanied, was 1500 strong, and commanded by. Lieutenant-Colonel Craigie, H.M.'s 55th regiment. The second column, 1050 strong, was under Lieut.-Colonel Morris, H.M.'s 49th regiment.

The force of the tides caused some delay in getting the troops on shore, and heavy fire was kept upon the boats from all points. H.M.'s 55th was the first to land. The enemy for some time kept under cover, and their guns had been silenced by the fire from the ships. But immediately our men landed, they again made their appearance on the brow of the hill; they crowded every height, and opened a galling fire of ginjalls and matchlocks upon the 55th, who were drawn out on the beach. The shot came upon them so thick, that it was judged prudent at once to advance up the hill, and drive the enemy off. The sight now became very animating, Major Fawcett leading his men up a steep and rugged ascent, and the enemy, with an infinitely superior force, drawn out in good order, and pouring down a heavy and well-sustained fire upon them. As our men approached, the Chinese came down to meet them in the most determined way. The gallantry of some individuals was most conspicuous—one man in particular attracted universal attention; standing on the peak of the hill while the shot from the Phlegethon and Nemesis plunged every moment within a few feet of him, he waved a flag, and the hearer the shot came, the more he waved; at last a 32 pounder shot finished his career. Another waririor quickly took his place, and was in like manner disposed of.

By this time, the 55th were close on the Chinese; the latter waited till they were within spears' length, and not much liking the steady appearance of a prepare to charge bayonets wheeled to the right about and retreated. This gallant corps had one officer and twenty men put *hors de combat* ere they reached the top of the hill.

By this movement we obtained command of a bridge which flanked the whole line of sea defence, and completely turned the right of the enemy's position. The artillery brought their light guns to enfilade the long line of sea battery, and on the 18th being landed, they pushed on at once to the attack, under Lieut.-Colonel Adams. Every foot of this long line was contested with more than ordinary spirit by a very large force, led apparently by one of the principal mandarins. Many of the enemy who were retiring along a causeway, seeing our men enter the battery, quickly returned and joined the main body. For some time it was a fair stand up fight, and the hardest hitters, holding out longest, had it. This, in a short time, proved to be the Royal Irish. The enemy took to their heels, but re-assembled again close to some brass guns. In their haste, however, they fired too high to do much injury. Some of the officers in advance saved their lives by making good use of their pistols; and the men advancing, shot or bayoneted every one of the enemy. It was here that General Keo, the chief naval and military commander, was killed, and his officers and men, sticking to him to the last, also fell with him. The 18th now pushed on and occupied Pagoda hill, which the well-directed fire from Trunball island had compelled the enemy to evacuate.

During these operations, the 55th regiment, which had now been joined by the Madras Artillery, Rifles, and Sappers (the latter with escalading ladders), moved on and occupied the heights overlooking the city to the north-west. The light field-guns which, with infinite labour, had been brought to the summit of the heights, opened their fire on the walls and town. The 55th proceeded to escalade, while the Rifles passed rapidly down a deep wooded ravine, and cut off the enemy's retreat, which was already seen to have commenced at the north and east gates. Captain Pears, of the Engineers, was the first in the city, and the colours of the 55th simultaneously waved on the walls of Tinghae, with those of the Royal Irish on the Joss-house hill, above the suburbs.

The right column, unfortunately, in consequence of the strong currents and scarcity of boats, was prevented from landing in time to take part in the action.

The casualties on our side amounted to thirty, including one officer killed; that of the enemy was calculated to be about 1500, including many officers of rank. There were thirty-six: brass guns captured; these were quite new, and admirably constructed, and some of the gun carriages far superior to those generally in use among the Chinese; two large twenty-four pounders,

The Joss-house hill from Chusan harbour. Drawn on wood by E. T. Wigan, c1844

brass, were on traversing carriages, similar to those in use in our steamers.

The suburbs of the city, since our evacuation of it, had been occupied entirely as a military post, the inhabitants evidently not being allowed to enter. The names on the streets marked by us—nay, even those written on the doors in chalk, were just as we left them. The beach, however, was so altered by the extensive works thrown up, that no one could possibly again recognise it.

As soon as Tinghae was fully occupied, various parties of troops scoured the country, in order to capture or drive off any body of the enemy still lurking on the island. A military government was formed, and 400 men.left as a garrison; and Sir Henry Pottinger, on the day after the engagement, issued a circular, in which he declared, "That under no circumstances will Tinghae and its dependencies be restored to the Chinese government, until the whole of the demands of England are not only complied with, but carried into full effect."

On the 7th of October, the wind having veered to the desired point, no time was lost in embark. ing the troops intended for the attack upon Chinhae. The plenipotentiary, in company with the naval and military commanders-in-chief, proceeded on the following day in the Nemesis and Phlegethon steamers to reconnoitre the enemy's positions, where every preparation for resistance appeared to have been made.

The city of Chinhae is situated on the left bank of the Tahae or Ningpoo river. It is about three miles in circumference, and is surrounded by a wall twenty-two feet high. At its southeastern extremity is a very commanding rocky height, which forms the entrance of the river; on the summit of this rocky eminence is the joss-house, or citadel. It is about 250 feet high, and is encircled by a strong wall, which is loop-holed and connected by turrets, and has three batteries mounting twenty-one guns at its east end, outside the wall, to defend the entrance of the river. The north and south approaches to this citadel are exceedingly steep, indeed, almost inaccessible. A causeway connects it with the city by a barrier gate at the bottom of a hill; on the isthmus between the two, and on the side facing the river, are several batteries which flank its entrance. By accounts received, the citadel was said to be occupied by 400, and the city by 3000 brave Tartar troops.

On the right or south bank of the river the enemy's force was posted in great strength. Field redoubts crowned the summits, and every defensible position bristled with ginjalls. Opposite the principal landing-place on this side of the river, were four batteries, mounting thirty-one guns, which flanked the entrance. The river had been so effectually staked by rows of piles driven into the ground, that with difficulty only could a landing be effected. On this side of the river a range of heights and steep hills overlooked the city and joss-house. All these were fortified, and presented a military position of great strength, consisting of a continued chain of entrenched camps on all the prominent points difficult of approach. A deep and wide canal also separated these strong posts of the enemy from the sea and landing-place. But at a short distance from the mouth of this canal it was ascertained that there were two bridges.

On the evening of the 9th, the whole of the squadron was anchored off Chinhae; and at an early hour the following morning, the Wellesley, Blenheim, Blonde, and Modeste, took up their positions, so as to cannonade the citadel and eastern part of the city walls,—the steamers Sesostris and Queen so as to shell the citadel in flank, and enfilade any batteries their guns could bear upon. The flat-bottomed steamers at the same time receiving on board the troops, proceeded to land them on the right bank of the river.

Sir Hugh Gough had divided his forces into a left, centre, and right column. The two former he himself accompanied; the latter was placed under Captain Sir Thomas Herbert, R.N., to be made available on the left bank so soon as the concentrated fire from the shipping had begun to affect the garrison of the citadel and city, or a practicable breach had been made in the walls. The landing of the troops on the right bank was opposed by a body of the enemy about 300 strong; but these soon fell back before a few volleys of grape and shrapnel from the steamers. The very great advantage of the iron steamers was on no occasion so clearly exemplified as on this; there being a scarcity of boats, and dispatch being a great desideratum, the steamers at once run their bows on the mud bank, and then permitted the men to wade on shore in water barely knee deep. After the troops had been landed, the two small steamers joined the rest of the squadron for the purpose of throwing shell into the citadel.

The left column was 1070 strong, and consisted of detachments of H.M's. 18th and 55th regiments, Madras Artillery, Sappers and Rifle Company, four light howitzers, and two five-and-a-half-inch mortars. It was commanded by Lieutenant-Colonel Craigie. The centre column consisted of H.M.'s 49th regiment, and detachments of Royal and Madras Artillery and Sappers, amounting altogether to 460 men, with two twelve-pounder howitzers, and two six-pounder field guns,—all under the command of Lieutenant-Colonel Morris. This column was landed about a mile to the right of the left column, on the opposite bank of the canal, and immediately in front of the enemy's position, and separated from it by a long low flat of ground. The left column was completely concealed from view of the enemy by a succession of steep hills. The force of the enemy in this position was supposed to be not less than 10,000, who, on seeing our small centre column only, turned out to give battle. About the same time that the left column reached the bridges across the canal, removed only a short distance from the enemy's strongest position, the right had also approached to within gun-shot range. The bridges were built up with masonry so as merely to permit one man to pass at a time. The enemy was drawn out in good order, and seemed determined on giving us a warm reception. They cheered, and waved us to approach, keeping up a constant though not a very effectual fire. The arrangements on the part of the general had been so admirably concerted, that the advance was hardly sounded when both columns poured in their volleys of musketry simultaneously, and with such admirable precision, as at once to check and paralyze the assailed. They were so hemmed in that they knew not which way to turn, and so thunderstruck with the suddenness of attack, that they lost all nerve even to reload their guns. Our rockets and musketry Continued for some time to mow them down by hundreds. Nothing could withstand the gallant and rapid advance of our small force. Field-work after field-work was cleared, and in very short time the British colours were displayed on the principal fortress.

Further to the left, the 18th were still engaged with a large body of the enemy who would not yield themselves. By order of Sir Hugh Gough, two flags were displayed to them, on which were inscribed in Chinese, "Yield and be saved," "Resist and perish." A few took the first friendly advice, but the majority preferred either seeking safety in flight or being shot down. Many were drowned in attempting to swim across the river, among these was Yu-keen, the imperial envoy; many officers committed suicide; one man, a Tartar general of high rank, he who boasted when the British were formerly at Chusan, that if permitted, "he would catch all the barbarians in a net, give their flesh to the wild beasts, and prepare their skins for the celestial troops to sleep upon," was caught in the act of cutting his throat, but a wound in the arm prevented his accomplishing his purpose with the usual expertness of the Chinese. The operations on this bank of the river had all terminated by eleven o'clock; upwards of 500 prisoners had been taken; these suffered only the loss of their tails, and were set at liberty.

On the left bank, the bombardment still continued; about noon, the walls of the citadel came crumbling down the rock on all sides. The city defences were also reduced to almost a ruinous state. The enemy, too, were evidently abandoning their guns, for their fire began to slacken. The right column, 700 strong, now landed; the seamen immediately dashed up the precipitous rock, and planted the union jack on the citadel walls. From thence they proceeded to the city, where our troops on the right bank had turned some of the enemy's guns, and in a short time cleared the ramparts. Several mines had been sprung in the course of the day, doing serious damage to some of our men. Thus, in a few hours, and with a mere handful of men, fell the stronghold of Chinhae, the chief military depot, the great arsenal of this district, and the key to the large and opulent city of Ningpo, at a loss of life to the Chinese of about 2000, while our casualties in killed and wounded amounted only to nineteen. There were sixty-seven brass guns captured, besides numberless iron ones. The former were of very superior manufacture, and some worked on a pivot with the greatest ease.

The city of Chinhae, being entirely a military post, did not present many attractions. The joss-house was a mere apology for a temple. Here their hideous idols, shattered and broken by the shot, lay indiscriminately on the ground, with the mangled corpses of those who worshipped them. In one house in the city a poor woman was found with her leg shot off, and in another, four little children were lying dead, the effects of a shell that had burst over them; unfortunately, the disasters of war do not fall upon the guilty or contending parties alone!

CHAPTER XX

British troops enter Ningpo—Loss of the steamer Madagascar, and ships Nerbudda and Viscount Melbourne.

The batteries and several forts at the mouth of the Ningpo river being in our possession, it was determined to push into the city of Ningpo, the second in importance of the province of Chekeang, and removed from Chinhae fifteen miles. With this view, the admiral proceeded in the Nemesis to ascertain the depth of water, and whether the river was free from obstructions. He met with no impediment in his progress, and actually reached the very walls of the city without any attempt at opposition.

On the morning of the 13th of October, a garrison of about 500 men having been left at Chinhae, the remnant of the force was placed in steamers, and proceeded up the river. No enemy appeared, and it was evident that no treachery was intended. The peaceable inhabitants thronged the banks of the river and a floating bridge of boats that connected the city on the left bank with the suburbs on the right. The troops landed, and advanced to the gates, which were found barricaded; the walls were soon escaladed and the gates opened from within, the Chinese assisting in removing the obstructions placed against them; all around was still and quiet, there was no appearance of resistance or show of force. The enemy, placing the utmost confidence in the defences of Chinhae, which, in their opinion, neither celestial nor terrestrial power could destroy, had taken no precautions for the protection of this rich and populous city. It was ascertained that the Tartar troops had positively refused again to face ours, in consequence of which the mandarins had all fled from the city about a couple of hours before the arrival of the squadron off its walls. Our little force of soldiers, sailors, and marines, not amounting, in all, to 1000 men, marched quietly into the city, the band of the Royal Irish playing "God save the Queen." A *feu de joie* and three hearty cheers sounded from the ramparts; this was returned from the shipping moored in the river, not 100 yards from the walls, upon which the troops proceeded to the quarters assigned to them.

Ningpo is a beautiful city. It is nearly five miles in circumference and surrounded by a high wall,—fully two-thirds the size of Canton, and equally densely populated. The number of its inhabitants is supposed to be not less than 600,000. They did not appear at all to be alarmed at our approach—the majority satisfying themselves with merely closing the doors of their houses, and marking over them the words "submissive people." For some days the streets were deserted, except by the victors; gradually, however, the people regained confidence, many of the shops were re-opened, and provisions of every description became cheap and plentiful. Many hundred tons of copper coin were found in the treasury, but the sycee and dollars had, in great part, been removed to a safer place during the period we were carrying on operations against Chinhae. Quantities of valuable silks and China ware were discovered, and the granaries were stored with a couple of years' supply of grain.

The country around Ningpo is rich and fertile and the banks on each side of the river a perfect garden. Parties who have proceeded up the river, about forty miles above the city, in the light steamers, describe the scenery on each side as of surpassing beauty.

The duties of our troops, broke and scattered as they now were, and garrisoned in five distinct places—viz., Hong-Kong, Amoy, Chusan, Chinhae, and Ningpo, were, it will easily be supposed, arduous and harassing. All, however, continued very healthy, which may be attributed to the praiseworthy conduct of the men, the total absence of every description of intemperance, the abundant supply of good food, and the comfortable barracks provided them. The artillery were quartered in the hall of audience, where Captain Anstruther used to be examined before the Chinese officers. Here he found the identical cage in which he was confined. He was immediately recognised by the turnkeys about his old prison-house, and was now enabled to oblige and assist those who had previously been kind to him.

In the early part of the Chinese expedition, Sir Charles Adam, in pointing out the difficulties of carrying it through, remarked that no ship could possibly get from Singapore to Macao during the prevalence of the north-east monsoon. The passage is, no doubt, a difficult, and, to a certain extent, a dangerous one. But that the honourable member's argument was too sweeping, is clearly seen in the number of ships that almost daily reach Hong-Kong, from the several ports of India, and proceed to Chusan. In the month of December, 1841, the Jupiter troop-ship conveyed H.M.'s 26th regiment from Hong-Kong to Ningpo; and this she effected, in the very teeth of the monsoon, in little more than a month. That occasional accidents will happen must be expected. No accounts have ever been heard of the Golconda, and the supreme government have directed that the names of those unfortunate officers and men embarked on her be now struck off the strength of the army.

The loss of the steamer Madagascar, though not in any way owing to the

A 19th century Chinese scroll showing the iron steamship Nemesis and a British man-of-war.

influence of the prevailing monsoon, may be here enumerated among those other losses which have already occurred on the expedition. This steamer started from Hong-Kong in the month of September, 1841, and proceeded about ninety miles, when her coal was discovered to be on fire. The fire had communicated from the furnace late one afternoon. Every exertion was made to extinguish it, but without effect. It blew a gale the whole of this night, and at daylight on the following morning, the fire was found to have extended so near the magazine, that it became absolutely necessary at once to forsake the ship. To effect this, however, was a service of danger, in consequence of the boisterous nature of the weather, and the Lascar or native crew, who on any sudden emergency become perfectly apathetic and useless. The steamer was provided with four boats. The Lascars, finding that it was determined to risk all to them, resolved to have their share. Without the consent or knowledge of Captain Dicey, an able and experienced seaman, a portion of the crew rushed into and lowered a couple of the boats. These no sooner touched the water, than, from want of proper precaution, they were swamped, and all on board perished. The other two boats, being properly manned, kept company for some time, but at length separated in a storm, and never met again. When about ten miles from the steamer, she was observed to blow up with a tremendous explosion, and go to pieces. The captain's boat, having on board the chief officer, the surgeon, Captain Gratton, 18th regiment, and forty of the crew, reached the shore the day after they forsook the wreck. They had not been long there when the Chinese took them prisoners. At first they were treated most unkindly; stripped of all their clothes, they were obliged to march many miles on their bare feet, until they arrived in the neighbourhood of Canton, where they were then kept close prisoners, but treated with greater kindness. They continued to pass themselves off as Americans; and after being nearly six months in the hands of the Chinese, through the local influence of that respectable firm, Messrs. Jardine, Matheson, and Co., they were at length liberated. This transaction reflects no great credit on Mr. Johnstone, in charge of the government of Hong-Kong, who throughout declined to exert himself in procuring their liberation, and after they had become free, actually refused to reimburse those who advanced a large sum of money to purchase their freedom, on the plea that they were not British subjects, but only servants of the East India Company!

The transport Nerbudda, also, sailed from Hong-Kong in September, bound for Chusan. She had on board, besides immense quantities of stores, thirty men and an officer of H.M.'s 55th regiment, and 150 public followers for the several corps in the north. The ship reached the Chusan group without accident; here, however, she experienced a most severe gale, which at once dismasted her; she drifted before the wind and tide until she reached the north end of the island of Formosa, where she struck upon a reef, but immediately going over it, she again floated in twenty fathom water, where she was anchored. The cutter and the two quarter-boats had been lost in the gale. The long-boat was therefore got out; into this, Lieutenant Hamilton, H.M.'s 55th regiment, commanding on board, the captain, all the officers, and every European in the ship, embarked for the purpose, if possible, of making Amoy, and procuring assistance for those left on the wreck. Finding this impossible, they bore up, and proceeded down the coast on the eastern side of Formosa Island. They had been at sea fourteen days, and had suffered great privations, when most fortunately they fell in with a junk, which supplied them with some water and rice, and on the following day they were picked up by a clipper, and brought into Hong-Kong harbour. H.M.'s ship Nimrod was immediately dispatched to the wreck, but not a trace of it was to be seen. In coasting down the inner, or western side of the island of Formosa, they discovered from some Chinese, whom they took on board, that a ship, answering the description of the Nerbudda, had gone down at her anchors, that a great portion of those on board had been lost, and that about 100 men who had come on shore in rafts had been sent by the inhabitants of Formosa to the Chinese coast.

The Viscount Melbourne sailed from Singapore in the end of December. On the fifth of January she struck on the Leuconia shoal, in the Chinese seas. Among other passengers on board of her was Lieutenant-Colonel Campbell, proceeding to take command of the 37th Madras Grenadier corps. The ship was fast settling, which rendered it necessary to have recourse to the boats as the only means of preservation. These were five in number; by mutual consent, they steered for Borneo Proper. On the 7th they came in sight of land. Here one of the boats, manned solely with Lascars, left the others, and, contrary to the directions of the captain of the ship, proceeded on shore, which, however, they had hardly reached when they were attacked by the

Malay pirates, and all taken prisoners. On the same evening the first cutter, in which Colonel Campbell was, became separated from the other boats in a gale of wind. The captain, who was in one of the latter, in consequence of the wind changing, altered his original intention, and steered for Singapore, which port they reached fourteen days after abandoning the wreck. Those in the first cutter were not so fortunate. This boat had been injured on the reef, and it was necessary to have two men day and night employed in baling out the water to prevent her from sinking. On the day after they had parted from the other boats, they were attacked by the Malay prows; but fortunately, being well-armed, they effectually resisted the attempts made to take them prisoners. From those prows, some of the Lascars who had been seized the previous day leaped overboard, and swam toward the boat, but only two men succeeded in getting on board. Finding it impossible to reach Borneo Proper, they steered for Sambas, a Dutch settlement on the coast of Borneo. Here, after suffering many privations from the want of water, the loss of rudder, the leaky state of the boat, and the dangerous nature of the coast, both from its imperfect scenery and the swarms of pirates frequenting it, they arrived in a state of extreme exhaustion on the 16th of January, when the Dutch authorities vied with one another in administering to their comforts during ten days they remained with them. The sultan of Sambas, who is friendly to the British government, was determined not to be behind hand in his attentions. He presented Colonel Campbell and the two officers in the boat with handsome gold rings, and ultimately sent them to Singapore in one of his own ships.

CHAPTER XXI

Opium and opium smoking.

It is well known that many high authorities at home as well as abroad have asserted, and still continue to assert, that the pending war between Great Britain and the celestial empire had its origin in the opium traffic. Now, in taking up this position, the expedition is made to appear in its most odious light, and were these arguments of its opponents once admitted as reasonable and founded on a true basis, England would, indeed, have cause to rue the events of the two past years. That the sale of the drug may have tended, in some degree, indirectly, to add a stimulus to the injuries inflicted upon foreigners trading to Canton, there is but little doubt; but the arrogance and insolence of the mandarins, acting under the orders of their emperor, had arisen to so great a pitch, independent of the opium trade altogether, that it required but little foresight to predict that a crisis was approaching between the two nations. Be this as it may, a work of this description would seem to be incomplete, were not a certain portion, however small, devoted to a subject so important and full of interest to the British and Indian governments. The opium for the Chinese market is procured solely from our Anglo-Indian possessions, the Patria and Benares from the corresponding districts of that name in Bengal, and the Malua from Bombay. The two former are exported in small cakes, the latter in balls, each about the size of a thirty-two pound shot. They are packed in the dried leaf and stocks of the poppy, and sent on to China in fast sailing clippers. It being a great object to be first in the market, there is at all times great competition amongst the several mercantile houses on this point. The clipper no sooner arrives at Macao, than she immediately proceeds to transfer a portion of her cargo to receiving ships, stationed at well-known positions on the coast of China. These ships are always effectively manned and armed to enable them to resist any sudden attack either by the mandarins or pirates who rove about this coast in great numbers. They for the most part lie at anchor some miles from land, and at stations where the Chinese opium merchant, from long habit, knows where to find them. Here they are always certain of obtaining a ready sale for the drug, and at prices which repay the original purchaser, at times, many hundreds per cent. There are but few firms, however, who can engage in the traffic to this extent, in consequence of the enormous floating capital required. The Chinaman comes with his bags of dollars and sycee, or pure native silver, and receives the opium in exchange. No credit is given or asked for; all dealings are carried on in ready money.

The opium is never used by the Chinese in its crude state, but it undergoes a process which separates the resin and other impurities, leaving a residuum somewhat analogous to the morphia used by us, though in a very impure state. This is retailed at most exorbitant prices, and is supposed to be used universally and indiscriminately throughout the empire. For medicinal purposes, it is employed by the Chinese both internally and externally, to a very great extent; and I have been informed by a native doctor, that a very few grains taken internally by the most confirmed opium smoker, is certain to lull him to sleep, and have a far more powerful effect upon his secretions than if ten times that quantity was introduced into the system by means of inhalation. The drug, when used for smoking, has the appearance and consistence of tar. The apparatus necessary for proceeding with the operation consists of a small lamp, fitted with a glass shade, a steel probe, a small brass box containing the drug, and an ebony pipe, about eighteen inches in length. At the further extremity of which is a large pear-shaped bowl, smooth and flattened on its upper surface, in the centre of which is a small hole capable of admitting a pin's head. The smoker now lies down on his bed, and drawing the table, on which the lamp is placed, close to him, with the probe he takes from the box a piece of opium about the size of a pea; this he applies to the flame until it swells and takes fire; instantly blowing the flame out, he rolls the opium for a short time on the bowl of the pipe, and then re-applies it to the flame, and repeats the same process until it becomes sufficiently burned to be fit for use. It is now introduced into the small aperture in the bowl, and the lungs having previously been emptied as much as possible of atmospheric air, the pipe is put to the mouth and the bowl applied to the flame, and in one long deep inspiration the opium becomes almost entirely dissipated. The fumes are retained in the chest for a short time, and then emitted through the nostrils. This operation is repeated until the desired effects of the drug are produced, the period of which varies according as the individual has been accustomed to its. effects. Some old stagers will smoke whole nights without being completely under its influence, whereas, to the beginner or to a person not used to the habit, a very small quantity is sufficient to stupefy.

I had the curiosity to try the effects of a few pipes upon myself, and must confess I am not at all surprised at the great partiality and craving appetite always present with those who are long accustomed to its use. From what I have myself experienced, as well as seen in others, its first effects appear to be that of a powerful stimulant. There are few who have not, at some period of their lives, experienced the powers of opium, either to soothe or mitigate pain, or drown cares and sorrows. But as with most other temporary stimulants, there follows a period of nausea and depression; the opium becomes partly digested in the stomach, and it deranges all the natural secretions. When introduced into the system through the lungs, this does not appear to follow. Its effects are then far more immediate and exhilarating, as well as more transient. The pulse vibrates, it becomes fuller and firmer, the face glows, the eyes sparkle, the temperature of the skin is elevated, and it becomes suffused with a blush; the organs of sense are exquisitely sensitive, perspiration flows profusely, respiration becomes quicker, the action of the heart is increased, the nervous energy is exalted, and a glow of warmth, and sensations similar to those which often attend highly pleasurable and agreeable feelings, overspreads the body; every organized tissue shares the impression, and the whole system becomes preternaturally excited, and assumes the characteristic of disease. The perceptions become more vivid, the imagination more prolific with ideas, and these of a more brilliant and exalted character. Fancy is awakened, and creates new and bright associations, the pleasurable scenes of former life are again recalled, events and circumstances long effaced from recollection, facts long forgotten, present themselves to the mind, the future is full of delightful anticipations, whilst the most difficult schemes appear already accomplished, and crowned with success. Under its operation every task seems easy and every labour light.

The spirits are renovated, and melancholy is dissipated; the most delightful sensations and the happiest inspirations are present when only partaken to a limited extent, and to those not long accustomed to its use. If persevered in, these pleasing feelings vanish, all control of the will, the functions of sensation and volition, as well as reason, are suspended, vertigo, coma, irregular muscular contractions, and sometimes temporary delirium, supervene.

From the earliest periods in every nation, and among every people, we find some description of stimulus in common use among them; and were we to be led away by the popular opinion that the habitual use of opium injures the health and shortens life, we should expect to find the Chinese a shrivelled, and emaciated, and idiotic race. On the contrary, although the habit of opium-smoking is universal amongst the rich and poor, we find them to be a powerful, muscular, and athletic people, and the lower orders more intelligent, and far superior in mental acquirements, to those of corresponding rank in our own country.

The Chinese themselves affirm that the use of the drug acts as a preventive against disease, and in this opinion, when smoked in moderation, I am inclined in part to agree with them. The particles, by their direct and topical influence on the nerves of the lungs, which carry the impres sions they receive to the heart, brain, and spinal cord, and, through them, to all parts of the body, may thus, to a certain extent, guard the system against disease, and, by its tonic influence, strengthen the several organs; this opium gains strength when we call to mind that a peculiar active principle in opium, the narcotic, has of late been employed with considerable success in Bengal, as a substitute for quinine. It may also be mentioned, that, at the time fevers prevailed so extensively among our troops at Hong-Kong, but comparatively few of the Chinese suffered,

though exposed throughout to the same exciting causes.

These facts would certainly, on the whole, rather tend to shew that the habitual use of opium is not so injurious as is commonly supposed; its effects, certainly, are not so disgusting to the beholder as that of the sottish, slaving drunkard. True, like all other powerful stimulants and narcotics, it must ultimately produce effects injurious to the constitution; and the unhappy individual who makes himself a slave to the drug, shuns society, and is indifferent to all around him; and, when deprived of his usual allowance, he describes his feelings as if rats were gnawing his shoulders and spine, and worms devouring the calves of his legs, with an indescribable craving at the stomach, relieved only by having recourse to his pipe—now his only solace.

There is no disease in which opium may not be employed; nor do we know of any substance which can supply its place. Yet here we find its use abused, like many others of the choicest gifts of Providence.

CHAPTER XXII

Troops enter winter quarters—Health of the force—Enemy threaten their position—Conclusion.

As the cold of winter approached, it became necessary to protect the troops as much as possible from its influence. Profiting, therefore, by last year's hard-bought experience, the most comfortable quarters procurable were provided them. In the months of December and January, the cold was most intense. At Ningpo, the thermometer was seldom above 16°, and very frequently as low as 10°. There were occasionally very heavy falls of snow, with severe frost; but such was the care and attention bestowed on the comfort of the men, that regimental hospitals, on an average, did not contain half-a-dozen patients, instead of the hundreds of last year's campaign, and a death was now quite a rarity amongst them. The navy, too, were equally healthy. For sportsmen, there was abundance of amusement—pheasant, woodcock, game and wild fowl in every variety abounded in the surrounding country. In the city of Ningpo, everything was going on quietly, the inhabitants were daily nocking back, and now openly expressed a wish to be taken altogether under British protection. Confidence was established; there was an excellent market, with supplies of all kinds, and the greater number of the shops have been re-opened.

The Emperor continued to fulminate forth edicts of extermination; the fall of Ningpo and Chusan had redoubled his wrath against us. In the same edict that he says he perused the reports of his officers on the subject "with fast-falling tears," he thunders vengeance against us, and directs his oldest and best generals to concentrate their forces, and advance upon us. In the statutes of the imperial council, the name of Great Britain is enrolled among the states tributary to China; and now that the rebellious subjects should prove so refractory was beyond endurance. Some intelligent men among the Chinese have actually revived an old prophecy, supposed to have been predicted by the great Confucius—"That China is to be conquered by a woman;" and believe that the period of its fulfilment is now approaching.

Our quiet and pacific mode of life at Ningpo had emboldened some few thousand Tartars, in the month. of January, to approach to within a few miles of the city, on one of the large branches of the river.. Intelligence of their movements having been brought to the British authorities, it was at once determined to attack them ere they could establish themselves close to our position. For this purpose, the two iron steamers were again called into requisition, and in the course of a very, few hours, the enemy were suddenly surprised, at the town of Yu-yao, by the appearance of 600 British troops. The Tartars attacked our men on landing, but were easily repulsed, with a loss of about 150 killed. Their encampment was destroyed, and their granaries opened to the populace; the troops then advanced to another position higher up the river, called Si-ke. Here, also, the enemy were easily repulsed, and their camp and granaries met the same fate as did those at Yu-yao, after which our troops returned to Ningpo. Subsequent to this period, no further annoyance was offered to us. Unfortunately, our force being so small, and so separated, no further active operations can be carried on until reinforcements arrive. Though this war has already dealt harshly with us, both in purse and in person, yet must it be proceeded with until the proud Chinese nation be brought to succumb to us, and that can only be done under the walls of Pekin. Like all our eastern wars, this one has been too much a war of negotiation, until we found the enemy were laughing at us. Two years' campaigning has at length convinced us of the utter inutility of obtaining a direct official intercourse with the emperor through his deceitful and lying mandarins, who, to cloak their own weakness, and consequently the weakness of the empire, wilfully misrepresent the true state of things. Henceforth, we must war, not only with the government, but with the people also, ere we obtain our object. By so doing will the Emperor, and the people too, be convinced that England must and will have her demands.

In this stage of the expedition we beg to take leave of our readers. Our narrative has now been brought to a conclusion, and the indulgence of critics is solicited for the errors of one unaccustomed to the intricacies of literature.

That coming events in China will be of a highly important and interesting nature, not only to Great Britain, but to the world at large, there can be but little doubt; and when we couple the warfare in this portion of the globe, with the fearful occurrences in Affghanistan, a vivid picture is indeed presented of our position in the east. Political experience, tact, and sound judgment, will now be called into play, and if, in the course of another year, tranquillity should reign over British relations with India and the Celestial Empire, let us hope that the consummation of such a peace may have added additional lustre to Old England's fame.

That qualities to work out such an end, with the help of Providence, are not wanting, we have ample proof in the present administration. To quote the words of the great Duke, "A great nation can never engage in a little war."

SUPPLEMENTARY CHAPTER

Barely four months had elapsed after the preceding pages were dispatched from India to England, when the most gratifying intelligence was announced that the arms of Great Britain had triumphed in Affghanistan and in China, and our hopes expressed in the conclusion of the last chapter most amply verified.

England is at peace with China! After many vain efforts on the part of the latter government to disturb our repose at Ningpo, in which our troops were always successful, we were at length left in uninterrupted possession.

Early in May, the long-expected reinforcements began to arrive. These consisted of H.M. ships Vindictive, 50; Thalia and Endymion, 44; Cambrian, 36; North Star, 26; Dido, 20; Pelican and Harlequin, 18; Childars, Clio, Hazard, Wanderer, Serpent, and Wolverine, 16; and Chameleon, 10; besides the war steamers Auckland, Tenasseriun, Pluto, Phlegethon, Proserpine, Ariadne, Medusa, Vixen, Driver, and Memnon, and several troop and surveying ships; H.M. 98th regiment, and a detachment of royal artillery from England; strong detachments of foot artillery, and sappers and miners; a troop of horse artillery, the 2nd, 6th, 14th, 39th, and 41st regiments of native infantry and rifles from Madras;—these, with a corps of Bengal volunteers and the marines and small-arms men, amounted to a force of nearly 20,000 men.

No time was now lost in recommencing active operations. The troops and ships of war moved northward, and on the 18th May stormed the citadel and city of Chappao. Here the Tartar troops fought bravely, and kept possession

Battle of Woosung, 16th June 1842, from an original drawing by Captain Wilson.

The capture of Chin-Keang-foo on 21st July, 1842

of one of their strongholds until the place was actually burned to the ground, firmly resolved to die rather than yield, and slaughtering indiscriminately their women and children to prevent their falling into our hands.

On the 13th June, the fleet entered the great Yang-tze-Keang river, at the spot where it joins the Woosung; and on the 16th, after a heavy and unceasing cannonade for two hours, took possession of an immense line of works erected to defend the entrances into both rivers. Here 364 large, handsome guns, 76 of which were brass, were captured. The casualties on both sides were trifling.

From this point the fleet advanced without encountering much opposition, save from adverse weather, until the 20th July, on which date the whole armament, consisting of seventy sail, anchored abreast of the city of Chin-Keang-foo, in the noble Yang-tze-Keang, upwards of a hundred miles from the sea, and about fifty from Nankin, the ancient and southern capital of China.

Chin-Keang-foo is a strongly fortified city, which commands the entrance into the great Imperial Canal. Here a sharp engagement was fought, in which, though the enemy were completely routed, we sustained considerable loss in killed and wounded. The Tartars, numbering about 5000, disputed every inch of ground with desperate valour, neither giving nor taking quarter.

A large British garrison was left at this important position, and the fleet proceeded towards Nankin, which was reported to hold a garrison of 14,000

Tartars. The bombardment of this enormous city, the outer walls of which were upwards of thirty miles in circumference, was fixed for the 13th August. The attack, however, was deferred in consequence of the unexpected appearance of a messenger, carrying in his hand a white flag. He was the bearer of a letter to the plenipotentiary, intimating that commissioners were approaching from Pekin, empowered by the Emperor to treat for peace. On the 15th, the Imperial High Commissioners Kee-Ying, a member of the royal family, Guse, a General, and Elipo, a Lieutenant-General, arrived. They immediately forwarded their credentials to Sir Henry Pottinger. The latter was soon satisfied of their powers to negotiate. Several visits of ceremony then passed on both sides, and matters being satisfactorily arranged, a treaty, of which the following are the most important provisions, was signed on board H.M. ship Cornwallis, on the 29th of August, 1842:—

1. Lasting peace and friendship between the two empires.
2. China to pay Twenty-one Millions of Dollars in the course of the present and three succeeding years.
3. The Ports of Canton, Amoy, Foo Chow Foo, Ningpo, and Shanghai, to be thrown open to British merchants, consular officers to be appointed to reside at them, and regular and just tariffs of import and export (as well as inland transit) duties to be established and published.
4. The island of Hong Kong to be ceded in perpetuity to her Britannic Majesty, her heirs and successors.
5. All subjects of her Britannic Majesty (whether natives of Europe or India), who may be confined in any part of the Chinese Empire, to be unconditionally released.
6. An act of full and entire amnesty to be published by the Emperor under his Imperial sign manual and seal to all Chinese subjects, on account of their having held service or intercourse with, or resided under, the British Government or its officers.
7. Correspondence to be conducted on terms of perfect equality amongst the officers of both Governments.
8. On the Emperor's assent being received to this treaty, and the payment of the first $6,000,000, her British Majesty's forces to retire from Nanking and the Grand Canal; and the Military Posts at Chinhai to be also withdrawn; but the islands of Chusan and Kulangsoo are to be held until the money payments, and the arrangements for opening the ports, be completed.

The Chinese flag then waved in amity with that of Great Britain, and a royal salute announced to all that lasting peace and concord was established between the two empires.

Our repeated victories on the coast of China, the noble display of so

The signing and sealing of the Treaty of Nanking, by John Platt, 1846.

many British ships close to the gates of the ancient capital, our possession of the great canal, the chief artery of the empire, and the extraordinary and unnatural powers imputed to our *devil's ships*, or steamers, have at length convinced the Emperor and his advisers of the utter futility of further resistance on their part; and, in dread of a nearer approach to the capital of the empire, they were glad to "bow gracefully," and conclude peace on any terms.

Our moderate demands will for ever redound to the credit of Great Britain. We have paved the way to the utter extinction of that exclusive-ness and idea of supremacy hitherto insisted on by the Celestial Empire, and we have laid open a most valuable mart of commerce to the world at large; and, with the help of Providence, we yet may be instrumental in sowing the seeds of Christianity amongst a skilful and intelligent people.

APPENDIX

I. NOTIFICATION.

Secret Department: Fort William, 7th Oct. 1840.

The Right Hon. the Governor General of India in council is pleased to direct, that extracts from a despatch from Major-Gen. G. Burrell, commanding the military force in the China seas, be published for general information, announcing the occupation of the island of Chusan, on the east coast of China, by a portion of the force under his command.

By order of the Right Hon. the Governor General of India in council.

H. Torrens, Officiating Secretary to the Government of India.

*

To his Excellency the Right Hon. Earl Auckland, G.C.B., Governor General of India, &c., &c., &c.

Brigade Head Quarters: City of Tinghse-heen, July 18th, 1840.

My Lord,—I have the honour to acquaint your lordship, that on the4th inst., H.M.'s ships "Wellesley," "Conway," and "Alligator," (to the former of which I had transferred brigade head quarters, in compliance with the wishes of Sir Gordon Bremer,) with the troop ship, "Rattlesnake," and two transports, arrived in the anchorage of Chusan harbour; the ships of war taking up a position in front of a hill, upon which there was a large temple, or joss house.

In the evening, a summons was sent to the admiral, who was also governor of the Chusan group of islands, calling upon him to surrender the island, and soliciting him to do so, that blood might not be shed in useless opposition.

The officers bearing the summons, returned with the Chinese admiral to the "Wellesley," accompanied by two mandarins, and although they acknowledged their incapacity to resist, they attempted, by evasion and requests, to obtain time, and left the ship without any satisfactory result; but perfectly understanding, that if submission was not made before daylight next day, hostilities must commence.

On the morning of the 5th, the hill and shore were crowded with a large body of troops, and from the mast-head of the ships, the city was seen at the distance of a mile from the beach, the walls of which were also lined with troops. On Temple Hill, the landing place, or wharf, and a round tower adjacent, there were twenty-four guns of small calibre, independent of a number of war junks; and from their proceedings it appeared that resistance was to be offered. As both wind and tide were against the transports, and only 350 men, including marines, were in the harbour, I availed myself of the time offered to reconnoitre the beach beyond Temple hill, with a view of landing at some distance from the batteries, but which I abandoned, as if opposed there, the shipping must have opened their fire on the different batteries, and the result have been the same with respect to loss of life, as of opening upon the batteries at once; besides which, it was not considered expedient to take from the ships of war, under the prospect of action, so many hands as were required to man the boats.

About two o'clock p.m., H.M.'s brigs, "Cruizer" and "Algerine," had got into position, and as the transports were then entering the harbour, the signal was given for landing in rotation, as boats could be supplied in the following order: —

First division.—18th Royal Irish; Royal Marines; two nine-pounders, and 26th regiment.

Second division.—Volunteer corps and 49th regiment, and detachment of Sappers and Miners.

On the 18th and Royal Marines quitting their ships for the boats, the waving of flags, and beating of gongs and drums, gave further intimation of decided hostile intentions on the part of the Chinese.

As previously arranged with his Excellency Sir Gordon Bremer, commander-in-chief, a gun was fired from the "Wellesley," after the 18th and Royal Marines were in the boats, with a view of ascertaining whether resistance was intended. The gun was fired at the round tower most correctly, and no individual injured thereby. As the whole of the guns on shore were manned, a return fire was instantly given from them and a number of war-junks, which brought a five upon the batteries and junks from the whole of the ships-of-war, but of very short duration—the guns and hills being abandoned, and suburbs evacuated in a very few minutes. The beach, and wharf, and Temple Hill being cleared, the troops landed without opposition, and I immediately took possession of the hill, from which a very good view of the city is obtained at the distance of about 1500 yards. As soon as the landing of the 26th regiment was completed, I pushed forward advanced posts from the 18th and 26th regiments, to within 500 yards of the walls of the city, which, although in a dilapidated state, are extremely formidable and difficult of access, being surrounded on three sides with a deep canal of about twenty-five feet wide, and a continued flat of inundated paddy land.

Having consulted with Lieutenant-Colonel Montgomerie, C.B., of the Madras Artillery, and Captain Pears, the senior officer of Engineers, I decided upon breaching the walls of the city near the west gate, and throwing shells into the N.W. angle, so that in the event of the ordnance being inadequate to breach the point already specified, the N.W. angle, which I meant to attempt by escalade, might be more easily carried, from the fire kept up on that point having weakened the defence. On the advance posts taking up this position, a fire was opened upon them from the walls of the city, and kept up at intervals until near midnight. A few shot, not exceeding eight or nine, were fired from our battery, which tended to silence their firing, without doing any injury. Whilst I was visiting them, several shot were fired without any other effect than proving that the Chinese were utterly ignorant of gunnery.

The second division, consisting of the Madras Sappers and Miners, Bengal Volunteers, and 49th regiment, were landed without delay, and, having taken up their position, threw out advanced posts to the front, the latter corps protecting the left of the suburbs.

Early on the morning of the 6th, I was happy to find, from the very great exertions of Lieutenant-Colonel Montgomerie, that during the night he had, in addition to the two nine-pounders landed with the troops, got into position six other guns of the same size, two five and-a-half inch howitzers, and two mortars, making a total of ten guns, in a position within four hundred yards of the walls. From the stillness in the city, I apprehended a change had taken place there, and I waited for daylight before issuing orders for offensive operations; on the first dawn, the flags were seen on the walls as they were the preceding evening, but, as the light increased, there did not appear a single person, where there had been thousands the preceding evening, which gave reason to suppose that the city was evacuated; and I sent forward Lieutenant-Colonel Montgomerie, Major Mountain, Deputy Adjutant-General, and Captain Pears, field engineer, with a small escort, to reconnoitre as closely as possible the state of the works, and endeavour to ascertain whether the city was abandoned or not.

These officers passed the canal (the bridge over which had been broken up) by throwing spars across, and with Captain Bethune, of the "Conway," who had now joined them, scaled the wall by means of a ladder found amongst the buildings outside. One or two unarmed Chinese, who appeared above the gate, hung a placard over the wall, and refused by signs to admit them, but offered no other opposition.

The gate was found strongly barricaded within by large sacks of grain, and by the time that a few planks had been thrown over the canal, a company of the 49th, which I had sent for, took possession of the principal gate of the city of Ting-hae-heen, upon which the British flag was hoisted.

Guards were quickly posted at the whole of the gates, and every protection given to life and property. I lament that several houses in the city had been plundered by the lower order of the Chinese people before we took possession, and that it was carried to considerable extent in the suburbs, by the same class, during the nights of the 5th and 6th, from their occupying houses which were ultimately proved not to belong to parties claiming them. Order is now restored: but a large portion of the people, who went into the country, have not yet returned.

A return of the ordnance captured on shore is herewith transmitted; that on board the war junks was considerable, but of which I have not a return.

The loss of the Chinese is estimated at about twenty-five killed; the number wounded I cannot learn, but it must be very small, from round shot having been fired. The admiral is said to be among the latter. I am happy to say, her Majesty's troops escaped without loss of any description, and are prepared for any further services required.

The city of Ting-hae-heen is extensive, the walls being about six miles in circumference; they are built of granite and brick, of inferior quality, and with the exception of a hill, where the defences are unusually high, there is a deep ditch or canal, about twenty-five feet wide, carried round the walls at the distance of a few yards. There are numerous bastions in the works, and with good troops, in its present state, the city is capable of making a good defence.

This dispatch will be delivered to your lordship by the Hon. Capt. Osborne, to whom I beg to refer you for further particulars respecting the island of Chusan and our position here.

I have the honour to be, &c,

(Signed) *Geo. Burrell, Brigadier, Commanding Eastern Force.*

True Extracts.

H. Torrens, Officiating Secretary to the Government of India.

*

Return of Ordnance captured at Chusan (on shore) by the combined naval and military force, under the command of Commodore Sir J. G. Bremer, C.B. and K.C.H., &c., and Brigadier Burrell, on the 5th July, 1840.

Ordnance: Where found	Guns, Iron				Guns, Brass	
	2 to 3 pdrs	4 to 6 pdrs	6 1/2 pdrs to 8	9 pdrs	6 1/2 pdrs	Total
On Sea Face	9	10	3	1	1	24
On walls of the Town	6	9	8	0	0	23
In the Arsenals	15	21	4	4	0	44
Grand Total	-	-	-	-		91

The guns, with the exception of the brass one, are all apparently of Chinese manufacture, and of a very inferior description. The brass gun has the date of "1601, made by Richard Phillips," place not mentioned.

A considerable quantity of gunpowder has been found, and three magazines, containing an extensive supply of iron shot, ginjals. matchlocks, swords, bows and arrows, &c, with steel helmets, and uniform clothing for a large body of men, the particulars of which have not yet been ascertained, but of which an inventory is being made. With the exception of the ordnance, most of the articles are packed and stored with much method and are in very good order.

(Signed) *P. Montgomerie, Lieut.-Col., Comdg. Arty. Eastern Expedition.*

(Signed) *Geo. Burrell, Brigr. Comdg. Camp, Chusan, 10th July, 1840.*

Republished by order of the Right Hon. the Governor in Council.

Hy. Chamier, Chief Secretary.

II. GENERAL ORDERS.

Fort William: Secret Department, the 24th February, 1841.

The Right Hon. the Governor-General of India, having received an official communication of the destruction, on the 7th of January, of Chuenpee and Ty-cock-tow, in an attack made upon those fortifications by the sea and land forces under the personal command of his Excellency Commodore Sir J. J. G. Bremer, C.B. and K.C.H., naval commander-in-chief on the coast of China, is pleased to order the publication of the following official account of the action.

By order of the Right Hon. the Governor-General of India.

T. H. Maddock, Secretary to the Government of India.

*

At eight o'clock this morning, the Royal Marines of the squadron, the detachments of the 26th and 49th regiments, and the 37th Madras Native Infantry, and Bengal Volunteers, were landed, accompanied by the detachment of Royal Artillery, with one 24-pounder howitzer, and two 6-pounder field-guns, together with a division of seamen belonging to the "Wellesley," "Blenheim," and "Melville," in all, about 1400 men, the land forces under the command of Major Pratt, of the 26th Cameronians, a copy of whose report will explain the details of military operations, which were admirably executed.

The "Queen"and "Nemesis" steamers were placed in position for throwing shells into the upper fort, by Commander Belcher, of the "Sulphur," and soon made an impression; a division of ships, consisting of "Calliope," "Hyacinth," and "Larne," under Captain Herbert, attacked the lower fort on the sea face, and, in less than an hour, silenced the guns, although a number of troops remained within the walls; by ten o'clock the troops had advanced, and carried the entrenchments with their field batteries; Major Pratt himself and two or three Marines were in possession of the upper fort, and the British colours hoisted; the lower fort was speedily surrounded, and stormed by the entrance, as well as the wall, by a party of Royal Marines, and the union jack displayed in the ramparts.

The management of Ty-cock-tow was entrusted to Captain Scott, of H.M.S. "Samarang," accompanied by the "Druid," Modeste," and "Columbine," and in one hour it was silenced; but the Chinese remained in it until it was stormed by the boats, in which operation Lieutenant Bowers, senior of the "Samarang," was severely wounded; the guns in all the forts have been destroyed, the magazines blown up, and the barracks and houses burnt; eleven large war junks were anchored in the shoal water to the eastward of the position; the "Nemesis," under Commander Belcher, accompanied by Lieutenant Killett, of the "Starling," attacked them in admirable style, assisted by the boats of the "Calliope," under Lieutenant Watson, senior of that ship; they were all set on fire and blown up—one with all her crew on board, a rocket having gone into her magazine. This ended the operations of the day.

His Excellency the naval Commander-in-Chief expresses his high admiration of the gallantry and zeal which animated every officer and man in the force, returns his thanks to Captains Sir Le Fleming Senhouse, of the "Blenheim," and the Hon. R. Dundas, of the "Melville," and Captain Maitland, of the "Wellesley." Captains Herbert and Scott carried their divisions into action with their accustomed gallantry, and they were ably seconded by Captains Smith and Blake, and Commanders Warren, Eyres, and Clarke, under their immediate orders. The Commanders Pritchard, Paget, and Fletcher, of the "Blenheim," "Melville," and "Wellesley," the commanders of the steam vessels, and every officer and man employed, deserve the highest praise for their zealous exertions on every point. Major Pratt, of the 26th, conducted the operations on shore, in the most able and gallant manner; he speaks in the highest terms of the conduct of every officer and man employed.

This service has been performed with trifling loss on the part of H.M.'s forces, although it is but justice to the Chinese to say that they defended themselves, especially in the batteries, with the greatest credit and devotion; they have suffered severely; their loss, including that on board the war junks, cannot be estimated at less than from five to six hundred, out of a force calculated at 2000 men. The slaughter in the lower fort, when carried by storm, was considerable.

*

To His Excellency Sir J. J. Gordon Bremer, C.B., K.C.H., Commodore of the First Class, Commander-in-Chief, &c.
H.M.S. "Wellesley," Chuenpee, January 8, 1841.

Sir, — I have the honour to report to you that the troops under ray command, consisting of a detachment of Royal Artillery, having one twenty-four pounder howitzer, and two six pounder field guns, aided by a party of seamen from H.M. Ships "Wellesley," "Blenheim" and "Melville," detachments of the 26th and 49th Regiments, a battalion of Royal Marines, the 37th Madras Native Infantry, and a detachment of Bengal Volunteers, in all 1400 men, landed yesterday, at nine o'clock, two miles below Chuenpee Point, for the purpose of capturing the several forts and batteries on Chuenpee.

The troops landed without opposition; and having formed them, I sent forward an advance of two companies of Royal Marines, under Captain Ellis; the guns were then moved on, supported by the detachments of the 26th and 49th Regiments, followed in column by the Marine Battalion, the 37th Native Infantry, and the Bengal Volunteers.

After advancing a mile and a half, on reaching the ridge of a hill, we came in sight of the upper fort, and of a very strong entrenchment, having a deep ditch outside, and a breast-work round it, which was prolonged upwards, connecting it with the upper fort; it was also flanked by field batteries, having deep trenches in the rear of the guns for the purpose of shelter; the whole was strongly lined with Chinese soldiers, who immediately on seeing us, cheered, waved their flags in defiance, and opened a fire from their batteries; our guns were promptly placed on the crest of the ridge, and commenced firing. This was duly returned by the Chinese for about twenty minutes; and indeed in this, as well as our other encounters with them, it is but justice to say, they behaved with courage. During this time, the advance crossed the shoulder of the hill to the right, driving before them the Chinese, who had lined it in considerable numbers; then, descending into the valley, took possession of a field battery placed there. I had previously ordered two companies of the 37th N. I., under Captains Bedingfield and Wardroper, to scour round a hill to the right of the advance, where they encountered the Chinese in some force, and drove them away with much loss. Captain Duff, commanding the corps, speaks highly of the conduct of these companies, which he had supported by another under Lieutenant Hadfield.

Seeing that the fire from our guns was causing the Chinese to fly from the entrenchments and batteries, I moved the column down the slope, causing the two leading companies of Marines, under Captain Whitcomb, to clear the wooded hill in front. I took a subdivision of them, got into the entrenchment, and proceeded up inside the breastwork to the upper fort, in which there was still a number of men. These were speedily dislodged by the two Marines who first reached it; the fort was entered, and the British ensign hoisted by a Royal Marine.

The attack on the Chinese war junks at Chuenpee creek.

The lower fort, which had sixteen guns facing the sea, and was surrounded by a high wall, and a small battery between, was, from this, completely exposed; but the fire of these, as well as of the upper fort, had been silenced by the ships attacking on the sea face. They were still in considerable numbers in the lower part of the fort, and had locked the gate; a fire was therefore kept up from the hill, and the advance coming round the lower side to the gate, forced it by musketry. On entering, they met with considerable resistance, which was speedily subdued; some men then entering an embrasure on the flank, the fort was taken, and our flag hoisted.

The whole of the forts and batteries being now in our possession, we proceeded to render the guns unserviceable, and dismantle the fort, setting their encampments on fire; and, on re-embarking, the magazine in the lower fort was blown up.

I am happy to say that the loss on our side has been small, and would have been less, but for the explosion of an expense magazine in the fort after the capture. The Chinese, however, suffered severely; between three and four hundred were killed and wounded, including amongst the killed the 'Heptai,' an officer with rank equivalent to our Brigadier-General. About 100 prisoners were taken, who were released at the close of the day.

I have great pleasure in stating to your Excellency the admirable manner in which the whole Force behaved, and I beg to recommend to your notice Major Johnson, 26th Regiment, commanding detachments of the 26th and 49th Regiments. I must particularly mention Captain Ellis, commanding the Marine Battalion, an old and previously distinguished officer, who conducted the advance during the whole day with the greatest gallantry and judgment, and he speaks in the highest terms of the men forming the advance; Captain Knowles, R.A., who placed his guns admirably, and dismantled the forts after their capture; Captain Duff, commanding the 37th N.I., and Captain Bolton, commanding the detachment of Bengal Volunteers. From Lieut. Stransham, Adjutant of the Royal Marines, who acted as Brigade Major, I received most valuable assistance during the day, and gladly availed myself of the services of your Military Secretary, Lieut. Stewart Mackenzie, 90th Regiment, who volunteered to act on my staff, and took charge of a party of skirmishers of the advance the better part of the day.

Lieutenant Wilson, H.M.S. "Blenheim," commanded the seamen, and the guns were dragged forward in good style; and the disembarkation and re-embarkation of the troops was ably managed by Lieutenant Symons, H.M.S. "Wellesley."

I enclose the list of guns captured and destroyed, and also the return of casualties.

I have, &c.

(Signed) *J. L. Pratt, Major, 26th Cameronians, Commanding the Force.*

*

List of Casualties in the Force employed at the Assault and Capture of the Forts and Batteries on Chuenpee, on the 7th January, 1841.

WOUNDED.

- 2nd Lieutenant White, Royal Marines, slightly.
- Assistant-Surgeon McPherson, 37th Madras Native Infantry, burnt by explosion.
- Mr. Arthur Vyner, Mate, R.N., (H.M.S. "Blenheim,") severely.
- Royal Artillery, 1 gunner and driver, slightly.
- Royal Marines, 2 sergeants, 7 privates, severely.
- 2 privates, slightly—18th Royal Irish.
- 2 privates, ditto—37th Madras Native Infantry.
- 2 havildars, 1 naique, 10 privates, severely.—Total, 30.

(Signed) *A. B. Stransham, Acting Brigade Major.*

*

- Calliope: 1 seaman, severely.
- Samarang: 1 Lieutenant Bowers, severely. 1 boy, 1st class, severely.
- Hyacinth: 2 seamen, severely. 3 seamen, slightly.

Total: 8

Of the force employed on shore: 30

Grand Total wounded: 38

*

(Copy.) H.M.S. "Blenheim," off the Bocca Tigris, Jan. 8th, 1841.
Return of Ordnance mounted in the Fort and Entrenchments at Chuenpee, when Stormed and Captured on the 7th January, 1841.

- In the Upper Fort — Guns, iron: 9
- Lower Fort — Guns, iron: 19
- In the Intrenchments — Guns, iron: 15
- Total: 43
- Guns, iron, not mounted: 23

  Grand Total: 66

The guns in the forts were nearly of the same calibre as the British 18 and 12-pounders. Those in the entrenchments, 6-pounders.

The guns were all rendered unserviceable and the carriages destroyed.

(Signed) *J. Knowles, Captain, Commanding Royal Artillery.*

- On Ty-cock-tow: 25

These guns were of the same calibre as those on Chuenpee, also rendered unserviceable.

- In the junks about 82, from 12 to 4-pounders.

  Recapitulation.
- On Chuenpee and its dependencies: 66
- On Ty-cock-tow: 25

  Grand Total: 173

*

To Commodore Sir J. J. G. Bremer, C.B., K.C.H, Commander in Chief, &c. &c. &c.

Sir,—In obedience to your instruction of yesterday, I proceeded with the ships placed under orders off Ty-cock-tow. The fort commenced its fire upon us at twenty minutes past ten o'clock, which I did not reply to until I took up my anchorage, ten minutes after, abreast of it, about two hundred yards distant, which was as near as the depth of water would permit of our approach. The "Modeste," "Druid," and "Columbine" anchored in succession, and in a few minutes so destructive and well-directed was the fire of the ships, that that of the enemy's was silenced, with the exception of an occasional gun or two. At 11.20 a.m., observing that we had effected a practicable breach in the southern end of the fort, I directed the boats, manned and armed, to proceed to storm it. Lieutenant Bowers (first of this ship) immediately landed, supported by the boats of the "Modeste;" those of the "Druid" and "Columbine," under the command of Lieutenant Goldsmith (first of that ship) proceeded to the north end.

At attempt at resistance was made by the enemy at the breach, against Lieutenant Bowers and his party, but was instantly overcome by the gallant and determined rush onwards of our men, which so appalled the garrison that they instantly made a hasty retreat over the hill wall, leaving us masters of the fort.

The guns, amounting to twenty-five longs, of different calibre, were then spiked, the trunnions knocked off, a shot, wrapped round with wet canvas, driven hard home in each, and they were then thrown into the sea, their carriages burnt, as well as the whole of the buildings and magazines blown up; previous to which latter operation, all the wounded of the enemy were carried away clear of the fort. Their loss, judging from the number of killed lying in every direction, must have been most severe.

My best thanks are due to Captain Smith and Commanders Eyres and Clarke, for the efficient and able support they have afforded me. It is impossible to say too much in favour of all those under my command, their conduct merits my warmest approbation. Of Lieutenant Bowers (first of this ship) I cannot speak too highly. In the attack of the breach he received a severe sabre wound across the knee, which I fear will deprive me for some time of his services; I beg leave to recommend him most strongly to your favourable consideration, as well as Mr. Luard, mate, who behaved most gallantly in the breach—the zealous conduct of this promising young officer has repeatedly drawn forth my commendations.

Our damages are very trifling, being merely some of the standing rigging cut away, and a shot through our hull, the fire of the enemy passing all over us.

Enclosed, I beg leave to return a list of wounded on board the "Samarang."

I have, &c,

(Signed) *James Scott, Captain. Her Majesty's Ship "Samarang,"*

Canton River, 8th Jan., 1841.

(True copies.) *T. H. Maddock, Secretary to the Government of India.*

Republished by order of the Right. Hon. the Governor in council.

Robert Clerk, Secretary to Government.

III. CIRCULAR BY CAPTAIN ELLIOT.

To Her Britannic Majesty's subjects resident at Macao.

Negotiations having been interrupted, the positions of Chuenpee and Ty-cock-tow were simultaneously attacked this morning by sea and land, and have both fallen to her Majesty's arms.

It will be very satisfactory to her Majesty's subjects to learn that this gallant achievement was effected with trifling loss, not withstanding an obstinate and honourable defence on all points.

(Signed) *Charles Elliot, Her Majesty's Plenipotentiary in China.*

Her Majesty's Ship "Wellesley," Anson's Bay, 7th Jan., 1841.

IV. CIRCULAR.

To Her Britannic Majesty's subjects.
Her Majesty's Ship "Wellesley," off Anunghoy, 8th Jan. 1841.

A communication has been received from the Chinese commander-in-Chief, which has led to an armistice, with the purpose to afford the high commissioner time to consider certain conditions now offered for his acceptance.

(Signed) *Charles Elliot, Her Majesty's Plenipotentiary in China.*

V. GENERAL MEMORANDUM.

"Wellesley," off Anunhoy, 21st Jan., 1841.

The Commander-in-Chief having received a communication from his Excellency her Majesty's Plenipotentiary, acquainting him that a treaty of peace had been entered into between the Chinese imperial commissioner and himself, hastens to make the same known to the fleet and force.

*

CIRCULAR.
To Her Britannic Majesty's subjects.
Macao, 20 Jan., 1841.

Her Majesty's Plenipotentiary has now to announce the conclusion of preliminary arrangements between the imperial commissioner and himself, involving the following conditions:—

1. The cession of the island and harbour of Hong-kong to the British crown. All just charges and duties to the empire upon the commerce carried on there to be paid as if the trade were conducted at Whampoa.
2. An indemnity to the British government of six millions of dollars, one million payable at once, and the remainder in equal annual instalments, ending in J 846.
3. Direct official intercourse between the countries upon an equal footing.
4. The trade of the port of Canton to be opened within ten days after the Chinese new year, and to be carried on at Wampoa till further arrangements are practicable at the new settlement.

Details remain matter of negotiation.

The Plenipotentiary seizes the earliest occasion to declare that her Majesty's government has sought for no privilege in China exclusively for the advantage of British ships and merchants, and he is only performing his duty in offering the protection of the British flag to the subjects, citizens, and ships of foreign powers that may resort to her Majesty's possession.

Pending her Majesty's further pleasure, there will be no port or other charges to the British government.

The Plenipotentiary now permits himself to make a few general observations.

The oblivion of past and redressed injuries will follow naturally from the right feeling of the Queen's subjects. Indeed, it should be remembered that no extent of modification resulting only from political intervention can be efficacious in the steady improvement of our condition, unless it be systematically seconded by conciliatory treatment of the people and becoming deference for the institutions and government of the country, upon the threshold of which we are about to be established.

The Plenipotentiary can only presume to advert very briefly to the zeal and wisdom of the Commander of the expedition to China; and to that rare union of ardour, patience, and forbearance, which has distinguished the officers and forces of all arms at all points of occupation and operation.

He is well assured the British community will sympathize cordially with him in their sentiments of lasting respect for his Excellency and the whole force, which he is ashamed to express in such inadequate language.

He cannot conclude without declaring that next to these causes, the peaceful adjustment of difficulties must be ascribed to the scrupulous good faith of the very eminent person with whom negotiations are still pending.

(Signed) *Charles Elliot, Her Majesty's Plenipotentiary, China.*

*

DOCUMENT.

"Keshen, a great minister of state, and imperial high commissioner of the second order of hereditary nobility, and acting governor of the two Kwang provinces, writes this despatch for the full imformation of the Tungche, or Keunmingfoo of Macao.

"The English barbarians are now obedient to orders, and, by an official document, have restored Tinghae and Shaheo, invoking me with the most earnest importunity, that I should for them report, and beg (the imperial) favour.

"At present, all affairs are perfectly well settled. The former order for stopping their trade and cutting off the supplies of provisions it is unnecessary to enforce; it is for this purpose that I issue these orders to the said Tungche, that he may obey accordingly, without opposition. A special despatch."

VI. CIRCULAR.

Circumstances have induced the Commander-in-Chief to announce to her Majesty's Plenipotentiary his intention to move the forces towards the Bocca Tigris. The Plenipotentiary will afford the earliest information in his power of the future course of events.

(Signed) *Secretary and Treasurer to the Superintendents. Macao, 10th Feb. 1841.*

VII. CIRCULAR.

To Her Majesty's Subjects.

The imperial minister and high commissioner having failed to conclude the treaty of peace, lately agreed upon with her Majesty's Plenipotentiary within the allotted period, hostilities were resumed yesterday afternoon. A Chinese force employed under cover of a masked and strong field-work, in blocking up the channel of the river at the back of Annanhoi, was dislodged, and the obstruction effectually cleared away; the guns in battery and deposit, amounting to about eighty, of various calibre, rendered unserviceable; and the whole of the military material destroyed. This effective service was accomplished in about two hours, by Captain Herbert, of H.M.S. "Calliope," having under his command the steam-vessel "Nemesis," and the pinnances of H.M.S. "Calliope," "Samarang," "Herald," and "Alligator." The extent of the Nemesis' loss has not been ascertained.

(Signed) *Charles Elliott, Her Majesty's Plenipotentiary.*

On board H.M.S. "Calliope," off South Wang-Tong, 24th Feb. 1841.

VIII. NOTIFICATION.

Secret Department, 20th April, 1841.

The Right Hon. the Governor General in council, has great satisfaction in publishing, for general information, the following details of brilliant successes which have been recently achieved in China, ending in the entire destruction of the defences of Canton, and in the placing of that city at the mercy of her Majesty's forces.

His lordship in council has directed a royal salute to be fired in honour of this occasion.

T. H. Maddock, Secretary to Government.

*

To the Right Hon. George Earl of Auckland, G.C.B., &c., Governor General of India.
Wellesley, off North Wang-Tong, March 10th, 1841.

My Lord,—It is with feelings of gratification I have the honour to announce to you that the forts of the Bocca Tigris, together with every other of the Chinese defences with which we are acquainted, have fallen to her Majesty's arms; the British flag flying on the fortress of Wang-Tong, in which is a garrison, and all the other batteries have been blown up, and utterly destroyed; and as I am aware of the intense interest which is felt by your lordship, I avail myself of the earliest opportunity of forwarding to you a detail of the events which have led to this result.

On the 20th of January, the preliminaries of a treaty of peace were agreed upon by her Majesty's Plenipotentiary, under the seal of the Chinese commissioner, one of the conditions of which was, the cession of the island of Hong-Kong to her Majesty, and the restoration of Chuenpee and Ty-cock-tow to the Chinese, together with the evacuation of Chusan at the earliest possible period. His Excellency, in consequence, requested me to move the force from the immediate neighbourhood of the Bocca Tigris; and having made the necessary arrangements with the Chinese admiral commanding in chief, the forts were delivered to his officers, under the usual salutes, on the 21st, and the fleet proceeded to the anchorage off the west end of Lantao island.

Her Majesty's Plenipotentiary and the Imperial Commissioner have arranged to have a formal meeting at the second bar, in the river, on the 26th, I detached the "Calliope" and "Larne," and "Madagascar" and "Nemesis" steamers to the Bocca Tigris, under the immediate command of Captain Herbert, of the "Calliope;" a guard of honour, composed of 100 picked men of the Royal Marines, under the command of Captain Ellis, R.N., of the "Wellesley," and the band of that ship were embarked. Captains the Hon. It. S. Dundas and Maitland, of the "Melville" and "Wellesley," together with as many of the officers of the fleet as could be spared, accompanied his Excellency; the party was received with every possible mark of distinction and respect; the troops were drawn up on the ramparts of the forts, and salutes fired from all; a sumptuous entertainment had been prepared, to which the officers were invited, after having been presented to the High Commissioner, and the negotiations proceeded in a satisfactory manner, the particulars of which have been stated by the Plenipotentiary to H.M.'s government.

On the same day, I proceeded to Hong-Kong, and took formal possession of the island in her Majesty's name, and hoisted the colours on it, with the usual salutes and ceremonies. By the terms of the treaty, the port of Canton was to be opened to the trade of all nations, on the 2nd of February, and as a proof of the sincere desire on the part of the British functionary to evince good faith, I had, at his request, sent the "Columbine" to Chusan, and an overland despatch, by the hands of a Chinese special messenger, directing Brigadier Burrell and Captain Bourchier, of H.M.S. "Blonde," to use every effort to embark the stores and troops, &c, and to restore the island to the Chinese authorities.

The proclamation for opening the port on the 2nd did not appear, and on the 11th, the two ministers again met at the Bocca Tigris, and after a discussion of several hours, on this day and on the next, her Majesty's Plenipotentiary acceded to a further delay (not to exceed ten days), in order that the definitive treaty might be fairly prepared. I must confess, that from this moment my faith in the sincerity of the Chinese commissioner was completely destroyed; my doubts were also strengthened by the reports of the officers I sent up to the place of meeting, who stated that military works on a great scale were in progress, troops collected on the heights, and camps protected by entrenchments arising on both sides of the river, and that the island of North Wang-Tong had become a mass of cannon. These indications being decidedly warlike, I determined to move the light division of H.M.'s ships at once to Macao Roads, and proceeded thither myself on the 13th, to confer with his Excellency the Plenipotentiary, and await events. I found that the treaty, as agreed upon by the commissioner and her Majesty's minister, had been sent up to the Bocca Tigris, for transmission to Canton, by the "Nemesis," with orders to await an answer until the night of the 18th, the period the confidential person employed by the Chinese commissioner had named for the purpose. The accounts daily received by merchants and others, at Macao, from Canton, were of the most hostile character, and an edict, purporting to be from the Emperor, calling on all his officers to exterminate us, was published, together with a proclamation, the authenticity of which I have, however, been unable to establish, offering 50,000 dollars for my head, and a like sum for that of the Plenipotentiary. On the morning of the 19th, the "Nemesis" arrived from the Bocca Tigris without any reply, and all doubt was at an end, a shot having been fired at her boat from North Wang-Tong. I instantly detached the light division under Captain Herbert, of H.M.S. "Calliope," (who was accompanied by H.M. Plenipotentiary,) with directions not to run any unnecessary hazard until the body of the force came up, but to prevent, as much as possible, any further defensive preparations on the part of the enemy. I proceeded at the same time to Hong-Kong, and weighed with the ships of the line, the "Queen" and "Madagascar" steamers, leaving the "Druid," "Jupiter," and transports to follow.

Captain Herbert, with the ships under his orders, took up a position on the western channel off South Wang-Tong, on the 20th, and on the 22nd he proceeded in the "Nemesis," with some boats of the squadron, to the channel at the back of Anunghoy, and destroyed a masked battery of 20 guns, which opened on them whilst employed clearing the passage, which the Chinese had been endeavouring to obstruct, by driving down poles, and mooring rafts across. This service was performed without any loss on our side; the guns in the battery were disabled by knocking off the trunnions, together with sixty found dismounted; the magazines &c. were burnt; the enemy left about thirty of the number dead, and their colours were taken by Lieutenant Bowers, senior of H.M.S. "Samarang."

From the prevalence of light winds, the line of battle ships and "Druid" were not collected until the 24th. On the 25th, I arranged a plan of attack on the formidable batteries in our front, and of which it may be necessary for me to give some description. Partly surrounding the old fort of Anunghoy, and in advance of it to high-water mark, was a new and well-built battery of granite, forming a segment of about two-thirds of a circle; on it were mounted forty-two guns, some of them of immense weight and large calibre; several strong entrenchments extended to the southward of this battery, and the ridges of the hill were crowned with guns, up to a camp calculated for about 1200 men; at the north side was a straight work, of modern erection, mounting sixty heavy guns; about 150 yards of rocky beach intervenes between the end of this battery and the northern circular battery, on which forty guns were mounted; all the works were protected in rear by a high wall extending up the hill, on which were steps or platforms for firing musketry, and in the interior were the magazines, barracks, &c.

On the east end of the island of North Wang-Tong is a battery with a double tier of guns defending the passage on that side, and also partly flanking a number of rafts constructed of large masses of timber moored across the river (about twelve feet apart), with two anchors each, connected by, and supporting four parts of a chain cable, the ends of which were secured under masonry work, one on South Wang-Tong, the other on Anunghoy. On the western end of North Wang-Tong is a strong battery of forty guns, flanked by a field-work of seventeen; indeed, the whole island is one continued battery; on the extreme western side of the channel was a battery of twenty-two heavy guns, and a field-work of seventeen, protecting an entrenched camp, containing 1500 or 2000 men. South Wang-Tong was not occupied by the enemy; it was an excellent position, and I therefore caused a work to be thrown upon it during the night of the 25th, and mounted two eight-inch iron, and one 24-pounder brass howitzer; at daylight on the 26th, Captain Knowles, of the Royal Artillery, opened this battery with admirable effect, throwing shells and rockets into North Wang-Tong, and occasionally into Anunghoy, which fire was returned by the Chinese with great spirit, from a battery immediately opposite, having also kept up a fire during the greater part of the preceding night, during the erection of the work, which slackened towards two, a. m., and finally ceased.

At eleven o'clock, the breeze springing up, the signal was made, and the fleet stood in.

The attack on Anunghoy I entrusted to Captain Sir H. Le Fleming Senhouse, of H.M.S. "Blenheim," having with him the "Melville," "Queen" steamer, and four rocket boats. The "Wellesley," "Calliope," "Samarang," "Druid," "Herald," "Alligator," and "Modeste," were opposed to the batteries on the south, south-west, and north-west of Wang-Tong, and the forts on the western side of the channel.

In less than an hour the batteries on Wang-Tong were silenced and the troops, (under Major Pratt, of the 26th Cameronians,) which had been previously embarked in the "Nemesis" and "Madagascar" steamers, consisting of the detachments of H.M.'s 26th and 49th regiments, 37th Madras Native Infantry, and Bengal Volunteers, together with the Royal Marines, were landed, and in a few minutes were masters of the island without any loss; 1300 Chinese surrendered.

The Anunghoy batteries had now been silenced by the beautiful precision with which the fire of the "Blenheim," "Melville," and "Queen" had been directed; and perceiving that the enemy were shaken, Sir Le Fleming Senhouse, at the head of the Marines and small-arm men, landed on the southern battery, and drove them in succession from that and the two others, and at one o'clock the British colours were flying on the whole chain of these celebrated works; and the animated gallantry displayed by the whole force, convinces me that almost any number of men the Chinese could collect would not be able to stand before them for a moment.

Our casualties are trifling,—five wounded slightly in the whole force: the main topmast and fore-yard of the "Blenheim" were shot through, one 32-pounder gun rendered unserviceable, several shot in the hull, and the rigging much cut up; the "Melville's" main-topmast wounded, and rigging considerably injured; the "Calliope" was struck in several places, and the other ships had merely a few ropes cut. The loss of the enemy was severe, but not so heavy as at Chuenpee, 1300, as before stated, having thrown down their arms. I should estimate their killed and wounded at 250 in Wang-Tong; probably as many in Anunghoy, at which place the Chinese Admiral, Kwan, and several other mandarins of rank fell. The body of the admiral was recognised by his family, and taken away the day after the action, under a fire of minute-guns from the "Blenheim."

On the morning of the 27th, the light squadron proceeded up the river under the command of Captain Herbert, of the "Calliope;" and on the day following, I was gratified by receiving a dispatch from him, reporting, that on their arrival off the first bar, the enemy were observed strongly fortified on the left bank of the river, close to Whampoa Reach, with upwards of forty war-junks, and the "Cambridge," (formerly an East Indiaman of 900 tons.) On approaching within three miles, the "Madagascar" and "Nemesis" steamers, having on board his Excellency and Captain Herbert, proceeded to reconnoitre, and find out a clear passage, a number of vessels having been

The attack on First Bar battery on the Canton River.

sunk; on advancing, a heavy fire was opened on the steamers, which was returned with great effect; the ships were now brought up, and opened fire on the junks, "Cambridge," and batteries, which in an hour were nearly silenced, when the Marines and small-arm men were landed, and stormed the works, driving before them upwards of 2000 of the Chinese troops, and killing nearly 300. In about half an hour after landing, all the defences were carried, though in several places brave and obstinate resistance was made. In the meantime, the "Cambridge" was boarded, and carried by the boats of the "Calliope," "Nemesis," and "Modeste," and almost immediately set on fire; the explosion of this vessel's magazine must have been heard at Canton. The fort (mud) mounted on the river-front forty-seven guns; on the left flank, three; a field-work, four; the "Cambridge," thirty-four; besides ten mounted in a junk, making altogether ninety-eight guns.

The war junks escaped up the river, where the ships were prevented pursuing them by a strong raft placed across the passage. The guns and other munitions were destroyed. In this gallant affair, the casualties (considering the opposing force) are few: one killed; three dangerously and five slightly wounded.

On the morning of the 1st instant, I proceeded up the river, to join the advanced squadron in the "Madagascar" steamer, taking the transport "Sophia" in tow. Captain Maitland, with the boats and one hundred small-arm men, together with the Marines of the "Wellesley," accompanied me; the "Queen," taking the "Eagle" transport in tow, on board which ship I had embarked the marines of the "Blenheim," "Melville," and "Druid," also attended by the boats of those ships, all being armed with their guns and howitzers.

On arriving at Whampoa, I found from Captain Herbert's report, that the enemy were in considerable force at the end of "Junk Reach," having as usual sunk several large junks in the river, and further protected themselves by a strong double line of stakes across it, and large bamboos and branches of trees between them. On the following morning I detached Commander Belcher, in H.M.S. "Sulphur," up Junk River to reconnoitre, that ship being taken in tow by three of the "Wellesley's" boats, under command of Lieutenant Symonds, senior lieutenant of the latter ship; on rounding a point on the right bank, they came in front of a low battery of twenty-five guns, masked by thick branches of trees, which opened a heavy fire on them. Lieutenant Symonds instantly cut the tow rope, and gallantly dashed into the battery, driving the enemy before him, and killing several of their number. The "Sulphur" anchored, and some shot from her completely routed them from the thick underwood in the vicinity, in which they had taken shelter; the guns were destroyed, and the magazine and other consumable material set on fire.

The number of troops was probably 250, and they were of the chosen Tartars; their loss was about fifteen or twenty killed—ours was one seaman of the "Wellesley," mortally wounded (since dead), and the boats were repeatedly struck by grape-shot.

As soon as a cursory survey of the river was made, the "Herald," "Alligator," "Modeste," and "Eagle" and "Sophia" transports were pushed forward, within gun-shot of Howqua's Fort; and thus, for the first time, were ships seen from the walls of Canton. On the 2nd, the "Cruiser" joined me, having on board Major-General Sir Hugh Gough, who took command of the land forces. The "Pylades" and "Conway" also joined from Chusan, and the two first-named vessels were sent in advance. On the 4th, in concert with the major-general, an attack was planned for the next morning, but on approaching, the fort was found to be abandoned; the British colours were hoisted, a garrison of the 26th regiment was placed in it, and a company of Royal Marines, under the command of Captain Ellis, R.M., took possession of a large joss house on the left bank (which the enemy were beginning to fortify), and rendered himself secure, while the seamen soon removed some of the stakes and_other impediments, and made a clear passage for ships. I may here describe the position.

On the right bank of the river, on the point formed by the mouth of a creek (which is a boat-passage to Whampoa), was Howqua's Fort, a square building, mounting thirty guns, from the northern angle; the stakes mentioned extended to the opposite bank, the ground on each side being low paddy fields, cut and intersected by canals in all directions. The Joss house rather projected into the stream, and consequently was a good position. The river here is about 500 yards wide; 2000 yards in front is a long low island, which divides the river into two branches, and on the extreme eastern point of which stood a fort, mounting thirty-five guns, built to commemorate the discomfiture and death of the late Lord Napier. From this fort a line of well-constructed and secured rafts (forming a bridge) extended to both sides of the river; on its right bank, flanking Napier's Fort and the raft, was a mud battery, intended for thirty-five guns; on the left was a battery, also flanking Napier's Fort, on which the enemy had forty-four guns, most of which they withdrew on the night of the 4th. In addition to these defences, stone junks were sunk in all parts of the river, between the stakes and the left of Napier's Fort, which raft also rested upon sunken junks, secured on either side within piles.

The position seemed, formidable, and on the 5th the major-general and myself prepared to attack it. He landed at the joss house, having with him the Royal Marines, and a detachment of the 26th, for the purpose of taking the battery on the left bank; the ships weighed, and dropped up with the tide. On the approach of the first ship, the enemy fired all their guns, and fled across the rafts and in boats. The British colours were then hoisted.

A paper was issued calling on the people to place confidence in us, and to avoid hostile movements, in which latter case protection was ensured to them. At noon the Kwang Chow Foo, or prefect, accompanied by the Hong merchants, came down, and after a long discussion with the Plenipotentiary, admitted that, Keshen having been degraded, and the newly-appointed commissioners not having arrived, there was no government authorized to treat for peace, or make any arrangements; they confessed the truth of the reports we had heard, that the greatest consternation existed in the city, and that every person who could quit it had done so; in fact, that it was at our mercy, and it has so remained, a monument of British magnanimity and forbearance. I fear, however, that the forbearance is misunderstood, and that a further punishment must be resorted to before this arrogant and perfidious government is brought to reason.

Her Majesty's Plenipotentiary being, however, desirous to try the effect of another proclamation, and to shew his desire for an equitable adjustment of affairs, addressed the major-general and myself, requesting that we would make no further movement towards the city until the disposition of the provincial government officers was put to the test, as far as regards their non-interference; and we have consequently remained in *status quo*; but reports (on which we can rely) arc daily reaching us, which state that fire vessels are fitting out about seven miles above Canton: forts in the rear of the city in course of erection, and the people are forbidden to bring us supplies, while the teas and silks, and every other valuable, are removing from it.

These proceedings, so directly contrary to the assurances of pacific intentions, (which they are ever ready to deal forth in profusion,) lead me to the conclusion, that we shall have to proceed, even at the risk of the destruction of the second city of the empire— an event exceedingly likely to occur, from its abandonment by the authorities, and the excesses of the lower classes of a community proverbially bad. The responsibility must, however, rest on the heads of those authorities.

I this day returned to Wang-Tong, accompanied by the major-general, in order that the arrangements in that garrison may be carried out, and plans devised for our further operations.

I have the honour to be, my lord, your lordship's most obedient humble servant,

J. G. Gordon Bremer, Commodore and Commander-in-Chief.

*

To the Right Hon. George Earl of Auckland, G.C.B., &c. &c. &c, Governor-General of India in Council.
Wellesley, off Wang-Tong, March 27th, 1841.

My Lord,—In continuation of my letter of the 10th instant, I have the satisfaction to inform your lordship, that on the 15th I received a report from Captain Herbert, of H.M.'s ship "Calliope," detailing a well-executed attack on the only remaining fort protecting the approaches to the city of Canton. This fort is situated about ten miles from the anchorage at Whampoa, up a narrow and intricate channel, which ends in the Broadway, or Macao passage from Canton. The attack commenced about five p.m., from the "Modeste," and "Madagascar" steamer, with the boats of the squadron, and in half an hour the works were in our possession, the Chinese keeping up a well-directed fire until the boats' crews were in the act of scaling the walls, when they gave way, and fled in all directions. They were devoting their whole attention to the strengthening of the defences of this post, and had rendered it one of the most formidable which had been encountered; I am therefore happy that it is in our hands. The loss of the Chinese is not correctly known; many were found dead in the fort. Our own casualties do not amount to more than three wounded.

The zealous desire of every officer and man in the squadron to seek occasions in which to distinguish themselves, has led to the performance of various well-executed services; amongst them is the forcing the inner passage from Macao to Whampoa, which was deemed by the Chinese impenetrable to foreigners. Her Majesty's Plenipotentiary having represented to the senior officer in Macao Roads the great advantages likely to accrue by this step, his views were at once acceded to by Captain Scott, and preparations made for carrying it into effect.

At three A. M. on the 13th, the "Nemesis," with the boats of the "Samarang" in tow, weighed from Macao Roads, and proceeded over the flats between Twee-lieu-shaw and Toi-koke-tow islands, to the Broadway River. At eight a. m. they came in sight of Motao Fort; and the steamer, having taken up an enfilading position, where not a gun of the enemy could bear upon her, opened her fire, whilst the boats proceeded to the attack. On their approach, the Chinese abandoned the place. Thirteen guns were found mounted, which were completely destroyed, the buildings set fire to, and a train laid to the magazine, which exploded before the boats returned to the "Nemesis." On reaching Point How—Hoak-tow—the river is divided into two channels; that to the right takes a sudden sharp turn, and becomes very contracted in its breadth. Here they discovered Tai-yat-kok, a field-battery (very recently constructed) of fourteen guns, very strongly posted, on a rising ground, situated on the left bank of the river, (surrounded by overflowed paddy fields,) which enfiladed the whole line of the reach leading up to it. As the steamer appeared round the point, the enemy opened an animated fire upon her, which was smartly kept up. It was most effectually returned by the two guns from the "Nemesis," which vessel threw her shot, shells, and rockets admirably. The boats advanced under the slight cover of the bank, but before a landing could be effected on their flank, they abandoned the guns, when possession of the work was taken by a narrow pathway, which could only be passed in single files. The guns were destroyed, and the buildings and material consigned to the flames, and blown up. Meanwhile a detachment of the boats had gone over to the opposite side of the river, and destroyed a military station, or depot. At noon, nine war junks were seen over the land, and chase immediately given. On entering the reach in which they were, Captain Scott observed on the right bank of the river a new battery, scarcely finished, with ten embrasures, but without guns, and Hochang Fort close to it, well built of granite, surrounded by a wet ditch, and mounting fourteen guns, and six ginjalls. Abreast of these (which they flanked) the river was strongly staked across, through the centre of which the last junk had passed, and the opening again secured. The enemy immediately commenced firing from the fort and junks, which was replied to by the "Nemesis" with good effect, while the boats opened a passage through the stakes, and dashed on to the attack of Hochang and the junks: the former was secured by wading the ditch and entering the embrasures, and the latter, seeing the fall of the fort, became so panic-stricken, that, on the approach of the boats, seven got on shore, their crews jumping overboard immediately they grounded, two junks alone escaping. Lieutenant Bower, in pushing to cut them off, discovered Fiesha-kok on the left bank of the river, within a hundred yards of the advanced junk aground, which fort, mounting seven guns, opened a heavy fire of grape upon him. Observing that the junks were abandoned by their crews, he turned all his attention to his new opponents, whom he drove out of their stronghold by passing through the adjoining town and taking them in reverse.

In the meantime, Mr. Hall dexterously managed in getting his vessel through the centre passage of the stakes, which fortunately was just sufficiently wide to admit of her passing. At 2-30 the boats returned to the steamer, after having destroyed all the guns, and set fire to Fiesha-kok Fort, and the seven war junks, which all blew up within a quarter of an hour. Chase to the two escaped junks recommenced, during which they passed two dismantled forts. At four p. m. they arrived off the large provincial town of Hiangshan, one of the large war junks preceding them about a mile. The dense population thickly crowded the banks, boats, junks, house-tops, the large pagoda, and surrounding hills. Both sides of the river were packed by the trading craft of the country in the closest possible order, the centre of the river (which is very narrow here) having merely sufficient space to allow the steamer's paddle-boxes to pass clear of the junks moored to its banks. Not the slightest fear was manifested by the people; but several mandarins took to their boats, and followed the war junks, which were closed so rapidly that one of them ran on shore, the crew jumping overboard. The steamer brought up abreast of her, and destroyed her. While thus employed, the fort of Sheang-chap, within two hundred yards, (but hidden by some intervening trees,) opened its fire, which was instantly returned, and the boats, with the Marines of the "Samarang," stormed it; its eight guns were destroyed. A number of Chinese troops coming down towards the fort made it necessary to fire two or three shot, which, going directly in the midst of the body, scattered and dispersed them in an instant. At six p. m. the junk and fort were fired, and the steamer passed on into a narrow, shallow channel, scarcely more than the breadth of a canal, when she anchored, head and stern, for the night.

At daylight on the morning of the 14th, they weighed, and proceeded up the river in the steamer's draught of water, and not broader than her own length, grounding occasionally on both sides. At 7-50 arrived at the large village of Hong-how, with a fort of the same name at the upper part, which flanked a strong and broad line of stakes, twenty feet wide, completely across the river, filled up in the centre by large sunken junks laden with stones. On discovering the fort, the "Nemesis" opened fire, which was instantly returned by the enemy. As in all the preceding actions, they fled the moment the boats landed to attack them. They had evidently expected to be assailed on the opposite side to that by which the "Nemesis" approached, the walls being piled up with sandbags outside in that direction; nine guns were destroyed here, and the fort blown up; after the "Nemesis" had made good her passage through the stakes, which was effected after four hours' incessant hard labour, assisted by the natives, who flocked on board and around in great numbers after the firing had ceased, all apparently anxious to aid in destroying the stakes.

At four p. m. they arrived off a military station; a shot was fired into the principal building, which drove out the garrison, who had screened themselves in it; the boats were then sent on shore, and the whole establishment, together with a mandarin boat, mounting one nine pounder and two ginjalls, were destroyed; and at six, the steamer anchored for the night.

At daylight on the 15th, the "Nemesis" continued her course upwards, and at 7-30 arrived off the large village of Zamchow, under the banks of which a number of soldiers with matchlocks were descried, endeavouring to conceal themselves, upon whom a fire of musketry was opened, which dispersed all those who were unhurt in less than a minute.

On moving up to Tsgnsi, a large town on the left bank of the river, three forts were passed, all dismantled and abandoned; the Custom-house of the latter place was destroyed, as well as a war junk mounting seven guns, which the crew had quitted on the approach of the steamer. On proceeding up to Whampoa, three more dismantled forts were observed, and at four p. m. the "Nemesis" came to in that anchorage, having (in conjunction with the boats) destroyed five forts, one battery, two military stations, and nine war junks, in which were 115 guns and eight ginjalls; thus proving to the enemy, that the British flag can be displayed throughout their inner waters, wherever and whenever it is thought proper by us, against any defence or mode they may adopt to prevent it. This service has been performed without the loss of a single man on our side, and only three seamen slightly wounded belonging to H.M.S. "Samarang." The greatest praise is due to Mr. W.H. Hall, R.N., commander of the "Nemesis," for the cool, unwearied, and zealous performance of his duties (under circumstances of frequent danger and difficulty) at all times, more especially in thus traversing a navigation never before passed by a European boat or vessel.

On the 19th, I was gratified by receiving a report from Captain Herbert, of H.M.S. "Calliope," commanding the advanced squadron, detailing the various operations of that force in the attack and capture of the forts, defences, and flotilla off Canton, and the hoisting of the union jack on the walls of the British factory: the guns of the squadron commanding all the approaches to the city from the western and southern branches of the river, thus placing in our power the great provincial capital.

This was brought about by the Chinese having fired upon a flag of truce, sent with a chop to the Imperial Commissioner, at the desire of his Excellency the Plenipotentiary. The flotilla of boats of the squadron formed into four divisions, under the command of Captains Bourchier and Bethune, of the "Blonde" and "Conway." Every arrangement having been completed, the force—consisting of the "Modeste," "Nemesis," "Madagascar," "Algerine," "Starling," "Young Hebe," and "Louisa," —moved in advance about noon, and engaged the batteries for about an hour, when the flotilla, with the Marines, under the command of Captain Bourchier, was brought up in admirable order, and upon the signal being given, stormed and completed the capture of the enemy's works, notwithstanding a most determined resistance on the part of the Tartar troops; 123 guns were mounted in the different forts. The loss of the enemy has been very considerable (upwards of 400 men): our casualties, I am happy to say, do not exceed six wounded.

This blow was followed by an agreement on the part of the High Commissioner to a suspension of hostilities, and afterwards by the publication of an edict, declaring the trade to be opened, and that all British and other merchants, proceeding to the provincial city, shall receive due and perfect protection.

I endeavoured to push forward to the scene of action in the "Hyacinth's" gig, but only arrived towards its close—in sufficient time, however, to be gratified by the hoisting of the British colours. Thus, for the first time in the history of China, have ships been brought under the very walls of Canton, and by channels and branches on which a foreign ship never before floated. I believe the Chinese were not acquainted with the capabilities of their splendid river; assuredly they had no idea that the second city in the empire could be assailed by ships of war on its waters. I trust that the fact will have its due influence on the authorities; and I have no doubt that the forbearance displayed towards a city so completely at our mercy as this is, will be appreciated by the better classes of the community who have everything to lose, and the benevolence of the British character more fully understood than it ever yet has been in this country.

The gratifying spectacle of our ships in this position is solely attributable to the unwearied exertions of the captains, officers, and men belonging to them, in sounding the various inlets through which they passed, not a single Chinese pilot having been employed throughout.

In conclusion, we may on this, as on former occasions, congratulate ourselves on this service having been performed without any loss of life on our side, and only seven wounded (severely;) amongst whom is that gallant officer, Lieutenant Stransham, Royal Marines, of H.M.S. "Calliope," acting Brigade-Major.

I have the honour to be, &c.

J. J. Gordon Bremer, Commodore of the First Class, Commander in Chief.

*

The report from Captain Herbert, of H.M.S. "Calliope," to His Excellency Sir Gordon Bremer, referred to in the preceding

Despatch, is annexed:—

(copy.) To Commodore Sir J. J. Gordon Bremer, K.C.B., K.C.H. Commander-in-Chief, &c.

British Factory, Canton, March 18, 1841.

Sir,—This day the force enumerated below, (Vide subjoined List) under my orders carried and destroyed, in succession, all the forts in the advance and before Canton, taking, sinking, burning, or dispersing the enemy's flotilla, and hoisted the union jack on the walls of the British factory, the guns of the squadron commanding all the approaches to the city from the western and southern branches of the river; thus placing in our power the great provincial capital, containing upwards of one million of inhabitants.

I found myself forced to make this attack without your instructions, for the reasons so strongly expressed in Her Majesty's Plenipotentiary's note, (March 17, 1841;) considering it my duty to resent, with all the promptitude in my power, the insult offered the day before to the flag of truce, sent with a chop to the Imperial Commissioner, at the desire of his Excellency.

I forward the accompanying sketch, placing you in more immediate possession of the line of concentration which led to such an immediate result. In detailing the operations of the day, I feel myself inadequate to do justice to the gallant officers and men employed on this occasion.

The flotilla of boats, formed into four divisions, was under the command of Captain Bourchier, of the "Blonde"—Captain Bethune of the "Conway" assisting. Three divisions, under the immediate charge of Commanders Barlow and Clarke, and Lieutenant Coulson, of the "Blonde." Her Majesty's sloop "Hyacinth," (to whom too much praise cannot be given for the exertion displayed by Commander Warren, his officers and crew, in getting her through the intricate and difficult passes of the river, piloted by Commander Belcher, to be in readiness for operation,) and a division of boats, under the command of these officers, was placed at the southern entrance of the river, recommunicating with the main stream at Fatee, to meet any retrograde movement of the numerous flotilla that had taken part in the aggression on the 16th instant.

Every arrangement having been completed and understood, the whole force moved in advance about noon; the vessels, Marines, and three divisions of boats from the northward of the Macao Fort, and within gun-shot of the enemy's advance batteries, engaging them for about two hours and a half, when all opposition ceased, and the Factory within the defences was taken possession of.

The "Modeste" was placed within 300 yards, in front of the principal battery, and shortly gave proofs of her well-directed fire, flanked by the powerful guns of the "Madagascar," Captain Dicey, with artillerymen under the direction of Lieutenant Foulis, (Madras Artillery,) and "Nemesis," Mr. W. H. Hall, R.N., commanding, with artillerymen under the direction of Captain Moore, and Lieutenant Gabbett, (Madras Artillery,) who handsomely volunteered their services upon the occasion; the "Algerine," Lieut. Mason, and "Starling," Lieut. Kellett, passing ahead, cutting through the rafts on the right bank, and engaging a part of the war junks; the "Hebe" and "Louisa" tenders taking part at the same time, under cover of the ships' guns. The flotilla, with the marines, was brought up in admirable order by Captain Bourchier; and upon the signal given, stormed and completed the capture of this part of the enemy's works, notwithstanding a most determined resistance on the part of the Tartar troops. From this battery, the vessels and flotilla moved forward, and carried the other defences in succession, amounting in the whole to 123 guns.

By the great care of Captain Nias, his officers, and ship's company, the "Herald" was brought over the flats, and entered the reach during the engagement, which must have had considerable effect upon the enemy, by dividing their attention, not knowing what other force might be in reserve.

Of Captain Bourchier, whose high character is so well known to you, sir, and the service, I cannot speak sufficiently strong for the manner in which he conducted the forces under his immediate command, not only leading them into action in admirable order, but keeping them together in readiness for any outbreak of the immense population of such a crowded city, and I cannot refrain mentioning his conspicuous and energetic exertions in towing off the burning junks, which were drifting upon the suburbs of Canton, and soon would have evidently set fire to that part of the city, and involved the destruction of the whole, in which, he reports, he was ably assisted by the officers under his directions. My thanks are also due to that excellent officer, Captain Bethune, and to Commanders Belcher, Warren, Barlow, and Clarke, for their great zeal. The Royal Marines, under Lieutenant Stransham, of the "Calliope," assisted by Lieutenants Daniel, Hewitt, Marriot, and Polkinghorne, were, as usual, conspicuous for their gallant, steady, soldierly bearing. I have, however, to regret that Lieutenant Stransham, in exerting himself to destroy the works, was suddenly exposed to a heavy explosion, by which he has been considerably burned, but continues at his post. To Lieutenants Kellett and Collinson, and Mr. Brown, master of the "Calliope," every favourable consideration is due, for having made themselves particularly useful in sounding, and afterwards conducting several men-of-war safely to an anchorage, off the city of Canton. Indeed, my sincere gratitude is due to every officer, seaman, and marine employed on this service, for their zeal and spirited conduct, from which it is to be hoped the most beneficial results will ensue.

His Excellency her Majesty's Plenipotentiary, ever on the alert, has done me the honour to be with me throughout these operations, and to whom my best thanks are due for his support and assistance on all occasions.

By Lieutenant Paul, who you kindly attached to me, I enclose a return of casualties, which I am happy to say are inconsiderable, and bring before you the officers employed in the flotilla on this service, with a return of ordnance destroyed in the defences near Canton.

Your presence at the close of the action releases me from going further into detail.

From the various reports brought in, we have been able to ascertain that the enemy's loss has been about 400 men. I have the honour to be, Sir,

Your most obedient servant,

(Signed) *T. Herbert, Captain.*

List of the Skips., Steamers, Boats, &c., employed at the capture of Canton, on the 16th instant.

- H.M. ship. Herald, Captain Nias.
- H.M. sloop, Modeste, Commander Eyres.
- H.M. sloop, Hyacinth, Commander Warren.
- H.M. brig, Algerine, Lieutenant Mason.

TENDERS

- H.M. schooner, Starling, Lieutenant Kellett.
- H.M. schooner, Hebe, Mr. Quin, Mate.
- H.M. cutter, Louisa, Mr. Carmicliael, Mate.

STEAMERS.

- H.C. steamer, Madagascar, Captain Dicey.
- H.C. steamer, Nemesis, Captain Hall.

BOATS.

First Division.

Commander Barlow; Lieutenant Williams; Lieutenant Stewart; Lieutenant Drury; Lieutenant Dewes, Actg.; Mr. Walter Kendall, Mate; Mr. Purver, Mate; Mr. Woolcome, Mate; Mr. Baker, Mate; Mr. Kator, Mate; Mr. Comber, Midshipman; Mr. Scott, Vol. 1st class.

Second Division.

Commander Clarke; Lieutenant Hamilton; Lieutenant Beadou; Lieutenant Shute; Mr. King, Master Actg.; Mr. Miller, Mate; Mr. Fitzgerald, Mate; Mr. Pearse, Mate; Mr. Head; Mate; Mr. Turnour, Mate; Mr. Crofton, Midshipman.

Third Division.

Lieutenant Coulson; Lieutenant Ingram; Mr. Christopher, Mate; Mr. Walker, Mate; Mr. Anderson, Mate; Mr. Purvis, Vol. 1st Class; Mr. Coke, ditto, Mr.

Lyons, ditto; Mr. Stanley, Assistant Surgeon.

Western Division

Commander Warren; Commander Belcher; Lieutenant Haskoll; Lieutenant Watson; Lieutenant Hay; Lieutenant Moorshed; Lieutenant D'Eyncourt; Lieutenant Wood; Lieutenant Hayes; Mr. Airy, Master; Mr. Daly, MAte; Mr. Rivers, Mate; Mr. Jeffreies, Mate; Mr. Le Vesconte, Mate; Mr. Egerton, Mate; Mr. Drake, Mate; Mr. St. Leger, Mate; Mr. Bryan, Mate; Mr. Brown, Mast. Assistant; Mr. Butler (M.D.) Assistant Surgeon, Mr. Tweedale, Assistant Surgeon

VOLUNTEERS.

Lieutenant Mackenzie, H.M. 90th regiment, Acting Military Secretary to the Naval Commander-in-Chief; Mr. Johnson, Master, H.M. ship, Conway; Mr. G. Ramsden, Clerk, H.M. ship, Calliope; Lieutenant Giffard, H.C. 12th regiment.

*

Return of Ordnance destroyed in the defences near Canton.

- Lower Battery, left bank, Macao passage: 22 Guns
- Upper Battery: 9 Guns
- Sand-bag battery, on wharf: 9 Guns
- Western Fort, Canton suburbs (Shaween): 10 Guns
- Red Fort, opposite Canton factories: 20 Guns
- Dutch Folly: 25 Guns
- Sand-bag battery, above arsenal: 13 Guns
- Two Junks moored off Admiral's house: 15 Guns

Total: 123 Guns

Besides those destroyed in Lin's and the mandarin war boats.

(Signed) *Thos. Herbert, Captain.*

*

A List of casualties in the force employed in the attack and occupation of the defences of the City of Canton, on the 18th day of March, 1841.

- Lieutenant Stransham, R.M.—severely.
- Calliope—two wounded slightly.
- Hyacinth—two ditto: one slightly, one severely.
- Modeste—two wounded slightly.

(Signed) *Thomas Herbert, Captain.*

*

To the Right Hon. the Earl of Auckland, G.C.B. &c. &c. &c. Governor-General.

H.M.S. "Wellesley," Bocca Tigris, 11th March, 1841.

My Lord,—I have the honour to,report to your lordship my arrival on.the

1st instant in the Canton River, and of my having joined and assumed the military command of the expeditionary force on the 2nd at Whampoa Reach, where I found Commodore Sir Gordon Bremer and her Majesty's Plenipotentiary, Captain Elliot, with the advanced division of the fleet and transports, except 200 men of the 37th Madras N. I., left at North Wang-Tong as a protecting, force.

2. The Commodore will have communicated to your lordship the operations up to that period, embracing the capture of the Bogue Forts, at either side the Bocca Tigris, on the 26th February; the forcing the barrier at the first bar, on the following day; together with the assault and capture of a heavy battery which flanked it, and the destruction of the ship "Cambridge."

3. Having unfortunately arrived too late to participate in those operations, I cannot refrain from expressing my admiration of the noble, daring, and judicious execution which thus reduced, within a few hours and almost without loss, what were considered by the Chinese as impregnable, and what, in the hands of almost any other nation, would have been nearly so. It is a great satisfaction to me to find Sir Gordon Bremer speak most favourably of the conduct of Major Pratt, of her Majesty's 26th, and the troops employed on this occasion.

4. Having communicated with the Plenipotentiary and the Commodore, I found it was proposed to continue the operations in advance the following day, (the 3rd,) by attacking the last defences on the Canton river, consisting of a square stone-built fort, mounting thirty-two guns, in front of which the river was barricaded by a double row of strong piles firmly driven in with an intervening space of about thirty feet, which the Chinese had filled, by sinking junks and placing masses of bamboos, together with timber of every description. Seventeen hundred yards further up, the river divides itself into two branches, forming a low, narrow island, which extends to within about a mile of Canton; at the lower point of this is Napier's Fort, a regular half-moon enclosed work of stone masonry, mounting thirty-six guns; at this point the river was again strongly-barricaded, connecting Napier's Fort with two strong newly-constructed field works, thrown up on either bank of the river by a planked platform placed over the barricade; these latter works shewed embrasures of from forty to fifty guns each.

5. On the morning of the 3rd, having made my arrangements with the Commodore for a conjoint attack on the enemy's works, I proceeded with him up the river in the "Nemesis" steamer; but a communication having been made that Yu, the Quang-chow-foo, was approaching, bearing a flag of truce, the white flag was hoisted by her Majesty's Plenipotentiary. Captain Belcher, of the "Sulphur," having reported that he could perceive no persons in How-qua Fort, (the before-mentioned work flanking the nearest barricade,)

I proceeded in the "Calliope's" boat with the Commodore and Captain Herbert, when we found it had been abandoned. I had it immediately occupied by the detachments of H.M.'s 26th and 49th regiments, under Major Pratt. At the same time I took possession of a joss house, at the opposite side of the river, (here about 800 yards wide,) where a five-gun mud field-work had been commenced, in which I placed Captain Ellis with his company of the Royal Marines.

6. An armistice, until noon of the day but one following, having been agreed upon, I had an opportunity of reconnoitring the Chinese defences, accompanied by a party of the Royal Marines under Captain Ellis. In performing this duty, I had to pass through a very large and populous village, the inhabitants appeared to view our approach towards Canton without the remotest ill-feeling, and I have no doubt would have shewn me the road, could I have made myself understood.

7. A further communication having been received from Canton, an extension of twenty-four hours was granted to the armistice, and at noon on the 6th, the time having expired, the troops were landed on the left bank of the river, consisting of the detachments of H.M.'s 26th and 49th regiments, under Major Pratt, and the Royal Marines of the fleet, under Captain Ellis, the light squadron and the flotilla getting under weigh at the same time. On the first vessel passing the barrier the Chinese fired off the guns in the centre battery, and retired; the guns in the two flank works, it appears, had been previously withdrawn, and these defences were instantly occupied by the seamen of the fleet. Thus the last defences of one of the richest towns in China, with a population of upwards of one million of inhabitants, were abandoned, without a shot having been fired on our side, and Canton lay at British mercy, and remains a memento of British forbearance.

8. Her Majesty's Plenipotentiary having forwarded me the accompanying letter, (No. 1,) the troops were re-embarked. On the receipt of the letter (marked No. 2) arrangements were made for the transports to fall down the river, and rendezvous here. All the forts have been destroyed by the indefatigable exertions of the seamen, the guns rendered unserviceable, and the barricades have been mostly removed, leaving open the free navigation of the river between Canton and Macao.

9. Major-General Burrell and the staff arrived three days back, and all the force from Chusan, with the exception of the Bengal Volunteers, has reached this river. I am using every exertion for the military occupation of North Wang-Tong, and when completed, or in a forward state, the fleet will proceed to the island of Hong Kong, which it is the intention of her Majesty's Plenipotentiary to occupy.

10. I shall not fail, when the troops are assembled at Hong-Kong, to give

my earnest attention to their location, so as to reestablish, by every means within my power, their health, and fit them for"ulterior operations; no want of supplies need, I conceive, be apprehended, nor do I believe, from all I can learn, that any exertions on the part of the Chinese authorities can prevent their being procured.

I have the honour to be, my lord, your lordship's most obedient humble servant,

H. Gough, Major-General, Commanding the Expeditionary Force.

Republished by order of the Right Hon. the Governor in Council.

Robert Clerk, Secretary to Government.

IX. PROCLAMATION.

By Charles Elliot, her Britannic Majesty's Plenipotentiary in China.

A PROCLAMATION.

People of Canton!—Your city is spared, because the great sovereign of Great Britain has commanded the high English officers to remember that the good and peaceful people must be tenderly considered.

But if the high officers of the Celestial Court offer the least obstruction to the British forces in their present stations, then it will become necessary to answer force by force, and the city may suffer terrible injury. And if the native merchants be prevented from buying and selling freely with the British and foreign merchants, then the whole trade of Canton must be immediately stopped. The high officers of the English nation have faithfully used their best efforts to prevent the miseries of war, and the responsibility of the actual state of things must rest on the heads of the bad advisers of the Emperor. Further evil consequences can only be prevented by wisdom and moderation on the part of the provincial government.

Dated off the Fort of Espumeo, near to Canton, 6th March, 1841.

X. GENERAL ORDERS.

Head-quarters, Marion, Canton River, May 24th.

1. The period has now arrived, so long looked for by the military portion at large of the China expedition, when it may have an opportunity, in co-operation with our gallant associates of the royal navy, of proving what can be effected by discipline and bravery.

2. Major-General Gough feels a confident assurance that every man will do his duty, that he will have the gratifying task, not only of recording and bringing to notice acts of gallantry, but (what is of infinitely more consequence

in the present instance, and will afford stronger proof of devotedness to our country's honour and our professional character) of unshaken discipline and undeviating attention to the orders issued by the officers in the command of columns of attack.

3. The nature of the position to be carried, and the probable necessity of subdividing the force into separate columns of attack, which may be led through the town and suburbs, make it the more necessary to enforce the most rigid discipline, and to guard against any man leaving the ranks upon any pretence whatever. The man who does so will most probably be cut off; but even should he escape, his name should be branded as a disgrace to his corps.

4. The Chinese system is not one to which the British soldier is accustomed, but if the Chinese have not bravery and discipline, they have cunning and. artifice. They have had ample time to prepare, and we may be well assured that their system of stratagem will be called into full play on the present occasion. But though such a system may be effectual against a mob, which every broken body is, it must fail before the steady advance of disciplined soldiers. The Major-General will only add, that Britain has gained as much of fame by her mercy and forbearance, as by the gallantry of her troops. An enemy in arms is always a legitimate foe, but the unarmed, or the supplicant for mercy, of whatever country or whatever colour, a true British soldier will always spare.

5. The troops will be prepared with cooked provisions for two days, to land this day at twelve o'clock, in two columns.

(Signed) *A. S. H. Mountain, Lieut-Col., D.A.G.*

XI. GENERAL ORDERS.

Head Quarters, Choultry Plain, 25th August, 1841.

The following general orders by the right honourable the Governor in Council having been addressed to the officer commanding the army in chief, Major-General Sir R. Dick has much gratification in publishing to the army the sentiments expressed by the highest authorities in India upon a series of brilliant operations, in which the Artillery, Sappers and Miners, and 37th regiment N.I. of this presidency, have contributed to success which is so honourable to the united services engaged.

Upon Captain Duff, 37th regiment N.I., Captain Anstruther of the Artillery, and Lieutenant and Brevet Captain Cotton of the Engineers, has devolved the honour of commanding in their respective corps those officers and men who have so creditably upheld the established reputation of the army to which they belong.

The Major-General notices with much pleasure the praise that has been bestowed upon the steady bravery of the C. company 37th regiment N.I., under command of Lieutenant Hadfield, who, with Lieutenant Devereux, Ensign Berkeley, Subadar Shaik Homed, and a band of sixty-six brave non-commissioned and Sepoys, repulsed the repeated attacks of superior numbers of Chinese.

*

General Orders by the Right Honourable the Governor in Council. Fort St. George, 20th August, 1841.

No. 148 of 1841.—The right honourable the Governor in Council, in promulgating to the army of this presidency the following notification in the secret department by the right honourable the Governor-General of India in council, has much gratification in publishing at the same time a dispatch to the address of his lordship from Major-General Sir Hugh Gough, K.C.B., commanding the forces in China. The high testimony borne by so distinguished an officer to the soldierly qualities of the detachments of Madras troops which have the good fortune to be employed on service in China, will be as gratifying to the army at large as it is honourable to those upon whom the well-merited praise has been bestowed.

To the Right Hon. Lord Elphinstone, G. C. H., &c. &c. &c. Head Quarters, Ship "Marion," off the Bocca Tigris, June 6, 1841.

My Lord,—My public despatch to the Governor-General will communicate the operations of this force before Canton, from the 24th of May to the 1st of June, but I cannot permit that despatch to go forward without conveying to your lordship, as head of the government of Madras, the high sense I entertain of the gallantry and exemplary conduct of that portion of the Madras army, which forms a part of this force.

The practice of the two companies of the Madras Artillery was most creditable, and their indefatigable exertions in getting the guns and ammunition to the heights, called for my best thanks. I feel it a duty to assure your lordship, that Captain Anstruther, and every officer, non-commissioned officer, and Lascar, most creditably did their duty.

To Captain Cotton, senior engineer officer, my best thanks are due; and it has afforded me no small gratification to record these sentiments in my public despatch, as also the expression of my thanks to every officer of Engineers present, from whom I received the most ready assistance. The two companies of Sappers merited and received my warmest approval.

I feel peculiar pleasure in bringing to your lordship's notice the spirited and steady conduct of the three companies of the 37th M.N.I., under Captain

Duff. It fell to the lot of one company, under Lieutenant Hadfield, to display these qualities in the most praiseworthy manner. Having become disengaged and unable to rejoin his corps during a violent thunder-storm, he was surrounded by some thousand Chinese militia, and maintained his ground, although, from the heavy fall of rain, the men's arms would not go off, until reinforced by two companies of the Royal Marines with the percussion locks.

Lieutenant Hadfield speaks very highly of the cheerful assistance he received from Lieutenant Devereux and Ensign Berkeley; the latter of whom, I regret to say, was severely wounded. This company had two Sepoys killed; one officer, one Havildar, nine Sepoys, and one Bhistie wounded.

I have, &c.

(Signed) *H. Gough, Major General, Commanding Expeditionary Force.*

NOTIFICATION.

Fort William, Secret Department, 7th August, 1841.

The right honourable the Governor-General of India in council, having this day received intelligence of the happy result of the joint operations of her Majesty's and the Honourable Company's naval and military forces in an attack upon the Chinese forces in front of the city of Canton, on the 25th and 30th of May last, is pleased to direct the publication for general information of the following dispatch from Major-General Sir Hugh Gough, K.C.B., commanding the land forces, and extracts from a dispatch addressed by Captain Sir Henry Le Fleming Senhouse, K.C.H., the senior naval officer of the fleet at Canton, to his Excellency the naval Commander-in-Chief in India, which has been communicated to the "supreme Government.

These accounts of the brilliant successes of the British arms have been received with the highest gratification by the Governor-General in council, who, in expressing his admiration of the gallant conduct of every portion of the forces employed in this service, has deeply to lament the loss which has been sustained by the death of Captain Sir H. Le Fleming Senhouse, who is reported to have subsequently sunk under the fatigue and exhaustion caused by his exertions in the actions with the Chinese.

The Governor-General in council is pleased to direct that in honour of this victory of the British arms, a royal salute be fired from the ramparts of Fort William, and at the principal military stations of the army of India.

By order of the right honourable the Governor-General of India in council.

(Signed) *T. H. Maddock, Secretary to Government of India.*

*

To the Right Honourable the Earl of Auckland, G.C.S., Governor-General, &c, &c, &c.

Head Quarters, Ship "Marion," Canton River, Proceeding to Hong-Kong, June 3, 1841.

My Lord,—My letter of the 18th from Hong-Kong will have made your lordship aware of the temporary abandonment of the movement on Amoy, in order to resume active operations against Canton, consequent upon the constant arrival and concentration of a large force from the several provinces, and other demonstrations indicative of an interruption to our friendly intercourse with the provincial government.

2. From the judicious and unwearied exertions of Sir Le Fleming Senhouse, the senior naval officer, the fleet of men-of-war and transports were prepared to sail on the 18th, but in consequence of light and variable winds, the whole did not get under weigh until the 19th. H.M.S. "Blenheim" took up her position within six miles of Canton, in the Macao passage, on the 21st ultimo, but the whole of the force was not assembled until the morning of the 23rd, when I proceeded, with Sir Le Fleming Senhouse, to the vicinity of the suburbs of the city, for the double object of meeting her Majesty's Plenipotentiary, and ascertaining, as far as possible, the extent of the enemy's preparations.

3. It being the anxious wish, both of Sir Le Fleming Senhouse and myself, to commence active operations on so auspicious an epoch as the anniversary of the birth of our Sovereign, every exertion was made, and the troops were placed, by 2 p.m. on that day, in various craft, procured during the previous day and night by the great exertions of the royal navy.

4. From all the sources from which I had been enabled to collect information, or rather from the conjectures of persons who have long resided in China, (for no European had been permitted to see the country above the factories, and the Chinese would give no information,) I was induced to decide on making my principal point of debarkation to the north-west of the city, while another column was to take possession of the factories, drawing the attention of the enemy to that quarter, and at the same time to cooperate with the naval force which was to attack the river defences, in order to silence numerous new works, recently erected by the Chinese, along the whole southern face of the city. A most spirited and judicious reconnoissance made by Captain Belcher, of H.M.S. "Sulphur," the previous evening, established the practicability of effecting a landing at the point I had selected.

5. Every arrangement having been completed by two o'clock, and the boats and other craft placed in tow of the steamers, the force moved to the point of attack as follows:—

Right column to attack and hold the factories, in tow of the Atalanta, consisting of her Majesty's 26th regiment, as below;[1] an officer and

1 Officers, 15; other ranks, 294

20 rank and file of the Madras Artillery, with one 6-pounder, and one 6j-inch mortar, and thirty Sappers, with an officer of Engineers, under Major Pratt, of H.M. 26th.

Left column—towed by the Nemesis, in four brigades, to move left in front.

		Officers.	**Other ranks.**
4th (left) brigade under Lieut.-Colonel Morris, 49th regt.	H.M. 49th, commanded by Major Stephens	28	273
	37th M.N.I., Captain Duff	11	219
	One company Bengal Volunteers, Captain Mee	1	114
3rd (Artillery) brigade, under Capt. Knowles, R.A	Royal Artillery Lieutenant Spencer	2	33
	Madras Artillery, including gun Lascars, Captain Anstruther	10	231
	Sappers and Miners, Capt. Cotton	4	137
Ordnance: four 12-pounder howitzers—four 9-pounder field guns—two 6-pounder ditto—three 5 1/2-inch mortars—one hundred and fifty-two 32-pounder rockets.			
2nd naval brigade under Captain Bourchier, H.M.S. Blonde	1st naval battalion, Captain Maitland, H.M.S. Wellesley	11	172
	2nd naval battalion. Com. Barlow, H.M.S. Nimrod	16	231
lst (right) brigade (reserve) under Major General Burrell.	Royal Marines, Captain Ellis	9	372
	18th Royal Irish, Lieutenant-Col. Adams	25	494

6. The right column reached its point of attack before 5 p.m., and took possession of the factories, when Major Pratt made the necessary arrangements for strengthening his post, holding his men ready for offensive or defensive operations.

7. The left column towed by the "Nemesis," from the difficulties of the passage, with such a fleet of craft as she had in tow, did not reach the "Sulphur" until dusk, which vessel Captain Belcher had judiciously anchored close to the village of Tsing-hae, the point of debarkation, about five miles by the river line above the factories. I could therefore only land the 49th regiment, with which corps I made a reconnoissance to some distance, meeting a few straggling parties of the enemy. After placing the picquets, the corps fell back on the village of Tsing-hae to protect and cover the landing of the guns, which was effected during the night, by the zealous efforts of the artillery. The following morning the remainder of the column landed, and the whole proceeded soon after daylight.

8. The heights to the north of Canton, crowned by four strong forts, and the city walls, which run over the southern extremity of these heights, including one elevated point, appeared to be about three miles and a half distant; the intermediate ground, undulating much, and intersected by hollows under wet paddy cultivation, enabled me to take up successive positions, until we

approached within range of the forts on the heights and the northern face of the city walls. I had to wait here some time, placing the men under cover, to bring up the Rocket Battery and Artillery.

9. I have already informed your lordship that I was totally un acquainted with the country which I had to pass over, the amount of the enemy's force, or the difficulties that might present them selves at every step; but I had the proud consciousness of feeling that your lordship had placed under me a band, whom no disparity of numbers could dishearten, and no difficulty could check. They nobly realized by their steadiness under fire, their disciplined ad vance, and their animated rush, my warmest anticipations.

10. Having, at 8 o'clock, got up the rocket battery, with two 5 1/2-inch mortars, two 12-pounder howitzers, and two 9-pounder guns, a well directed fire was kept up on the two western forts, which had much annoyed us by a heavy fire. I now made the disposition for attack in Echellon of columns from the left, and directed the 49th regiment to carry a hill on the left of the nearest eastern fort, supported by the 37th Madras Native Infantry and Bengal Volunteers, under Lieutenant-Colonel Morris, of the 49th regiment. The 18th Royal Irish, supported by the Royal Marines, under Major-General Burrell, I directed to carry a hill to their front, which was strongly occupied, and flanked the approach to the fort just mentioned. This movement was to cut off the communication between the two eastern forts, and cover the advance of the 49th in their attack and storm of the nearest. Major-General Burrell had directions to push on and take the principal square fort, when the 49th made their rush. Simultaneous with these attacks, the brigade of seamen was to carry the two western forts, covered by a concentrated fire from the whole of the guns and rockets.

11. During the whole of the advance,,, my right had been threatened by a large body of the enemy, which debouched from the western suburbs, and, just as I was about to commence the attack, a report was made that heavy columns were advancing on the right, I was therefore compelled to detach the Marines, under Captain Ellis, to support the brigade of seamen, and to cover my right and rear.

12. At about half-past nine o'clock, the advance was sounded, and it has seldom fallen to my lot to witness a more soldier-like and steady advance, or a more animated attack. Every individual, native as well as European, steadily and gallantly did his duty. The 18th and 49th were emulous which should first reach their appointed goals; but, under the impulse of this feeling, they did not lose sight of that discipline which could alone ensure success. The advance of the 37th M.N.I. and Bengal Volunteers, in sup port, was equally praiseworthy.

13. The result of this combined movement was that the two forts were

captured with comparatively small loss, and that, in little more than half an hour after the order to advance was given, the British troops looked down on Canton, within 100 paces of its walls.

14. The well-directed fire of the artillery in the centre was highly creditable, and did great execution.

15. In co-operation with these attacks, I witnessed, with no ordinary gratification, the noble rush of the brigade of seamen, under their gallant leader, Captain Bourchier, exposed to a heavy fire from the whole of the north-western rampart. This right attack was equally successful; and here also the British standard proudly waved on the two western forts, while the British tars looked down upon the north-western face of the city and its suburb.

16. During the greater part of the day, a very spirited fire from heavy pieces of ordnance, ginjals, and matchlocks, was kept up on the different columns occupying the heights and forts.

17. A strongly entrenched camp of considerable extent, occupied apparently by about four thousand men, lay to the north-east of the city, upon rising ground, separated by a tract of paddy land from the base of the heights. Frequent attacks were made upon my left by bodies.sent from this encampment, but were as frequently repulsed by the 49th. This, however, exposed the men to a heavy fire from the walls of the city.

18. About two o'clock, perceiving that mandarins of consequence were joining this force from the city, and had occupied a village in rear of my left, I directed the 49th to dislodge them. This was instantly effected in the same spirited manner that had marked every movement of this gallant corps. About three o'clock, it was evident that some mandarin of high rank had reached the encampment, (I have since understood that it was Yang, the Tartar general,) and that preparations were making for a fresh attack. I ordered down the 18th, therefore, with one company of the Royal .Marines, to reinforce the 40th, and directed Major-General Burrell to assume the command, to repel the projected attack, and instantly to follow up the enemy across a narrow causeway, the only approach, and take and destroy the encampment. This duty was well and gallantly performed, but I .regret to say with rather severe loss from the difficulty of approach, exposed to a heavy fire from the guns and ginjals on the north-east face of the city wall. The enemy were driven at all points and fled across the country; the encampment was burnt; the magazines, of which there were several, blown up; and the permanent buildings of considerable extent set on fire. I had as much pleasure in witnessing, as I have in recording, my approval of the spirited conduct of Captain Grattan, who commanded the two leading companies of the 18th, across the causeway. These companies were closely followed by

the 49th, the remainder of the 18th, and company of the Royal Marines, who passed along a bank of the paddy fields to their left. The enemy not appearing inclined to move out of the town to support this point, I directed the force to return to the heights.

19. Having reconnoitred the walls and gates, I decided on taking the city by assault, or rather upon taking a strong fortified height of considerable extent within the city wall, before the panic ceased, but the hill in our rear being peculiarly rugged, and its base difficult of approach, on account of the narrowness of the path between wet paddy fields, I had only been enabled to get up a very few of the lightest pieces of ordnance and a small proportion of ammunition. I therefore deemed it right to await the arrival of this necessary arm to make the assault.

20. The following morning, the 26th, at 10 o'clock, a flag of truce was hoisted on the walls, when I deputed Mr. Thorn (whom Captain Elliot had sent to me as interpreter) to ascertain the cause. A mandarin stated that they wished for peace. I had it explained that, as General commanding the British, I would treat with none but the General commanding the Chinese troops—that we came before Canton much against the wishes of the British nation, but that repeated insults and breaches of faith had compelled us to make the present movement, and that I would cease from hostilities for two hours, to enable their general to meet me and Sir Le Fleming Senhouse, who kindly accompanied me throughout the whole operation, and to whose judicious arrangements and unceasing exertions for the furtherance of the united services (and I am proud to say they are united in hand and heart) I cannot too strongly express my sense of obligation. I further explained that Captain Elliot, her Majesty's Plenipotentiary, was with the advanced squadron to the south of the city, and that if I did not receive a communication from him, or had not a satisfactory interview with the general, I should, at the termination of the two hours, order the white flag to be struck.

21. As the general did not make his appearance, although numerous messages were received between this time (about noon) and 4 p.m., I hauled down the white flag. The enemy, however, did not, which was rather convenient, as it enabled me to get up my guns and ammunition, without exposing my men to fire.

22. During the night of the 26th, everything was prepared on our side, with the exception of one 12-pounder howitzer, the carriage of which had been disabled; the guns, by the indefatigable exertion of the officers and men of the Royal Artillery and Madras Artillery and Sappers, were placed in position. All was ready, and the necessary orders were given for opening the batteries at 7 o'clock on the morning of the 27th, and for the assault at 8, in four columns.

23. The right column, composed of the Royal Marines, under Captain Ellis, had directions to pass through a deserted village to the right of the north gate, to blow the gate open with powder bags, if possible, and if not, to escalade a circular work thrown up as a second defence to that gate.

24. The second column on the right, consisting of the brigade of seamen, under Captain Bourchier, was directed to make the assault, by escalade, on the opposite side of the circular defence, where the wall appeared comparatively low, covered by a heavy fire of musketry from the hill, within pistol-shot of the walls. This column would have been exposed only to the fire of a few flanking guns, which I calculated would have been kept under by the fire of the covering party.

25. The 18th Royal Irish, under Lieutenant-Colonel Adams, were ordered to advance from the rear of a hill close to the five-storied pagoda, and to escalade the walls behind this pagoda, (which was not flanked except by one gun,) although they were very high, from twenty-eight to thirty feet, but I hoped, by the concentrated fire of the guns, to have reduced an exceedingly high and apparently slight parapet. The escalade of this corps was to be covered by the Bengal Volunteers, and a company of the 37th M.N.I.

26. The left assault was to be made by the 49th, under Lieut.-Colonel Morris. This corps was directed to escalade by a bastion directly in front of, and commanded by, the principal fort in our possession, called by the Chinese, Yung-Kang-Tai, the fire of musketry from which would have prevented the enemy from making use of their guns. To strengthen this attack, two companies of the 37th M.N.I. were to occupy the heights, and keep up a rapid fire upon the wall.

27. The ground was peculiarly favourable for these several attacks, and for the effective fire of the covering parties, without a chance of injuring the assailants. The heights which we occupied are from 90 to 250 paces from the city wall, with a precipitous glen intervening. On making a lodgment on the walls, each column was to communicate with and support that on its inner flank, and, when united, to make a rush for the fortified hill within the walls, on which the artillery was directed to play from the moment the advance was sounded. I directed Captain Knowles to ascertain, as far as practicable, by the fire of heavy rockets and shells, whether it was mined, which alone I apprehended—the Chinese usually forming their mines so as to make them liable to explosion by such means.

28. The flags of truce still appeared upon the walls at daylight on the 27th, and at a quarter past six o'clock I was on the point of sending the interpreter to explain that I could not respect such a display after my flag had been taken down, and should at once resume hostilities. At this moment, an officer of the royal navy, who had been travelling all night, having missed his

way, handed me the accompanying letter from her Majesty's Plenipotentiary. Whatever might be my sentiments, my duty was to acquiesce— the attack, which was to have commenced in forty-five minutes, was countermanded, and the feelings of the Chinese were spared. Of the policy of the measure I do not consider myself a competent judge; but I say feelings, as I would have been responsible that Canton should be equally spared, with exception of its defences, and that not a soldier should have entered the town further than the fortified heights within its walls.

29. At ten o'clock, Yang, the Tartar general, requested a conference, when Sir Le Fleming Senhouse accompanied me, and a long and uninteresting parley ensued, in which I explained that her Majesty's Plenipotentiary having resumed negotiations with the local authorities, I should await a further communication from him. At twelve, Captain Elliott arrived in camp, and all further active operations ceased.

30. The following day, at twelve, in a conference with the Kwang-chow-foo, under the walls, every arrangement was made for the evacuation of the city, by as large a portion of the Tartar troops as could be got ready, and I permitted a mandarin of rank to pass through my lines to procure quarters for them. I was now given to understand that the force amounted to 45,000 men from other provinces, exclusive of the troops belonging to the Quang-Tung province. At the request of Captain Elliot, I acquiesced in the former passing out of the N.E. gate, to the left of my position, and permitted them to carry away their arms and baggage, on condition that no banner should be displayed, or music sounded.

31. About twelve the following day, I perceived numbers of men, apparently irregulars, and armed for the most part with long spears, shields, and swords, collecting upon the heights, three or four miles to my rear. As they continued rapidly to increase, detaching bodies to their front, I directed General Burrell to take charge of our position, and hold every man ready, in case a sortie, or other act of treachery, under cover of a flag of truce, should be intended; and I advanced with a wing of the 26th, (which corps I had withdrawn two days previously from the factories,) three companies of the 49th, the 37th Madras N.I., and the company of Bengal Volunteers, supported by the Royal Marines. The two latter corps I kept in reserve, ready to return, and act on the flank, should an attack be made on our position from the town. When I descended the heights, about 4000 men appeared in my front. I directed the wing of the 26th, under Major Pratt, supported by the 37th M.N.I., to advance, and drive them from rather a strong position they had taken up behind an embankment along the bed of the stream. This duty the 26th and 37th performed most creditably; and as the Chinese made a rally at what appeared to be a military post in my front, I directed

that it should be destroyed, which was instantly effected by the 26th, and a magazine, unexpectedly found in the village, blown up. These duties having been performed without the loss of a man, the Chinese throwing away their spears, and flying the moment a fire was opened upon them, I directed the 49th, Royal Marines, and Bengal Volunteers, to fall back on our position, and remain with the wing of the 26th and 37th M.N.I., (about 280 men,) to watch the movements of the Chinese, who had retreated to a range of heights in my front, having no banners, and apparently but few matchlocks amongst them. Within two hours, however, from 7000 to 8000 men had collected, and displayed numerous banners. When I first moved, I had ordered Captain Knowles, of the Royal Artillery, to bring out a few rockets, but our advance was so. rapid that he did not get them up until after the repulse of the first body.

32. At this moment the heat of the sun was hardly supportable, and both officers and men were greatly exhausted. I must here state, and with sincere sorrow, that Major Beecher, Deputy Quarter Master General, a most estimable and willing officer, whose services throughout the previous operations were as creditable to him as they were satisfactory to me, fell by my side from over-exertion, and expired within a few minutes. My aide-de-camp, Captain Gough, was also alarmingly unwell from the same .cause, and I ordered him back to camp, when the enemy were repulsed, but hearing that the Chinese were again assembling, he returned, and meeting the Bengal Volunteers, very judiciously brought them back.

33. The Chinese having advanced in great force, some rockets were fired at them, but although thrown with great precision, appeared to have little effect, and as the approach of a thunderstorm was evident, I became anxious, before it broke, to disperse this assemblage, whose approach bespoke more determination than I had previously witnessed. I ordered Major Pratt to attack a large body who were advancing through the paddy fields on his left, and to clear the hills to his front. Captain Duff, with the 37th M.N.I., supported by the Bengal Volunteers under Captain Mee, I ordered to advance direct to his front, and dislodge a body, which had re-occupied the post that we had previously burned, and then push forward and clear the hills to his front. I witnessed with much satisfaction the spirited manner in which these officers executed my orders, and the enemy were driven in at all points. The right of the 37th being threatened by a military post at the foot of the hills to our right, the Bengal Volunteers dispersed the occupants. This, however, separated them from 37th M.N.I., and perceiving that this latter corps was advancing further than I intended, I requested Captain Ommaney, of the 3rd Madras Light Cavalry, (who with Lieutenant Mackenzie, of H.M.'s 90th regiment, accompanied me as amateurs, and both were most zealous and

useful in conveying my orders,) to direct the Bengal Volunteers to move up to its support. Captain Duff meanwhile, to open his communication with the 26th on his left, had detached a company under Lieutenant Hadfield for that purpose.

34. The thunder-storm was now most awful, and finding that as our men advanced, the Chinese retired, I considered that it would be injudicious to follow them further, and directed the whole to fall back. The rain continued to fall in torrents, and most of the firelocks had got wet; at one time the 26th had been unable to fire a single musket; this emboldened the Chinese, who, in many instances, attacked our men hand to hand, and the 26th had frequently to charge bodies that advanced close to them.

35. As the Chinese, even in this mode of warfare, could make no impression, they retreated, and the 26th and 37th M.N.I. and Bengal Volunteers fell back. Understanding from Captain Duff that his detached company was with the 26th, I directed the whole, after a short halt, to return to our position, and was exceedingly annoyed, on the force concentrating, to find that the detached company, under Lieutenant Hadfield, had never joined the 26th. I immediately ordered two companies of marines, with the percussion locks, to return with Captain Duff to the scene of this day's contest. It gives me no ordinary gratification to say, that a little after dusk they found Lieutenant Hadfield, with his gallant company in square, surrounded by some thousand Chinese, who, as the 37th firelocks would not go off, had approached close to them. The sepoys; I am proud to say, in this critical situation, nobly upheld the high character of the native army, by unshrinking discipline and cheerful obedience, and I feel that the expression of my best thanks is due to Lieutenant Hadfield, and to Lieutenant Devereux and Ensign Berkeley, who zealously supported him during this trying scene. The last-named officer, I regret to say, was severely wounded. The marines, with Captain Duff, fired a couple of volleys into this crowd, which instantly dispersed them, with great loss.

36. At daylight, the next morning, I felt myself called upon to send into the city, and inform the Kwang-chow-foo, that if, under existing circumstances, a similar insult was offered, or any demonstration made, indicative of hostile interruption to the negotiations pending under a flag of truce, for the evacuation of the city by the Chinese troops, and a ransom for its deliverance, I would at once haul down the white flag and resume hostilities. At twelve, Captain Elliott joined me, and a communication was received, that the Kwang-chow-foo would meet us under the walls. Previous to his arrival, vast numbers of Chinese appeared on the hills from which we had driven them the night before, and which, during the early part of the morning, had been clear. Guns and ginjalls were fired in all directions,

various banners displayed, and large parties thrown out in advance. About 7500 Tartar troops had marched out of the city that morning, and were still moving with their arms, but, as stipulated, without music or banners. I felt some doubt whether treachery was not contemplated, and I therefore made such a disposition of our troops as to ensure its defeat. By two o'clock, from 12,000 to 15,000 men, evidently the same description of force that we had met the preceding day, had assembled on the same heights.

37. The Kwang-chow-foo now arrived, and it became evident, as he was perfectly in my power, that no combination existed between the troops in the town or those marching out, and the assemblage in my rear. I therefore ordered the wing of the 26th—the other wing had been left at Tsing-hae—to keep up the communication with the rear, and a wing of the 49th, with the 37th M.N.I., and the Royal Marines, to be prepared to disperse the assailants. On joining the Kwang-chow-foo, and explaining my determination to put my threat in force if the enemy advanced, he assured me that this hostile movement was without the knowledge, and against the wishes, of the Chinese authorities; that there were no mandarins with this militia in our rear; that it had assembled to protect the villages in the plain, and that he would instantly send off a mandarin of rank, (his own assistant,) with orders for its immediate dispersion, if I would depute an officer to accompany him.

38. Captain Moore, of the 34th Bengal N.I., Deputy Judge Advocate General, volunteered this hazardous duty. This officer had accompanied me as one of my personal staff throughout all the operations, and he and Major Wilson, paymaster to the expedition, who kindly volunteered to act in the same capacity, had, by their zealous service, been most useful to me, in a country where all my orders were to be conveyed by officers on foot through an intricate line of communication. Captain Moore was quite successful, as the whole body instantly retreated and entirely dispersed, as soon as he and the mandarin had made known to the leaders the object of their coming.

39. Finding that five millions of dollars had been paid, and that her Majesty's Plenipotentiary was perfectly satisfied with the security for payment of the remaining million for the ransom of Canton; that upwards of 14,500 Tartar troops had marched out of the town under the terms of the treaty, without colours or banners flying, or music beating; that 3000 had gone by water, and that the remainder were prepared to follow, when carriage was provided, I acceded to the wish of her Majesty's Plenipotentiary to embark the troops, the Chinese furnishing me with 800 coolies to convey my guns and ammunition. These coolies being furnished soon after daylight on the 1st instant, I sent all the guns and stores to the rear, covered by the 26th Royal Marines, 37th M.N.I., and Bengal Volunteers, and at twelve o'clock the British flag was lowered in the four forts, and the troops and brigade of

seamen marched out and returned to Tsinghae.

40. By the excellent arrangements, and under the active superintendence, of Captain Bourchier, of H.M.S. "Blonde," and Captain Maitland, of H.M.S. "Wellesley," the whole were re-embarked by three o'clock, without leaving a man of the army or navy, or a camp-follower behind, and, under tow of the "Nemesis," reached their respective transports that night.

41. I have now, my lord, detailed, I fear at too great length, the occurrences of eight days before Canton. I might have been very brief, perfect success attending every operation; but by a mere statement of the leading facts, I should not have done justice to the discipline of the small but gallant band whom it was my good fortune to command, and whose devotedness was worthy of a better foe.

42. I have not touched upon the brilliant conduct of the royal navy in their attacks and various operations to the south of the city, as these will be detailed by their own chief, to whom, as I have said, I cannot too strongly express my obligations.

43. In a body, where all have done their duty nobly and zealously, it would be invidious to particularize: I will, however, entreat your lordship's favourable notice of the commanding officers of brigades and corps, from whom I have received the most able assistance, and to whom my best thanks are due. To Major-General Burrell, commanding the right brigade, who was zealously supported by Lieutenant-Colonel Adams, commanding 18th Royal Irish, and Captain Ellis, commanding the Marine Battalion; to Captain Bourchier, of H.M.S. "Blonde," commanding the brigade of seamen, supported most ably by Captain Maitland, of H.M.S. "Wellesley," and Captain Barlow, H.M.S. "Nimrod;" to Lieutenant-Colonel Morris, commanding the left brigade, whose good fortune it was first to carry the heights and place the colours of the 49th in the first fort taken, gallantly seconded by Major Stephens, who commanded the 49th in the first operation, and Major Blythe, who commanded that corps during the latter part of the day; to Captain Duff, commanding 37th M.N.I.; and Captain Mee, commanding the Bengal Volunteers.

To Major Pratt, commanding H.M.'s 26th regiment. This corps, though not at first much engaged, from the nature of its position at the factories, proved on the 30th, by its spirited and steady conduct, which nothing could exceed, how valuable its services would have been throughout.

To Captain Knowles, of the Royal Artillery, senior officer of that arm, my best thanks are due for his valuable services. Lieut, the Hon. R. C. Spencer, with the detachment of Royal Artillery, well supported the high character of that distinguished corps. The zeal of Captain Anstruther, commanding the Madras Artillery, was indefatigable, as were the efforts of every individual of that valuable body in bringing up the guns and ammunition.

To Captain Cotton, field engineer, I feel under the greatest obligations, arid I experienced the most ready support from every Officer under him. Of one of them, Lieutenant Rundall, I regret to say, that I shall probably lose the services for some time, in consequence of a severe wound. The useful labours of the Sappers called for my best thanks; they were cheerfully prepared to place the ladders for the escalade.

I feel greatly obliged to all the General Staff; all accompanied me on shore, and to their indefatigable attention in conveying orders on foot, at times to a considerable distance, I was much indebted. To Lieutenant-Colonel Mountain, Deputy Adjutant-General, my best thanks are due, for his unwearied exertions and valuable services, not only upon the present, but upon every occasion. The exertions of Major Hawkins, Deputy Commissary-General, were unceasing, and by his judicious arrangements, (and those of his assistant,) the troops were amply supplied. The excellent arrangements made by Dr. Grant, the officiating Super-intending Surgeon, and Medical Staff of corps, call also for my acknowledgment. I beg to bring to your lordship's particular notice my aid-de-camp, Captain Gough, of the 3rd Light Dragoons, from whom I have upon this, as upon every occasion, received the most active and unremitting assistance.

44. Having now conveyed my approval of the conduct of the commanding officers of brigades and corps, and the heads of departments, permit me to draw your lordship's special attention to the praiseworthy conduct of the sailors and soldiers under my command, which, in my mind, does them the highest credit. During the eight days this force was on shore, (and many of the corps were unavoidably placed in situations where sham-shu was abundant,) but two instances of drunkenness occurred; and I deem it but justice here to mention a strong fact. The soldiers of the 49th, finding a quantity of sham-shu in the village they had so gallantly taken, without order or previous knowledge of their officers, brought the jars containing this pernicious liquor, and broke them in front of their corps, without the occurrence of a single case of intoxication.

45. This dispatch will be presented by Captain Grattan, whose conduct I have already mentioned to your lordship, and whom I have selected for this duty alone, on account of that conduct. He is a most intelligent officer, and will be able to give your lordship any further information.

I have the honour to be, &c.

(Signed) *H. Gough, Major-General, Commanding Expeditionary Forces.*

P.S.—It is with deep regret that I have to mention the loss of Lieutenant Fox, of H.M.S. "Nimrod," a most promising young officer, attached to Captain Barlow's battalion of seamen, who fell at the storm of the western forts; Mr. Walter Kendall, mate of the same ship, a very deserving officer, lost his leg, I am sorry to add, at the same time.

I have the honour to forward a return of the killed and wounded, and a list of ordnance captured. Of the killed and wounded on the enemy's side, it is difficult to form a correct estimate; but the Kwang-chow-foo acknowledged to me, that of the Tartar troops, 500 had been killed, and 1500 wounded, on the 25th of May; and I conceive that the killed and wounded on the Chinese side, upon the 30th, and in the different attacks made upon my flanks and line of communication, must have been double those numbers.

To His Excellency Major-General Sir Hugh Gough, K.C.B., and Captain Sir H. Le Fleming Senhouse, K.C.H., &c. &c. &c. H.M.S. "Hyacinth," off Canton, May 26th, 1841, 10 p.m.

Gentlemen,—I have the honour to acquaint you that I am in communication with the officers of the Chinese government, concerning the settlement of difficulties in this province, upon the following conditions:—

1st. The Imperial Commissioner, and all the troops, other than those of the province, to quit the city within six days, and remove at a distance exceeding sixty miles.

2nd. Six millions of dollars to be paid in one week for the use of the crown of England,—one million payable before to-morrow at sunset.

3rd. British troops to remain in their actual positions till the whole sum be paid; no additional preparations on either side; but all British troops and ships of war to return without the Bocca Tigris as soon as the whole be paid. Wang-Tong also to be evacuated, but not to be re-armed by the Chinese government, till all the difficulties are adjusted between the two governments.

4th. The loss occasioned by the burning of the Spanish brig, "Bilbaino," and all losses occasioned by the destruction of the factories, to be paid within one week.

For the purpose of completing this arrangement, I have to request that you will be pleased to suspend hostilities till noon. I have the honour to remain, &c.

(Signed) *Charles Elliot, Her Majesty's Plenipotentiary.*

*

To His Excellency Major-General Sir Hugh Gough, K.C.B., and Captain Sir H. Le Fleming Senhouse, Knt., K.C.H., &c. &c. &c. H.M.S. "Hyacinth," off Canton, 27th May, 1841, three, p.m.

Gentlemen,—Herewith I have the honour to transmit to you an English version of the arrangement this day concluded with the officers of the Chinese government, and also of the full authority given to the Kwang-chow-foo to act for their Excellencies.

I shall take an early opportunity of communicating with you again upon this subject.

And I have the honour to be, &c.

(Signed) *Charles Elliot, Her Majesty's Plenipotentiary.*

Terms of Agreement granted to the Officers of the Chinese Government, resident within the city of Canton, on the 27th May, 1841.

1. It is required, that the three Imperial Commissioners, and all the troops, other than those of the province, quit the city within six days, and proceed to a distance of upwards of sixty miles.

2. Six millions of dollars to be paid in one week, for the use of the crown of England, counting front the 27th May; one million payable before sunset of the said 27th day of May.

3. For the present, the British troops to remain in their actual positions: no additional preparations for hostilities to be made on either side. If the. whole sum agreed upon be not paid within seven days, it shall be increased to seven millions; if not within fourteen days, to eight millions; if not within twenty days, to nine millions. When the whole shall be paid, all the British forces to return without the Bocca Tigris, and Wang-Tong and all fortified places within the river to be restored, but not to be re-armed till all affairs are settled between the two nations.

4. Losses occasioned by the plunder of the factories, and by the destruction of the Spanish brig "Bilbaino," in 1839, to be paid within one week.

5. It is required that the Kwang-chow-foo shall produce full powers to conclude this arrangement, on the part of the three Commissioners, the General of the Tartar garrison, the Governor-General, and the Fooyuen of Kwantung.

(Seal of the Kwang-chow-foo.)

Written the 26th, agreed to the 27th May, 1841.

(True copy - Signed) *J. Rob. Morrison, Acting Secretary and Treasurer.*

*

Yishan, Generalissimo—Lungwan and Yang Fang, Joint Commissioners—Atsinga, General of the Garrison—Kekung, Governor of the two Kwang—and Eliang, Lieutenant Governor of Kwang-tung—hereby issue instructions to the Kwang-chow-foo.

The Plenipotentiary of the English nation being now willing to observe a truce, and make arrangements for peace, the said Kwang-chow-foo will conduct the details of the pacific arrangement and settlement. He is not, upon any plea, to excuse himself-These are his instructions.

The foregoing to the Kwang-chow-foo, thus be it.

Twankwang, 21st year, 4th month, 7th day.

(27th May, 1841):

L. S of the Generalissimo, L. S. of the Joint Commissioners.

L. S. of the Governor of the two Kwang, L. S. of the Fuyain of Kwantung.

(True translation.) (Signed) *J. Rob. Morrison,*
Chinese Secretary and Interpreter.

(True copy - Signed) *J. Rob. Morrison, Acting Secretary and Treasurer.*

*

Return of Killed and Wounded in her Majesty's forces, at the attack on Canton, from the 23rd to the 30th of May, 1841.

Ships or Corps	Killed	Wounded	Remarks
Blenheim	2	9	1 Off., 1 R. Ay., 1 Act I R. M., and 8 Seamen.
Wellesley	0	6	3 Seamen, and 3 Royal Marines.
Blonde	1	1	1 Seaman, and 1 Royal Marine.
Calliope	0	1	1 Seaman.
Hyacinth	0	5	2 Officers, and 3 Seamen.
Nimrod	2	4	2 Officers, and 4 Seamen.
Modeste	1	9	2 Officers, and 8 Seamen.
Columbine	0	2	2 Seamen.
Algerine	0	4	1 Officer, 2 Seamen, and 1 R.M.
Nemesis	0	1	1 Officer.
Madras Artillery	0	1	
Sappers and Miners	0	1	
18th Royal Irish	2	19	
26th Cameronians	3	15	
49th Regiment	1	17	
37th Native Infantry	1	13	
Bengal Volunteers	0	1	
Camp followers	1	3	
Staff	1	0	
	15	**112**	
		+15	
	Total	**127**	

Officers killed—Major Beecher, Deputy Quartermaster-General, died from over-fatigue; Lieutenant Fox, her Majesty's sloop, "Nimrod," killed.

Officers wounded—Mr. Walter Kendall, mate of "Nimrod," (dangerously,) lost his leg; Mr. W. H. Bate, mate of "Blenheim," slightly; Lieutenant Morshead, of "Hyacinth," slightly; Mr. Peter Barclay, mate of ditto, slightly; Mr. E. Fitzgerald, mate of "Modeste," dangerously; Mr. W. Pearse, ditto ditto, slightly; Mr. Hall, commanding "Nemesis," severely burnt; Mr. Vaughan,

Assistant Surgeon of the "Algerine," slightly; Lieutenant Rundall, of the Madras Sappers and Miners, dangerously; Captain Serjeant, 18th Royal Infantry, severely; Lieutenant Millard, ditto, slightly; Lieutenant Edwards, ditto, severely; Lieutenant Pearson, 49th regiment, severely; Lieutenant Johnson, 26th Cameronians, slightly; Ensign Berkeley, 37th Native Infantry, severely.

*

Return of Killed and Wounded on the 25th and 30th May, before Canton, of the Force under the command of Major-General Sir Hugh Gough, K.C.B.

CORPS.	25th May.						30th May.						Total					
	Killed.			Wounded			Killed.			Wounded			Killed.			Wounded		
	Officers	NCOs & Privates	Camp Followers	Officers	NCOs & Privates	Camp Followers	Officers	NCOs & Privates	Camp Followers	Officers	NCOs & Privates	Camp Followers	Officers	NCOs & Privates	Camp Followers	Officers	NCOs & Privates	Camp Followers
Royal Artillery	–	–	–	–	1	–	–	–	–	–	–	–	–	–	–	–	1	–
Madras Artillery	–	–	–	–	1	–	–	–	–	–	–	–	–	–	–	–	1	–
Sappers & Miners	–	–	–	1	–	–	–	–	–	–	–	–		–	–	1	–	–
18th Royal Irish	–	2	–	3	16	–	–	–	–	–	–	–	–	2	–	3	16	–
26th Cameronians	–	–	–	–	4	–	–	3	–	1	10	–	–	3	–	1	14	–
49th Regiment	–	1	–	1	16	–	–	–	–	–	–	–	–	1	–	1	16	–
Naval Brigade	1	4	–	2	13	–	–	–	–	–	–	–	–	4	–	2	13	–
Royal Marines	–	–	–	–	5	–	–	–	–	–	–	–	–	–	–	–	5	–
Bengal Volunteers	–	–	–	–	1	–	–	–	–	–	–	–	–	–	–	–	1	–
37th Madras N.I.	–	–	–	–	1	–	–	2	–	1	10	–	–	2	–	1	11	–
Camp Followers	–	–	1	–	–	3	–	–	–	–	–	1	–	–	1	–	–	4
Total	**1**	**7**	**1**	**7**	**58**	**3**	**–**	**5**	**–**	**2**	**20**	**1**	**1**	**12**	**1**	**9**	**78**	**4**

- 25th May: 9 Killed, 68 Wounded
- 30th May: 5 Killed, 23 Wounded

Total: 14 Killed, 91 Wounded.

Armine S. H. Mountain, Lieut.-Col., Deputy Adjutant-General, Expeditionary Force.

Officers Killed and Wounded.

25th May.—Killed: Lieutenant Fox, H.M.S. "Nimrod."— Wounded: Lieutenant Rundall, Madras Sappers and Miners, dangerously; Mr. Kendall, mate, H.M.S. "Nimrod," ditto; Captain Serjeant, H.M. Royal Infantry, severely; Lieutenant Millard, ditto, slightly; Lieut. Edwards, ditto severely; Lieut. Pearson, H.M. 49th regiment, severely; Mr. Bate, H.M.S. "Blenheim," slightly.

30th May.—Wounded: Lieut. Johnson, 26th Cameronians, slightly; Ensign Berkeley, 37th Madras Native Infantry, severely.

*

Return of the Ordnance mounted in the Forts on the Heights above Canton, when stormed and captured on the 25th of May, 1841, by the forces under the command of Major-General Sir Hugh Gough, K.C.B., Commanding Expeditionary Force serving in China.

- Yung-Yang-Tai Fort: 13
- She-Ting-Paon Fort: 6 Guns of all Calibre
- Paon-Keih-Tai Fort: 11 Guns of all Calibre
- Kung-Keih-Tai Fort: 12 Guns of all Calibre

Total: 42 Guns

In each fort a number of ginjals and a considerable quantity of powder found.

(Signed) *J. Knowles, Captain, Commanding Artillery Brigade.*

(True copy - Signed) *Armine S. H. Mountain, Lieut.-Col., Dep. Adj.-Gen. Expeditionary Force.*

(True copies - Signed) *H. Gough, Major-General, Commanding Expeditionary Force.*

*

Extracts from a Despatch from Captain Sir H. Le Fleming Senhouse, K.C.H., &c, to Commodore Sir J. J. Gordon Bremer, C.B., and K.C.H., Commander in Chief, &c. &c.

Dated Heights above Canton, May 29th, 1841, continued on board H.M.S. "Blenheim," French River, June 2nd, 1841.

I closed my former letter with the details of our proceedings up to the moment the expedition was about to leave Hong Kong for Canton. I have now the gratification to enter upon the details of a succession of operations, highly honourable, I trust, to her Majesty's arms, and by which the large and populous city of Canton has been laid in complete submission at the feet of the Queen's forces.

No overt act of hostility had taken place up to the 21st May, except remounting the guns in the Shamien battery, but the Chinese appear to have been perfectly ready for attack. All remained quiet in the river until about eleven o'clock, p.m., when an attempt was made with fire rafts to burn the advanced vessels. This attack not only totally failed, but was followed up by a gallant attack on the Shamien battery, and the silencing of it by the vessels of the squadron, under the immediate superintendence of Captain Herbert, of the "Calliope," and the destruction of a large flotilla of fire vessels, which the Chinese had been preparing, and had brought out of the branch of the river which leads north of the town. About the same time, though later in the night, the "Alligator" was attacked off Howqua's Fort; and to shew how necessary it was to have been always on our guard, the fire junks came up with the flood tide in a direction with the merchant vessels at

Whampoa, where all seemed to sleep in security. Captain Kuper's account of his prompt and decisive conduct in repelling the attack, I have also the honour to forward, (No. 1.)

Opinions were uncertain as to the feasibility of entering the northward branch of the river, and of floating at low water. To determine this, I availed myself once more of the zeal and great ability of Commander Belcher, who most handsomely volunteered to explore it with his own boats, assisted with three others from the "Pylades," "Modeste," and "Algerine," all placed under the command of that gallant and judicious officer, Lieutenant Goldsmith, of the "Druid," who was attached to the "Blenheim," in that ship's launch, and who had orders to protect Commander Belcher in his surveying operations.

The Major-General and myself went to Canton to make a reconnoissance and a personal inspection on the same day, the 23rd. In our progress we observed a firing and explosions in the direction of Captain Belcher's party; and Commander Belcher's letter, a copy of which I enclose (No. 2,) gives the detail of a gallant and spirited affair which took place in the creek. At eleven at night, Commander Belcher returned with the gratifying intelligence that he had discovered an excellent landing-place on a pier, with water enough for the "Sulphur," close to it, at low water. The ground directly around it rose in low hills, and a line of hills appeared to continue to the height near the city, although there might-be swampy ground in the small valleys dividing them.

Our united force consisted of the ships and vessels named below, comprising, in their crews, officers, seamen, and Marines, inclusive, about 3200 men, out of which about 1000 officers, seamen, and Marines were landed to serve with the army. The military force under that gallant, distinguished, and experienced officer, Major-General Sir Hugh Gough, comprised her Majesty's 49th regiment, 311 in number; 37th Madras Native Infantry, 240; Bengal Volunteers, 79; Royal Artillery, 38; Madras Artillery, 232; Sappers and Miners, 171; her Majesty's 18th Royal Irish, 535; and her Majesty's 26th Cameronians, 317; making about 2223.

Forming the Macao Fort Division:

- Blenheim, Cruiser, Blonde, Columbine, Sulphur, Algerine, Hyacinth, Starling, Nimrod, Modeste, Pylades, Atalanta and Nemesis steamers.

Forming the Whampoa Division:

- Calliope, Herald, Conway, Alligator.
- Wellesley, at Wang-Tong, in the Bocca Tigris, sent up her marines and 160 seamen.

Captain Herbert was stationed at Whampoa with the "Calliope," "Conway," "Herald," and "Alligator," and was directed on the 24th to take the command of the force, afforded by the four vessels under his orders, and pushing up with the flood-tide with such vessels as could proceed, or with the boats of the ships endeavour to take possession of and secure the arsenal. I informed him that the ships near the factory would drop down and secure the Dutch fort, and to keep up an enfilading fire on the face of the works thrown up in front of the city, where I understood many guns were mounted. I left it to his own judgment to act according to circumstances, in endeavouring to drive the enemy from the French fort, and to endeavour to open the communication with the ships of war to the westward, and with the commanding officer of the left column stationed at the factories. I beg to enclose a letter I have received from Captain Herbert (No. 3), detailing the part he took in the affair that followed, where the usual gallantry and zeal were displayed by her Majesty's seamen and Royal Marines, Commander Warren, with his gig's crew, placing his colours first on the walls of the French fort. Commander Warren was also ordered, with the ships under his command, to take up his anchorage in line along the town from the western fort as far as the factory, and to cannonade the exterior to prevent the enemy from firing on the right column as it passed. After the enemy's fire had been silenced, he was to leave the "Nimrod" and another vessel to keep the enemy in check at that quarter, and to detach the rest of his force to secure the Dutch fort, and, to place them with the "Atalanta," so as to enfilade the line of batteries in front of the city, but he was not to expose his ships to the front fire of the heavy guns said to be placed there until the enemy were shaken in their position.

The landing of the left column was placed under his particular charge, and it was not to land until he had made the signal.

So effectually and vigorously did Commander Warren execute these instructions, that when the right column passed his station everything had been completed, and all was still. The detail of this gallant affair is annexed in a copy of his letter (No. 4), where I regret to observe the loss of men was more than had been ordinary.

A return of the killed and wounded is here added (No. 5), and although it may appear strange to see the wounded of the army in the naval report, yet the two corps had been so entirely mingled together, their services so blended, and such intimate harmony has existed, that it would be difficult to make any separation between the acts of either, or the circumstances that concerned them. The two officers who had fallen, Major Beecher, of the Indian Army, Deputy Quarter Master General, a very old officer, who had served ably in the Burmese war, and Lieutenant Fox, first of the "Nimrod," have united the regret of all by their characters and services. The same shot took off the legs of Lieutenant Fox, and of Mr.Kendall, his shipmate, the gunnery mate of the "Nimrod;" the former fell a victim to his wound, the latter has survived amputation. I thought it would gratify Mr. Kendall to give him an acting commission as lieutenant of the "Nimrod" in Lieutenant Fox's vacancy, on the field of battle, until your pleasure is known, though his wound will disable him from doing his duty perhaps for some time, and may oblige him to go home.

I have the honour to enclose lists of the officers who have been personally engaged in the operations on shore, and afloat in boats, but it must be remembered that the duties and the fatigues of Commander Pritchard, of the "Blenheim," and of those who remained on board their respective ships, were increased in the same ratio as their numbers were diminished, and that the ultimate success is the attainment of the whole body, each working in his particular sphere. The names of many will be seen who have already distinguished themselves at Chuenpee, Anunghoy, Wantong, and the many affairs in the Canton River, and no doubt, have already, like their brother officers at Acre, been so fortunate as to secure their country's notice. Never was there a finer set of zealous, able commanders. Commanders Belcher and Warren have only continued in that path of able and judicious service on which they have so long travelled; their own services will always attract attention. Of the lieutenants, Lieutenant Joseph Pearse, Lieutenant Goldsmith, Lieutenant Watson, Sir Frederick Nicholson, Lieutenant Moorshead, first of their respective vessels, may, perhaps, be named, without injury to all others who well played their parts; to Lieutenant Kellett, of the "Starling," I am much obliged; and Lieutenant Mason, of the "Algerine," has won his promotion by a long series of gallant and brave services. I beg to acknowledge the zeal and the assistance I have had from every captain and officer of the squadron whom I have had the happiness to command.

*

No. 1.

To Captain T, Herbert, Commanding the advanced Squadron.

H.M.S. "Alligator," off Howqua's Folly, May 22, 1841.

Sir,—I have the honour to acquaint you that last night, shortly after twelve o'clock, an attack was made by the Chinese upon H.M.S. "Alligator," under my command, by fire rafts.

They were chained in pairs, and brought down in a direct line for the ships, on a flood tide. Owing to the confined position I was in, and the sunken junks, and line of stakes astern, I could not slip but by steering the ship; and, by the activity of Lieutenant Stewart, first of this ship, and Messrs. Woolcombe and Baker, mates in command of the boats, they were towed clear, although they passed within ten yards of the bows. As I had reason to believe that a considerable force was assembled in the vicinity, to take advantage of any accident that might occur, I fired several shot on both sides to clear the banks. No damage has been sustained.

I have the honour to be,

(Signed) *Augustus L. Kuper, Captain, (Actg.)*

*

No. 2.

To Captain Sir H. Le Fleming Senhouse, Kt., K.C.H., Senior Officer, &c. &c. &c.

H.M.S. "Sulphur," off Canton, May 23, 1841.

Sir,—In pursuance of your directions, I proceeded up the creek on the western side of Canton, in order to examine the nature of the country; our force consisting of the "Druid's" launch, Lieutenant Goldsmith, (first lieutenant of that ship,) the "Sulphur's" pinnace, and two cutters, "Modeste," "Pylades," and "Algerine's" cutters, the "Starling's" cutter, and my gig, the two first-named boats carrying guns.

On approaching Neishang, where the boats of the squadron were yesterday engaged, I observed the "fast boats" of the enemy collected in great numbers; part retreated by a creek to the left, but shortly after returned, and manifested a disposition to impede our progress, by firing guns, and drawing up across the creek. Our advance, and notice of our determination, by a round from each of the boats carrying guns, put them to flight, and in a very short period thirteen fast boats, five war junks, and small craft collected, amounting to twenty-eight in all, were in flames. Fire rafts were in readiness on the banks of the creek, but too well secured by chains, and therefore beyond our ability to destroy during our short stay.

The whole force behaved with their usual gallantry, and the commander of the division under my direction, (Lieutenant Goldsmith,) afforded me that steady determined support which so particularly distinguishes him, and which caused me to ask you for his co-operation.

The enemy being posted in force on a hill above us, prevented me, in obedience to your orders, from exposing my small party, by an attempt to dislodge them. But I fully succeeded in effecting my reconnoitre, by being hoisted to the mast-head of the largest junk, from whence I was able to survey the whole surrounding country.

From that examination, I am happy to acquaint you that landing on solid ground is perfectly practicable. That the advance to the batteries situated on the hills north of Canton, is apparently easy; and I have every reason to believe that our artillery will not meet with an extraordinary difficulty.

On my return, I landed at the mandarin temple at Tsingpoo, where I found sand bags and five small guns, which were spiked, and thrown into the sea. This temple, with other large commodious buildings, will afford ample quarters for the troops which may first be landed.

No casualties whatever occurred. I brought out with me one large fast boat of sixty oars, the boat from which the mandarin escaped; and in pursuance of your separate orders, collected vessels for the conveyance of 2000 soldiers.

I have the honour to enclose a list of boats and officers engaged, and am, sir,

Your most obedient servant,

(Signed) *Ed. Belcher, Commander.*

Return of Officers employed on the 23rd instant, off Tsingpoo.

Names	Rank	Ship	Boat	Guns	No. Of Boats
Lieut. Goldsmith	Lieut.	Druid	launch	1	1
W.C. Wood		Sulphur	pinnace	1	2
R.M.H. Richardson	Mate		cutter		3
Jasper Selwyn					4
John Richards	Mas. Asst.		gig		5
— Need	Mate	Druid	launch		0
— Pearce		Modeste	cutter		6
— Purver		Nimrod			7
— Sheddon	Mid.	Algerine			8
Peter Chown	2nd Mast.	Starling			9

(Signed) *Edwd. Belcher, Commander.*

*

No. 3.
To Captain Sir H. Le Fleming Senhouse, Kt., K.C.H., &c. &c. &c, Canton River.
H.M.S. "Modeste," off Canton, 26th May, 1841.

Sir,—I received your orders of the 24th instant, a little before noon on that day, and immediately proceeded with the boats and Marines of "Calliope" and "Conway," to the "Alligator," off Howqua's Fort, making the signal to "Herald" to close and send her boats.

I ordered Captain Kuper to move the "Alligator" up the right bank of the river, past Napier's Fort, where he anchored her in her own draught, and the boats were pushed up as far as possible, without exposing them to the enemy's fire. A little before sunset, I observed the "Algerine" moving down past the Dutch fort, and she shortly anchored and engaged a battery on the Canton side, which she silenced. Anxious to co-operate with her, I went a-head with Captain Bethune to reconnoitre, but was stopped by a shot through my boat from the French fort.

I remained under cover of the Point until dark, when I sent Captain Bethune with a division of boats to support her, and a concerted signal having been made, I joined her with the whole force at two a. m.

The arsenal being secured, I reconnoitred the line of defence, and perceived that it could not be attacked with advantage, without having heavier guns in position than those of the "Algerine." I therefore lost no time in ordering the other sloops down, and at the same time put myself in communication with Major Pratt, commanding H.M. 26th in the Factory.

Finding that the "Modeste" was the only vessel likely to be got across the bar, and there appearing even some doubt of her accomplishing the passage, I fitted shell guns in three of the captured war junks.

Captain Eyres having succeeded, by great exertion, in getting getting his vessel over the bar, I this morning moved her, "Algerine," and the gun junks on the French fort; the enemy deserted the upper defences, and about nine a.m. opened their fire from the fort, which was speedily silenced. I then cleared the beach by a few well directed broadsides, and made the signal to advance. Captain Bethune immediately landed on shore with the storming party, and the fort was carried in the most gallant style. The whole line of defence, extending about two miles from the Factory,—which, with the exception of the French fort, had been lately constructed in the strongest manner,—has been destroyed, and a communication is opened with the ships at Napier's Fort. The guns destroyed are sixty-four in number, including four of 10 1/2 inch calibre. The Dutch fort was not armed.

To that excellent and able officer, Captain Bethune, I feel particularly indebted; and my best thanks are also due to Commanders Warren and Gifford, who assisted in the attack. This is the sixth time I have had occasion to mention the gallant conduct of Commander Eyres. Lieutenant Mason, commanding the "Algerine," acquitted himself entirely to my satisfaction; and both Captain Eyres and himself speak in the highest terms of the assistance they received from Lieutenant Shute, and Mr. Dolling, mate, their seconds in command, and all the other officers and men.

Lieutenants Haskell and Hay, Senior of "Cruiser" and "Pylades," directed the guns in the junks with great ability. Captain Bethune speaks in the highest terms of Lieutenants Watson, Beadon, Coryton, Colinson, Morshead, Hayes, Hamilton, and Mr. Brown, Master; as also of Lieutenant Hayes, of the Bombay Marine, and of all the other officers and men employed more immediately under his orders, a list of whom is annexed. The party of Marines was commanded by Lieutenant Urquhart, assisted by Lieutenant Marriott, and Lieutenant Somerville, agent of transports, aided with some boats of the transports; Lieutenant Gabbett, of the Madras Artillery, threw shells with great effect from one of the junks; and Major Pratt offered in the handsomest manner to co-operate in the attack if required. I enclose a list of vessels captured, afloat, and building.

I have the honour, &c,

(Signed) *T. Herbert,*

Captain of H.M.S. "Calliope," and Senior Officer present.

*

List of Officers employed on the 26th May, 1841, off Canton.

Calliope: Mr. Watson, Lieutenant; Mr. D'Eyncourt, Lieutenant; Mr. Brown, Master; Mr. Daley, Mate; Mr. Rivers, Mate; Mr. Le Vescompt, Mate; Mr. Egerton, Mate; Mr. Taylor Mate; Dr. Butler, Asst. Surgeon.

Conway: Mr. Beadon, Lieutenant; Mr. Coryton, Lieutenant; Mr. Read, Mate; Mr. Kane, Mate; Mr. Forster, 2nd Master.

Alligator: Mr. Stewart, Lieutenant; Mr. Woolcombe, Mate; Mr. Baker, Mate

Hyacinth: Mr. Moorshead, Lieutenant; Mr. Barclay, Mate; Mr. Osborne, Mate; Dr. Robertson, Asst. Surgeon.

Cruiser: Mr. Haskell, Lieutenant; Mr. Hayes, Lieutenant; Mr. Drake, Mate; Mr. Bryant, Mate

Pylades: Mr. Hay, Lieutenant; Mr. Jeffrys, Mate; Mr. Sauley, Mate; Dr. Tweeddale, Asst. Surgeon

Columbine: Mr. Hamilton, Lieutenant; Mr. Miller, Mate; Dr. Crawford, Asst. Surgeon.

H.C.S. Atalanta: Mr. Grieve, Lieutenant; Mr. Eden, Midshipman.

Rattlesnake: Mr. Cowell, 2nd Master; Mr. Waddington, 2nd Master; Mr. Brodie, Voir. 1st class.

Lieutenant Somerville, with boats of the "Minerva, "Sulimany," and "Marion."

Lieutenants Urquhart and Marriott, of the Royal Marines, Conway" and Alligator."

Lieutenant Collinson, attached to the surveying department, was exceedingly active in getting the ships into their positions.

(Signed) *T. Herbert, Captain and Senior Officer present*

*

Return of war junks and row boats, &c. found in the Chinese naval arsenal, on the 27th of May, 1841.

Twelve war-junks, building; twenty-four row boats, and twelve war-junks, lying at anchor off the arsenal. A large quantity of timber, gun carriages, and various stores.

(Signed) *T. Herbert, Captain and Senior Officer present.*

*

No. 4.

To Captain Sir Humphrey Le Fleming Senhouse, Kt., K. C.H., &c. &c. &c. Senior Officer in the China Seas.

Her Majesty's Sloop "Hyacinth," off Canton, May 26th, 1841.

Sir,—I have the honour to acquaint you, that immediately on the receipt of your letter of the 24th instant, I weighed with the advanced squadron, and ordered H.M.'s sloop "Nimrod" to attack the Samien Fort, on the west end of the suburbs, supported by H.M.'s sloop "Pylades;" her Majesty's sloop under my command being placed abreast of the English factory, to silence and dislodge any troops that might be there, and also with a view of covering the landing of H.M.'s 26th regiment; her Majesty's sloops, "Modeste," "Cruiser," and "Columbine," taking up a position to attack the Dutch Folly Fort, and to enfilade the line of batteries lately thrown up in front of the city to the eastward of that fort. On the ships taking up their position, three fire-vessels were sent adrift, and, although the tide was running very strong, by timely despatch of boats they were enabled to clear the ships and tow three on shore, and set fire to the suburbs.

In the performance of this service they opened their fire on the boats and shipping. In half an hour, the enemy were completely silenced to the eastward of the Dutch Folly Fort. After reconnoitring the Factory, and finding it quite deserted, I immediately ordered the preconcerted signal for H.M.'s brig "Algerine," and "Atalanta" steamer, to approach with H.M.'s 26th regiment, when they landed and took possession of the Factory without the slightest casualty. This service being completed, I ordered Lieutenant Mason, commanding H.M.'s brig "Algerine," to proceed to attack a fort to the eastward, which I feel much pleasure in reporting to you was done in a particularly spirited and gallant style by that officer; but perceiving the firing to be so heavy from the forts, I ordered the boats of H.M.'s ships to her support:—H.M.'s sloop "Hyacinth's," under Lieutenant Stewart, and Mr. Peter Barclay, mate; "Modeste's," Mr. Fitzgerald, mate; "Cruiser's," Lieutenant Haskell, and Mr. Thomas J. Drake, mate; "Pylades'," Lieutenant Hay; and "Columbine's," Lieutenants Hamilton, Helpman, and Mr. Miller, mate. It is gratifying to me to inform you, by half-past seven the fort of eleven guns was silenced and the guns spiked, under a heavy fire of ginjalls and musketry from the houses; at the same time, I regret to add, it was not done without considerable loss. It would be impossible to particularize upon an occasion where every officer and man engaged against an enemy defending themselves with much vigour at all points, but in addition to my best thanks and acknowledgments to Commanders Barlow, Eyres, Gifford, Anson, and Clarke, and Lieutenant Mason, I hope you will give me leave to recommend to your particular notice my own first lieutenant, W. H. Moorshead, who was wounded in the hand in a personal engagement with a mandarin. Lieutenant Mason, of the "Algerine," speaks in the highest terms of the conduct of Mr. Dolling, mate, and Mr. Higgs, second master of that vessel. I cannot conclude without expressions of my approbation of the steadiness of Commander Rogers, of the Indian navy, in conducting the "Atalanta" to her station.

I beg leave to attach a statement of the killed and wounded, and damage sustained by the ships engaged.

I have the honour to be, &c,

(Signed) *Wm. Warren, Commander.*

*

No. 5.

General Return of Killed and Wounded in her Majesty's forces, at the attack Canton, from the 23rd to the 30th of May, 1841.

Ships or Corps	Killed	Wounded	Remarks
Blenheim	2	9	1 Off., 1 R. Ay., 1 Act I R. M., and 8 Seamen.
Wellesley	0	6	3 Seamen, and 3 Royal Marines.
Blonde	1	1	1 Seaman, and 1 Royal Marine.
Calliope	0	1	1 Seaman.
Hyacinth	0	5	2 Officers, and 3 Seamen.
Nimrod	2	4	2 Officers, and 4 Seamen.
Modeste	1	9	2 Officers, and 8 Seamen.
Columbine	0	2	2 Seamen.
Algerine	0	4	1 Officer, 2 Seamen, and 1 R.M.
Nemesis	0	1	1 Officer.
Madras Artillery	0	1	
Sappers and Miners	0	1	
18th Royal Irish	2	19	
26th Cameronians	3	15	
49th Regiment	1	17	
37th Native Infantry	1	13	
Bengal Volunteers	0	1	
Camp followers	1	3	
Staff	1	0	
	15	**112**	
		+15	
	Total	**127**	

Officers killed and wounded.

Killed:—Major Beecher, Deputy-Quarter-Master-General, died from over-fatigue; Lieutenant Fox, of the "Nimrod."

Wounded:—Mr. Walter Kendall, mate of the "Nimrod," (lost his leg,) dangerously; Mr. W. T. Bate, mate of the "Blenheim," slightly; Lieutenant Moorshead, of the "Hyacinth," slightly; Mr. Peter Barclay, mate of the "Hyacinth," slightly; Mr. E. Fitzgerald, mate of the "Modeste," dangerously; Mr. Wm. Pearse, ditto, slightly; Mr. Hall, commanding the "Nemesis," severely burnt; Mr. Vaughan, Assistant-Surgeon of the "Algerine," slightly; Lieutenant Rundall, of the Madras Sappers and Miners, dangerously; Captain Serjeant, H.M. 18th Royal Irish, severely; Lieutenant Hilliard, ditto, slightly; Lieutenant Edwards, ditto, severely; Lieutenant Pearson, 49th, severely; Lieutenant Johnstone, 26th, slightly; Ensign Berkeley, 37th, M.N.I.

severely.

(Signed) *H. Le Fleming Senhouse, Captain and Senior Officer, China Coast.*

(True Extracts and Copies.)

(Signed) *T. H. Maddock, Secretary to the Government of India.*

(Signed) *S. W. Steel, Lieutenant-Colonel, Secretary to Government.*

By order of the officer commanding the army in chief. R. Alexander, Lieutenant-Colonel, Adjutant-General of the Army.

XII. BY THE GOVERNOR-GENERAL IN COUNCIL

Fort William, 24th Dec. 1841.

No. 289 of 1841.—The following paragraphs of a military letter from the Hon. the Court of Directors to the Governor of Bengal, No. 9, dated 27th October, 1841, are published for general information:—

Para. 1. We have much gratification in announcing to you, that her Majesty has been graciously pleased to promote the undermentioned officers of our service, by special brevet, in the East Indies, for their services during the late operations near Canton, their commissions bearing date the 26th May, 1841—viz.

To be Lieutenant-Colonels—Major Roger Williamson Wilson, of the 65th regiment of Bengal Native Infantry; Major Francis Spencer Hawkins, of the 38th regiment of Bengal Native Infantry.

To be Majors—Captain Daniel Duff, of the 37th regiment of Madras Native Infantry; Captain George Augustus Mee, of the 58th regiment of Bengal Infantry; Captain Philip Anstruther, of the Madras Artillery; Captain Henry Moore, of the 34th regiment of Bengal Native Infantry.

2. The conduct of Lieutenant and Brevet Captain Frederick Conyers Cotton, of the Madras Engineers, and of Lieutenant Hadfield, of the 37th regiment of Madras Native Infantry, is considered to have entitled them to a similar distinction; but the regulations of her Majesty's army do not admit of the grant of brevet rank to subaltern officers for services in the field. The General Commanding in Chief has, however, announced his intention of recommending the grant of the brevet rank of Major to these two officers on their attaining the regimental rank of Captain.

3. We have to express our entire approbation of the conduct of the whole of our troops engaged on the above occasion.

4. In order to mark our sense of the gallantry and steadiness displayed by the 37th regiment of Madras Native Infantry, under most trying circumstances, we have resolved on constituting that corps a Grenadier regiment.

5. We further direct, that the name of each European and native

commissioned officer, non-commissioned officer, and sepoy, who composed the company of that regiment detached under Lieutenant Hadfield, and who, by their steady courage and discipline, successfully defeated the repeated attacks of a large body of the enemy, and thus nobly sustained the credit of the native army, be entered in the regimental order book of that corps, with a record of the transaction to which it refers. We also desire that the native officers, non-commissioned officers, and sepoys of that company, be granted an addition to their pay and pension on retirement, either by admitting them to the advantages of the "Order of Merit," or in any other manner which you may consider desirable.

6. You will publish in general orders our sentiments as expressed in this despatch.

XIII. NOTIFICATION.

Fort William, Secret Department, 20th Nov., 1841.

The Right Honourable the Governor-General of India in Council has the highest satisfaction in publishing, for general information, the annexed copies of despatches from the military and naval commanders-in-chief of H.M. forces in China, reporting the capture, on the 26th of August, of the town and fortification of Amoy.

By order of the Right Honourable the Governor-General of India in Council.

T. H. Maddock, Sec. to the Government of India.

To the Right Honourable the Earl of Auckland, G.C.B., Governor-General, &c. &c. &c.

Head quarters, ship "Marion," Amoy Harbour, Sept. 5th, 1841.

My Lord,—I am happy to be enabled to report to your lordship the complete success of the operations against Amoy with very trifling loss; my anticipations, in regard to the preparations of the enemy, have been fully realized, but I did not calculate on so feeble a resistance.

1. The expedition left Hong-Kong harbour on Saturday, the 21st of August, but in consequence of light winds, the fleet did not clear the Lemma passage until Monday the 23rd, and on the evening of the 25th we arrived in the outward anchorage of Amoy, a few shots only having been fired as we were running through a chain of islands which form the mouth of this anchorage, and most of which the Chinese had fortified. As it was blowing very fresh, I could not get oil board the flag-ship until the following morning, when I accompanied their Excellencies Sir Henry Pottinger and Admiral Sir William Parker, in the "Phlegethon" steamer, to reconnoitre the defences,

with a view to the commencement of immediate operations. The enemy allowed us to do so without firing a shot, and the plan of attack was at once decided upon, a summons having been previously sent in, requiring the surrender of the town and island of Amoy to her Majesty's forces.

2. The enemy's defences were evidently of great strength, and the country by nature difficult of access. Every island, every projecting headland, from whence guns could bear upon the harbour, was occupied and strongly armed. Commencing from the point of entrance into the inner harbour on the Amoy side, the principal sea-line of defence, after a succession of batteries and bastions in front of the outer town, extended for upwards of a mile, in one continuous battery of stone, with embrasures, roofed by large slabs, thickly covered with clods of earth, so as lo form a sort of casement, and afford perfect shelter to the men in working their guns. Between some of the embrasures were embankments to protect the masonry, and ninety-six guns were mounted in this work, which terminated in a castellated wall, connecting it with a range of precipitous rocky heights, that run nearly parallel to the beach at a distance varying from a quarter to half a mile. Several smaller works were apparent at intervals amid the rocks.

3. The entrance to the inner harbour is by a channel, about 600 yards across, between Amoy and the island of Koo-lang-soo, upon which several strong batteries were visible, and some of these flanked the sea-line and stone battery. It appeared expedient, therefore, to make a simultaneous attack on these two prominent lines of defence.

4. It was proposed that the two line-of-battle ships, with the two large steamers, should attack the sea defences on the island of Amoy, nearest the town, and that some of the smaller vessels of war should open their fire to protect the landing of the troops, which was to be effected below the angle formed by the junction of the castellated wall with the sea-line, while the remaining vessels should engage several flanking batteries that extended beyond these works.

5. At the same time, the two heavy frigates and the "Modeste" were to run in and open their fire upon the works of Koo-lang-soo, where I instructed Major Johnstone, with a company of Artillery and the three companies of the 26th regiment, supported by 170 Marines under Major Ellis, to land in a small bay to the left of the batteries, which they were to take in reverse.

6. About half-past one o'clock the attack commenced, the enemy having previously fired occasional shot at the ships as they proceeded to their stations. Sir William Parker will no doubt communicate to your lordship the very conspicuous part taken by her Majesty's ships on this occasion. From the difficulty of getting the boats collected in tow of the steamers, the troops did not land quite so soon as I could have wished, notwithstanding

the judicious arrangements of Captain Gifford, of H.M. sloop "Cruiser," who conducted the disembarkation. The 18th and 49th regiments, however, landed about three o'clock, with very little opposition. The former regiment I directed to escalade the castellated wall, while the 49th were to move along the beach, and get over the sea-face, or through the embrasures. These two operations were performed to my entire satisfaction, and the greater part of these corps were soon in position within the works, and rapidly moved along the whole line of sea-defence, the enemy flying before them. Upon reaching the outskirts of the outer town, they were joined by a party of marines and seamen, whom Sir William Parker had most judiciously landed in support, and whom I directed to occupy a rocky hill in our front, in the neighbourhood of which firing was still heard. This duty was promptly and ably performed by Captain Fletcher, of H.M.S. "Wellesley," and Captain Whitcomb, of the Royal Marines.

7. While these operations were going on upon the Amoy side, the island of Koo-lang-soo was ably attacked by the frigates, and the troops landed. Major Ellis, with some of the Marines and Cameronians, who first landed, climbed up the rocks to the left of the easternmost battery, and gallantly driving the enemy from the works on the heights, which were defended with some spirit, continued his progress to the north side of the island, while Major Johnstone, who closely followed up with the rest of the troops, proceeded across it, and carried the remaining works, thus putting us in possession of this very important position. Major Johnstone reports that Brevet-Captain Gregg had an opportunity of distinguishing himself in driving a large body of the enemy from a battery, upon which he came unexpectedly with a detachment of twelve men.

8. On Amoy, a chain of steep rocky hills, running from the range already mentioned transversely to the beach, still intercepted our view of the city, though the outer town lay beneath my advanced post. The guns having been landed, by the exertions of the Artillery and Sappers, and brought on far enough for support, had a strong force opposed our advance, I decided upon forcing the position in my front, which appeared extremely strong and well calculated to be held during the night. Having made the necessary disposition, I directed the 18th regiment to advance up a precipitous gorge, where the enemy had two small works, while the 49th were to pass through the outer town by the road to the same hills, extending their left, after gaining the pass, to the works above the beach, so as to open a communication with the shipping. This movement was also executed with spirit, the enemy merely firing off their guns and flying, and at dusk I found myself in position close above the city, and perfectly commanding it.

9. Owing to the boisterous state of the weather, and the delay in the return

of the steamers, the 55th regiment had not yet landed, but this was effected at daylight the following morning; I regret to say, not without loss, a boat having been swamped, and five men unfortunately drowned. Thus reinforced, I pushed strong parties of the 18th and 49th regiments down to the outskirts of the city, in the north-eastern quarter of which, upon irregularly rising ground, and closely surrounded by a dense mass of buildings, appeared the walled town or citadel. Having carefully reconnoitred the place, I satisfied myself that, although there was a concourse of people passing and repassing at the northern gate, the walls were not manned. I therefore thought it advisable to take advantage of the prevailing panic, and having sent a small party with Captain Cotton, the Commanding Engineer, to reconnoitre the approach to the eastern gate, which he promptly effected, I directed, upon his return, the 18th to advance, having the 49th in support, and the 55th in reserve. The advanced party of the 18th escaladed the wall by the aid of ladders found on the spot, and opened the east gate, which was barred, and barricaded from within by sacks filled with earth and stones. The remainder of the regiment passed through it and. manned the other gates, the enemy having previously abandoned the place, leaving it in possession of the mob, which had already began to plunder the public establishments.

10. I occupied the citadel with the 18th and Sappers, placing the 49th regiment in an extensive building without the public office of the intendant of circuit, from whence they could give protection to the northern suburb, and command the communication to the interior by the only road on this side the island. The artillery I placed in a commanding position upon the top of the pass between the city and the outer town, with the 55th in support, occupying a range of public buildings, in which the sub-prefect of Amoy held his court.

11. Amoy is a principal third class city of China, and, from its excellent harbour and situation, appears to be well calculated for commerce. The outer town is divided from the city by the chain of rocks I have mentioned, over which a paved road leads through a pass, that has a covered gateway at its summit. The outer harbour skirts the outer town, while the city is bounded in nearly its whole length by the inner harbour and an estuary, which deeply indent the island. Including the outer town and the north-eastern suburb, the city cannot be much less than ten miles in circumference, and that of the citadel, which entirely commands this suburb, and the inner town, though commanded itself by the hills within shot range, is nearly one mile. The walls are castellated, and vary, with the inequality of the ground, from twenty to thirty feet in height; and there are four gates, having each in an outwork a second or exterior gate at right angles to the inner gate. The citadel contained five arsenals, in which we found a large quantity of powder,

with store of material for making it; ginjalls, wallpieces, match-locks, and a variety of fire-arms of singular construction; military clothing, swords of all descriptions, shields, bows and arrows, and spears, were also found, in such quantity as to lead to the conclusion that these must have been the chief magazines of the province. Within the sea defences first taken there was a foundry, with moulds and material for casting heavy ordnance.

12. All these have been destroyed, and this so much occupied my time, considering, too, how much the troops were harassed by patroles to keep off Chinese plunderers, and by other duties incident to the peculiarity of our situation, that I abandoned my intention of visiting the interior of the island. These plunderers flocked into the city and suburbs to the extent, as the Chinese themselves reported, of many thousands, and I regret to say, that several gangs penetrated into the citadel, and committed much devastation. Indeed, with the prospect of leaving Amoy so soon, I doubt that our marching through the island might rather have frightened away the peaceable householders, and led to further plunder by the mob than have been of any advantage. Such, indeed, was the audacity of these miscreants, that I was in some cases obliged to fire, in order to disperse them; but I am glad to say but little loss of life occurred.

13. I am most happy to be enabled to state that the conduct of the troops has been exemplary; some instances of misconduct have no doubt occurred; but when it is considered that they were in the midst of temptation, many of the houses being open, with valuable property strewed about, and many shops in every street deserted, but full of sham-shu, it is matter of great satisfaction that these instances were so few.

14. During our stay upon the island, I did all in my power to prevail upon the respectable merchants and householders, who had so much at stake, to aid me in protecting property, which they readily promised; but their apprehension of appearing to be on friendly terms with us was so great, that I could obtain no effectual assistance from them, and was unable even to get a Chinese to remain with the guards at the gates, and point out the real owners of houses within the citadel, for the purpose of granting them free egress and ingress.

15. Our departure being determined upon, I could take, no measures for permanent occupation, and as the wind was strong against us, we were kept on shore four days in a state of constant watchfulness, until yesterday, at half-past two, p.m., when the preconcerted signal for embarkation was given by the Admiral. By half-past six, every soldier and every follower had been embarked (without a single instance of inebriety occurring) on board the steamer which transferred the troops on board their respective transports during the night.

16. The three companies of the 26th regiment have remained upon the island of Koo-lang-soo, which her Majesty's Plenipotentiary has determined to hold for the present; and I have strengthened Major Johnstone, who is in command, with a wing of the 18th regiment, and a small detachment of artillery. This little force, amounting to five hundred and fifty men, will, I trust, together with the ships of war also left behind, be sufficient to hold this small but important possession.

17. To the commanding officers of corps and detachments, Lieutenant-Colonel Craigie, 55th regiment, Lieutenant-Colonel Morris, 49th regiment, and Lieutenant-Colonel Adams, 18th regiment, Major Johnstone, 26th regiment, Major Ellis, Royal Marines, Captain Knowles, Royal Artillery, Captain Anstruther, Madras Artillery, and Captain Cotton, Commanding Engineer, my best thanks are due; and I have received the most cordial and active support from the officers of the general and my personal staff, Lieutenant-Colonel Mountain, Deputy Adjutant-General, Captain Gough, Acting Deputy Quartermaster General, Major Hawkins, Deputy Commissary General, Dr. French, Superintending Surgeon, and Lieutenant Gabbett, my A.D.C.

18. I cannot too strongly express to your lordship, in conclusion, my sense of obligation to his Excellency Rear Admiral Sir William Parker, for his ready support and judicious arrangements upon every occasion, as well as for having given me, at the disembarkation and embarkation, and during the whole period of our stay at Amoy, the able assistance of Captain Giffard, to whom my best thanks are due.

19. I have the honour to enclose a list of ordnance captured, and a return of the wounded on our side, upon the 26th ultimo, and have no means of correctly estimating the killed and wounded of the enemy, but it must have been severe, and we know that several mandarins were amongst the former.

I have the honour to be, my lord, your lordship's most obedient humble servant,

(Signed) *H. Gough, Major-General, Commanding Expeditionary Force.*

*

Return of Ordnance mounted on the Defences at Amoy, when stormed and captured on the 26th August, 1841.

Batteries on the Island of Amoy, extending from the suburbs of Amoy, nearly opposite the east end of the Island of Colonso, along the shore in a S. E. direction:—

Guns—Brass.

- 1 x Calibre 46 inches. Length 9 feet 5 inches.

Guns—Iron.

- 2 x 86 pounders.

- 1 x 8 pounders.
- 6 x 24 pounders.
- 12 x 18 pounders.
- 31 x 12 pounders.
- 49 x 9 pounders.
- 25 x 8 pounders.
- 12 x 6 pounders.
- 12 x 4 pounders.
- 1 x 3 pounders.
- 1 x ginjall.

Total 152

The guns were all of Chinese manufacture, except sixteen English, which were old, but without any date. Five iron guns had burst when fired by the Chinese. 153 iron guns, not mounted, were found, principally of small calibre, from 3 to 6-pounders.

Batteries on the south point of the Island of Amoy.

Guns—Iron.

- 7 x 18 pounders
- 3 x 16 pounders
- 10 x 12 pounders
- 5 x 9 pounders
- 4 x 8 pounders
- 7 x 4 pounders
- 15 x 10 inch howitzers
- 1 x 8.8 inch howitzers
- 1 x 7.1 inch howitzers
- 1 x 6.4 inch howitzers

Total 58

The guns were all of Chinese manufacture, except 11 English, which were old. Four iron 10-inch howitzers were found not mounted.

Batteries on the Island of Colonso.

No. 1, or Marine Battery.

Guns—Iron.

- 1 x 86 pounder.
- 2 x 18 pounder.
- 7 x 14 pounder.
- 6 x 12 pounder.

Total 16

No. 2 Battery, opposite the suburbs of Amoy.

Guns—Iron.

- 3 x 11 pounder.

- 7 x 9 pounder.

Total 10

No. 3 Battery, south side of the island.

Guns—Iron.

- 1 x 34 pounder.
- 2 x 12 pounder.
- 1 x 9 pounder.
- 2 x 8 pounder.
- 2 x 7 pounder.
- 14 x ginjalls

Total 22

In this battery a subterranean magazine was discovered, containing a vast quantity of powder, which was destroyed.

No. 4 Battery.

Guns—Iron.

- 3 x 8 pounders.

No. 5 Battery, S.W. extremity of the island.

Guns—Iron.

- 6 x 8 pounders.
- 8 x ginjalls.

Total 14

No. 6 Battery (quite new) on the N. W. angle of the island.

Guns—Iron.

- 1 x 12 pounder.
- 2 x 9 pounder.
- 1 x 8 pounder.
- 7 x 6 pounder.

Total 11

Batteries on the S. W. side of the Bay.

Guns—Iron.

- 1 x 86 pounder.
- 1 x 48 pounder.
- 1 x 32 pounder.
- 1 x 24 pounder.
- 2 x 18 pounder.
- 6 x 12 pounder.
- 12 x 9 pounder.
- 7 x 8 pounder.
- 10 x 6 pounder.

Total 41

The guns were all of Chinese manufacture, except four. One large gun had burst when fired by the Chinese.

Batteries on the Island of Little Gouve, S. W. side on entering.

Guns—Iron.

- 2 x 9 pounder.
- 12 x 8 pounder.
- 1 x 4 pounder.

Total 15

The guns were all of Chinese manufacture.

General Abstract.

- Island of Amoy: 211
- Island of Golong-soo: 76
- Batteries on S. W. side of Bay: 41
- Little Gouve: 15

Total: 343

Guns not mounted: 157

Grand Total: 500

The guns were all rendered unserviceable.

(Signed) *J. Knowles, Captain, Royal Artillery.*

N.B.—Fifty pieces of ordnance of small calibre, captured in the citadel, not included in the above.

(Signed) *Armine S. H. Mountain, Lieut.-Col., Deputy Adjutant General.*

*

EXPEDITIONARY FORCE.

Return of Killed and Wounded of the Force under the command of Major-General Sir Hugh Gough, K.C.B., &c, on the 26th of August, 1841, at the capture of the batteries, heights, city, and citadel of Amoy.

Head Quarters, Amoy Castle, Sept. 1st, 1841.

Rank and File.

- 18th Royal Irish Regiment: wounded 2
- 49th Regiment: wounded 7

Total: wounded 9

(Signed)

Armine S. H. Mountain, Lieut.-Col., Deputy Adjutant General Expeditionary Force.

Major-General Sir Hugh Gough, K.C.B., Commander-in-Chief, Expeditionary Force, China.

*

To the Right Hon. the Earl of Auckland, G.C.B., &c. $c. &c.

"Wellesley," in the Bay of Amoy, August 31st, 1841.

My Lord,—It is with much gratification that I have the honour of announcing to your lordship the capture of the city of Amoy and the island of Golong-soo, (which forms the west side of the harbour,) together with their strong lines of batteries and sea defences, mounting above 228 guns, by the combined forces of her Majesty, after a short, but vigorous attack, on the 26th instant, with very trifling loss on our part.

The expedition, comprising the ships of war hereafter named, and twenty-one transports containing the land forces, military and victualling stores, &c, under the command of his Excellency Major-General Sir Hugh Gough, sailed from the anchorage of Hong-Kong on the 21st, and fortunately arrived off the islands at the entrance of Amoy Bay, by sunset on the 25th; it was then beginning to blow strong, but favoured by a fair wind, and good moonlight, with the advantage of the local knowledge of Captain Bourchier, of the "Blonde," the fleet were pushed into the bay, and anchored in security for the night.

A few shots were discharged at H.M.'s ships as they passed between the fortified islands, but no mischief was done.

It blew too hard during the night to admit of any boats leaving the ships to sound, or make observations; but no time was lost after daylight in reconnoitring the Chinese positions, in which the General and Sir Henry Pottinger did me the favour to accompany me in the "Phlegethon" steam vessel.

We found the batteries and works of defence on the entire sea face strengthened by every means that the art of these active people could devise; presenting a succession of batteries and outworks, from the extreme outward points of this extensive bay, until within about three quarters of a mile of the entrance of the harbour, where a high barrier wall was constructed from the foot of a steep and rocky mountain to a sandy beach on the sea; and from this latter point, a strong casemated work of granite, faced with soil, and occasional small bastions with parapets of stone, to afford flanking defences, was continued to the very suburbs and entrance of the harbour, from whence were masked batteries with sand bags, until opposite the north-east point of Golong-soo island, altogether 152 guns.

On the island of Golong-soo, which is the key of Amoy, strong batteries, mounting in all seventy-six guns, were also placed in every commanding position for flanking the approach to the harbour, (which is scarcely half a mile wide at the entrance,) and protecting the accessible points of landing.

As it was of the utmost importance, with a view to ulterior operations, and the advanced period of the present monsoon, that we should be delayed as short a time as possible at Amoy, it was determined that the batteries within the barrier wall, and on the island of Golong-soo, should be immediately attacked by the squadron, and the troops landed within the barrier as soon as it might be practicable, to take the batteries in the rear; for this object the

"Wellesley" and "Blenheim" were ordered to anchor against the strongest batteries on Amoy, and as near the entrance of the harbour as possible, leaving the "Cruiser," "Pylades," "Columbine," and "Algerine," to engage the extreme point of the line and cover the landing of the troops, flanked by the heavy guns of the "Sesostris" and "Queen" steam vessels; the "Phlegethon" and "Nemesis" being appointed to receive the troops, and tow in the boats for landing them.

The attack of the island of Golong-soo, where we had reason to apprehend the water was shoaler, was assigned to Captain Bourchier of the "Blonde," with the "Druid" and "Modeste," 150 Marines under Captain Ellis, and a detachment of the 26th regiment under Major Johnston.

Pending the necessary preparations for disembarking the troops, and moving the ships into their appointed positions, a communication was received from the shore, requesting to know the object of our visit, to which the answer No. I. was returned.

About a quarter past one, a steady and favourable breeze having set in, the squadron weighed and proceeded to their stations. The "Sesostris," being the most advanced, received a heavy fire before any return was made; she was soon joined by the "Queen," and both commenced action with good effect.

The "Wellesley" and "Blenheim," after ranging along the line of works on Amoy, under a smart fire, were anchored by the stern about half-past two p.m., admirably placed by Captains Maitland and Herbert in ten fathoms water, within 400 yards of the principal battery, precisely in the position allotted them; and the "Cruiser," "Pylades," "Columbine," and "Algerine," took their stations with equal judgment.

The "Blonde," "Druid," and "Modeste" reached their positions against the batteries on Golong-soo, a few minutes earlier, but their captains found such difficulty, from the shallowness of the water, in placing them satisfactorily, that, to effect this object, they very spiritedly carried their ships into almost their own draught.

The "Bentinck" had been appointed to sound the channel ahead of the "Wellesley" as we ran in, which Lieutenant Collinson very skilfully performed, and then gallantly anchored the brig within the entrance of the harbour, where she was joined by the "Sesostris," which was placed by Captain Ormsby in a very judicious situation for relieving her and the other ships from a flanking fire.

The fire of the Chinese soon slackened under the excellent gun practice of the squadron. At half-past three, I had the satisfaction of seeing the Marines and the 26th regiment land on the island of Golong-soo, and the British colours planted on the batteries. The "Modeste" and "Blonde" then weighed and stood into the inner harbour, and after silencing, as they passed, the town batteries, which were out of our reach, they anchored completely inside, and abreast of the city, taking possession of twenty-six war junks, with 128 guns on board, in a state of preparation for sea, but deserted by their crews.

About the same time, the first division of troops were landed, under the able direction of Commander Giffard, of the "Cruiser," and headed by their gallant General, Sir Hugh Gough, escaladed and took possession of the works, at the barrier wall.

An outwork beyond this point (which had been previously silenced) was also entered, and the British colours hoisted by the crew of a boat from the "Phlegethon;" and the batteries immediately opposite the "Wellesley" and "Blenheim" being nearly demolished, a party of seamen and Marines were landed from those ships under the command of Commander Fletcher and the officers named below;[2] by whom the Chinese, who had taken shelter in adjoining buildings, were put to flight, after discharging their matchlocks, and possession taken of the works.

The General having cleared the intermediate space of such of the Chinese as remained, pushed forward, and occupied the heights immediately above the town for the night; every point being thus completely in our power.

In detailing this service to your lordship, I have the highest satisfaction in reporting the gallantry, zeal, and energy which has been manifested by every officer and man of her Majesty's navy and Royal Marines, as well as those of the Indian navy under my command; they have vied with each other in the desire to anticipate and meet every object for the public service, and are fully entitled to my best acknowledgments, and the favourable consideration of the Board of Admiralty and Indian Government. I have no less pleasure in witnessing the anxiety whicli pervades all ranks, to go hand in hand with our gallant companions of the army.

His Excellency Sir Henry Pottinger and suite were with me on board the "Wellesley," during the operations of the 26th.

Captain Bourchier's own report (Enclosure No. 2) will best describe the proceedings of the little squadron placed under his orders for the attack of Golong-soo, which was admirably executed, and I can only add my meed of praise on this additional instance of the gallantry of Captain Ellis, and the officers and men of the Royal Marines under his command, as well as of Major Johnston, and the detachment of the 26th, acting with them.

The accounts we have received of the force of the Chinese for the defence of Amoy, vary from 5600 to 10,000 troops; and it is with sincere pleasure I am enabled to transmit your lordship so small a list of casualties amongst

---

2 Wellesley: Acting-Lieutenant Carmichael L. White, R.M., Mates: Lord A. Beauclerk, S. S. L. Crofton, L. G. Halsted., Midshipman: W. F. F. Jackson.

Blenheim: Captain Whitcomb, R.M., Mates: R. C. Revern, T. A. St. Leger.

the crews, and masts and rigging of the squadron, (Enclosures Nos. 3 and 4.) The resistance made by our opponents would have justified the apprehension of greater injury. Under the protection of their well-constructed casemated works, they stood on some points firmly to their guns. We have no knowledge of their actual loss; more than sixty dead bodies were, I believe, found in the batteries; but nearly all the wounded, and many of the slain, were carried off by their countrymen.

His Excellency the Commander of the Forces will probably give your lordship an account of the munitions of war and government stores which have fallen into our hands, including a large quantity of gunpowder, and a foundry for cannon, where some guns, of very large calibre, newly cast, have been discovered.

We have been constantly employed in destroying the guns, (Enclosures Nos. 5 and 6;) and, as far as it has been practicable, the batteries taken on the 26th. The last two days, Commander Fletcher, with a party of seamen and Marines, has been also detached in the "Nemesis," and with very commendable zeal has completely disabled the guns on every battery on the north-east and south-west sides of the bay, and the fortified islands at the entrance, of which your lordship will find official returns enclosed.

The superiority of the bay and inner harbour of Amoy has much exceeded our expectations. The anchorage in the former appears excellent; and the latter, as far as our hasty surveys have gone, affords perfect security for ships of any class, and to a great extent, with a reasonable prospect of proving a healthy situation; Sir Hugh Gough and myself have therefore entirely concurred with his Excellency Sir Henry Pottinger, in the expediency of retaining possession of the island of Golong-soo, which will at any time give us the command of Amoy, until your lordship's wishes, or the pleasure of her Majesty's government is known. For this purpose, a sufficient garrison will be placed on the island by the General, and I propose to leave Captain Smith, of the "Druid," with the "Pylades" and "Algerine" for their support.

The wind is unfortunately at present adverse, but your lordship may be assured that the expedition will proceed to the northward, the moment it is practicable, in the further execution of our instructions.

I have the honour to be, my lord, your lordship's most obedient servant,

W. Parker, Rear Admiral.

*

Enclosure No. I.
On Board H.M.S. "Wellesley,"
Off Amoy, 26th August, 1841.

The undersigned, Sir Henry Pottinger, Bart., her Britannic Majesty's Plenipotentiary, Sir William Parker, commanding in chief the naval forces, and Sir Hugh Gough, commanding in chief the land forces of the British nation in these parts.

To his Excellency the Admiral commanding in chief the Naval Forces of the Province of Fukieon.

There being certain differences subsisting between the two nations of Great Britain and China, which have not been cleared up, the undersigned Plenipotentiary, and the Commanders-in-Chief, have received the instructions of their Sovereign, that unless these be completely removed, and secure arrangements made, by accession to the demands last year presented at Tieatsin, they shall regard it as their duty to resort to hostile measures for the enforcement of those demands.

But the undersigned Plenipotentiary and Commanders-in-Chief, moved by compassionate feelings, are averse to causing the death of so many officers and soldiers as must perish, and urgently request the Admiral, commanding in chief in this province, forthwith to deliver the town and all the fortifications of Amoy into the hands of the British forces, to be held for the present by them. Upon his so doing, all the officers and troops therein will be allowed to retire with their personal arms and baggage, and the people shall receive no hurt; and whenever these difficulties shall be settled, and the demands of Great Britain fully granted, the whole shall be restored to the hands of the Chinese.

If these terms be acceded to, let a white flag be displayed from the fortifications.

(Signed) *Henry Pottinger, Her Majesty's Plenipotentiary.*
William Parker, Rear Admiral.
Hugh Gough, Major-General.

*

Enclosure No. II.

To His Excellency Rear Admiral Sir William Parker, K.C.B., Commander-in-Chief, &c., &c., &c.

East Indian Station, Her Majesty's Ship "Blonde," Inner Harbour of Amoy, 27th August, 1841.

Sir,—The operations of the force you did me the honour to place under my command for the attack of the island of Golong-soo, were so immediately under your observation, that little remains to me beyond the agreeable duty of bringing to your Excellency's notice the admirable conduct of every officer and man I had the honour to command.

The squadron was led into action by Captain Eyres, commanding her Majesty's sloop "Modeste," with the most perfect skill and gallantry; the "Blonde" and "Druid" followed, and were placed as near as the shoalness of the water would admit to the three principal batteries, which they succeeded in silencing after a fire of one hour and twenty minutes, when the Marines under the gallant Captain Ellis were landed, and carried the heights with their accustomed bravery.

The distance of the transports prevented the 26th Cameronian regiment from being on shore at the same moment with the Marines, but they were promptly after them; and the detachment of that distinguished corps, under Major Johnston, assisted in clearing the remaining batteries, and dispersing the enemy.

From Captain Smith, of H.M.S. "Druid," I received the most able support; that ship was placed with excellent judgment, and her conduct such as was to be expected from her high state of discipline. This island being now completely in our possession, I left the "Druid" to protect it, and pushed the "Modeste" and "Blonde" into the Inner Harbour, silencing their war junks and batteries, on the opposite shore, as we passed; and I have herewith the honour to enclose a return of the vessels captured, and ordnance destroyed. The officers and crew of this ship merit my highest praise, as well as the party of Royal Artillery serving on board under the command of Lieutenant the Honourable R. E. Spencer. I should be wanting injustice, were I to close this letter without bringing to your notice the merits of Lieut. Sir Frederick Nicolson, first of this ship, to whose valuable assistance I am much indebted; and I must also beg to name to your Excellency the senior mates of this ship, Messrs. Walker, Rolland, and Anderson, young officers of much promise.

I have great pleasure in adding that this service was performed without loss of life on our part, although the ships have suffered considerably in their masts, sails, and rigging.

The Captains of the "Druid" and "Modeste" speak in the highest terms of their officers and ships' companies. I enclose the report of Captain Ellis, of the Royal Marines.

(Signed) *T. Bourchier, Captain.*

*

Enclosure in Captain Bourchier's Letter.
To Captain Bourchier, R.N., &c. &c, &c.
Military Quarters, Royal Marines, Island of Coronsou, near Amoy,
August 27th, 1841.

Sir,—Having yesterday received your directions to land from H.M. Ships "Blonde" and "Druid," under your orders, the detachments of Royal Marines of the ships named in the note,[3] and drive the enemy from the strong battery of Coronsou, which you had previously engaged, I have the

3 "Wellesley," "Blenheim," "Blonde," "Druid," and "Modeste."

honour to acquaint you, for the information of Rear-Admiral Sir William Parker, K.C.B., Commander-in-Chief, that, in furtherance of that object, I landed with them on a sandy beach to the right of the battery, and after some difficulty in climbing rocks, and other impediments, succeeded in gaining the ridge, and the flank of the Chinese position.

The enemy, before we had gained the level, opposed us courageously, attacking us with matchlocks, spears, and stones, but we soon drove them before us, cleared the battery, and dispersed them, the garrison retreating to the rear, many of whom effected their escape by boats on the beach, to Amoy opposite. Several men were killed in and about the battery, in following the retreating party, some of whom also were wounded. I made a detour of this large and populous island, and discovered, at its western extremity, a sand-bag battery of nine guns, and a few ginjalls; they were all loaded, but did not appear to have been recently discharged. No other armed party of the enemy was fallen in with. I am happy to add, that, in these operations, no casualty happened to the detachment I have the honour to command; moreover, I have great pride in reporting to you, that all the officers, non-commissioned officers, rank and file, throughout the day conducted themselves individually, as well as collectively, with a courage, zeal, and perseverance, far beyond my power to express.

(Signed) *J. B. Ellis, Captain, Royal Marines.*

*

Field state of Battalion, Royal Marines, Island of Coronsou, Harbour of Amoy, August 27, 1841.

	Sub.	Sergt.	Fifer.	Rank and File	Total
Wellesley	1	1	0	42	44
Blenheim	2	1	0	31	34
Blonde	2	2	1	26	31
Druid	2	2	0	42	47
Modeste	0	1	0	15	16
Total	7	7	2	156	172

- First Lieutenant Hewitt - Blonde
- First Lieutenant Maxwell - Druid.
- First Lieutenant Usher - Wellesley.
- Lieutenant Whiting - Blenheim.
- Lieutenant Harmar - Blenheim.
- Lieutenant Pickard - Druid.
- Lieutenant Polkinghorne - Blonde.
- First Lieutenant Maxwell - Adjutant.

- Assistant Surgeon Smith - Wellesley.
- Assistant Surgeon Stanley - Blonde.

(Signed) *J. B. Ellis, Captain, Royal Marines.*

*

Enclosure No. 3.

A Return of Killed and Wounded on board her Majesty's Ships and Vessels, and the Hon. East India Company's Steam Vessels, under the command of Rear-Admiral Sir William Parker, K.C.B., in Action with the Batteries and Defences of the Islands of Amoy and Golong-soo.—August 26th, 1841.

Killed.				Wounded.			
Ship.	**Name.**	**Rank or Station.**	**No.**	**Names.**	**Rank or Station.**	**No.**	**Nature of Wound.**
Wellesley			0	S.S.L. Crofton	Mate	0	Severely
Wellesley			0	Jno. Duncan	B.	2	Ditto
Blenheim	Wm. Barlow	Ordy.	1	Henry Turner	Boy, 1st class	1	Ditto - since dead
Modeste			0	—		1	Slightly
Bentinck			0	Chas. Johnstone	Ordy.	1	Dangerously
Phlegethon (steam vessel)			0	*W.H. Ryves	Acting Lieut., Indian Navy	1	Severely
Nemesis (steam vessel)			0	Henry Steers	Armourer	1	Slightly
		Total	**1**		**Total**	**7**	

** Appointed by Commodore Sir J. J. Gordon Bremer.*

W. Parker, Rear-Admiral.

Her Majesty's Ship "Wellesley," at Amoy, August 27th, 1841.

*

Enclosure No. 4.

An Account of Damages sustained in the Hulls, Masts. &c, of the Squadron under the command of Rear-Admiral Sir William Parker, K.C.B., in the Attack of the Defences and Batteries of Amoy.—August 26th, 1841.

Wellesley.

- Four shot holes in ship's hull.
- Mizen trysail badly wounded.
- Flying jibstay shot away.
- Starboard foremast swifter shot away.
- Starboard fore topmast backstay shot away
- Foresheet shot away.
- Main royal backstay shot away.
- Larboard fourth shroud of mizen rigging shot away.

- Mizen top bowline shot away.
- Mizen top-gallant brace shot away.
- Jib, three shot holes in it.
- Main topsail, two shot holes in it.
- Driver, four shot holes in it.

Blonde.

- One sponge with rammer head and wadhook.
- One 32-pounder gun struck.
- One fore topmast shroud shot away.
- One top-gallant lift shot away.
- One topsail buntline shot away
- Lower studding haulds and span shot away.
- Back rope of spritsail gaff shot away
- Maintop gallant backstay shot away
- Main sheet shot away
- Main topsail, two holes rent.
- Ensign shot in two places.
- Berthing of head shot away.
- The washboard of wastenettings blown away.
- Fore topmast very slightly struck.

Columbine.

- One shot starboard quarter.
- One in the copper under the gangway.
- One or two shots about the flying jib-boom gear.

Druid.

- Foremast wounded by a shot 18 feet above the deck.
- Fore topmast ditto below the cap. Fore topsail shot through in several places.
- The standing and running rigging much cut.

Sesostris.

- One 6-pounder in fore part of starboard sponson.
- Fore topsail braces cut through by shot.
- Main throat hauld, block cut through by shot.
- Fore trysail peak out haul cut through by shot.

Blenheim.

Cheeks of foremast starboard slightly wounded.

Cross jackyard larboard slightly splintered.

Main shroud, one shot away.

Various running rigging ditto.

(Signed) *W. Parker, Rear-Admiral.*

*

Enclosure No. 5.

H.M. Ship, "Wellesley," August 30th, 1841.

Dimensions of Guns Destroyed.—August 30th, 1841.

No. of Guns and Forts		Length.		Diameter.		No. of Guns and Forts		Length.		Diameter.	
		ft.	in.	in.	ths.			ft.	in.	in.	ths.
1 Fort	1	6	10	4	0	6 Fort, low. en.	22	7	0	4	2
	2	6	4	3	5		23	7	3	4	1
	3	6	10	3	8		24	7	10	4	5
	4	6	10	3	7		25	7	0	4	5
	5	6	5	4	3	7 Fort	26	8	0	4	6
	6	6	8	3	9		27	6	7	4	2
2 Fort	7	6	11	3	9		28	6	7	4	0
	8	6	9	3	7		29	6	9	4	0
	9	7	0	4	4		30	6	11	3	9
	10	7	9	4	3	8 Fort	31	7	10	4	8
	11	7	9	4	5		32	7	7	4	5
3 Fort	12	6	11	3	7		33	7	0	5	7
	13	7	9	4	5	9 Fort	34	9	0	5	0
	14	7	10	4	0		35	10	4	8	7
	15	7	0	3	9		36	9	10	5	9
	16	7	10	4	1		37	10	0	6	0
	17	8	10	5	3		38	(Burst)			
4 Fort	18	7	1	4	0		39	9	4	7	2
	19	7	2	4	5	10 Fort	40	7	0	3	6
5 Fort	20	7	3	3	6		41	7	0	3	8
6 Fort, low. en.	21	6	10	4	0		42	7	10	4	6

(Signed) *John V. Fletcher, Commander*

*

List of Chinese Ordnance Taken and Destroyed on the Island of Coulongsou.

In No. 1, on the Marine Battery.

	Average length		Number
	feet	inches	
86 pounders, iron	19	10	1
18 pounders, iron	9	7	2
14 pounders, iron	8	4	7
12 pounders, iron	7	6	6
		Total	**16**

In No. 2 Battery, opposite the suburbs of Amoy.

	Average length		Number
	feet	inches	
11 pounders, iron	7	0	3
9 pounders, iron	6	10	7
		Total	**10**

No. 3 Battery, south side of the island. In this battery a subterranean magazine was discovered, containing a quantity of powder, which was destroyed, as well as that discovered in the other batteries, by being thrown into the sea.

	Average length		**Number**
	feet	**inches**	
34 pounders, iron	9	6	1
12 pounders, iron	7	9	2
9 pounders, iron	7	4	1
8 pounders, iron	7	6	2
7 pounders, iron	6	9	2
Ginjalls 1/2 to 1 1/2			14
		Total	**22**

In No. 4 Battery, a short way to the right of the above.

	Average length		**Number**
	feet	**inches**	
8 pounders, iron	7	4	3

In No. 5 Battery, south-west extremity of the island, discovered on 28th of August.

	Average length		**Number**
	feet	**inches**	
8 pounders, iron	7	6	6
Ginjalls			8
		Total	**14**

In No. 6 Battery, quite new, on the north-west angle of the island.

	Average length		**Number**
	feet	**inches**	
12 pounders, iron	6	0	1
9 pounders, iron	7	3	2
8 pounders, iron	7	0	1
6 pounders, iron	6	6	7
		Total	**11**

Grand Total: 76 guns.

Destroyed by the "Modeste's" boats on the town of Amoy side, two batteries, containing eleven guns, making a total of 87.

Total number of guns destroyed by the light squadron, on shore, in the batteries, and in junks, 198.

(Signed) *W. E. S. Baker, Lt. In charge of artillery on the island. August 29, 1841.*

(Signed) *Thomas Bourchier, Captain.*

*

A List of Her Majesty's Ships and Vessels, and of the Honourable East India Company's Steam Vessels in Action with the Batteries and Defences of Amoy—August 26, 1841.

- Wellesley, Flag-ship, 72 guns, Capt. T, Maitland
- Blenheim, 72 guns, Capt. T. Herbert
- Blonde, 44 guns, Capt. T. Bourchier
- Druid, 44 guns, Capt. Henry Smith, C.B.
- Modeste, 18 guns, Capt Harry Eyres
- Cruiser, 16 guns, Commdr H.W. Giffard
- Pylades, 18 guns, Commdr. T.V. Anson
- Columbine, 16 guns, Commdr. T.J. Clarke
- Bentinck, 10 guns, Lieutenant R. Collinson
- Algerine, 10 guns, Lieutenant J. H. Mason
- Rattlesnake, Troop Ship, Master J. Sprent

Steam Vessels:

- Sesostris, 4 guns, Acting Com. Ormsby
- Phlegethon, 4 guns, Lieut. M'Cleverly, R.N.
- Nemesis, 2 guns, Master W.H. Hall, R.N.
- Queen, 2 guns, Ag. Mast. M'Warden, R.N.

*

Enclosure No. 6

Account of the Guns Destroyed.—August 31st, 1841.

No. of Guns & descriptions of Battery		Length.		Diameter.		No. of Guns & descriptions of Battery		Length.		Diameter.	
		ft.	in.	in.	ths.			ft.	in.	in.	ths.
1 Connette	1	8	0	4	9*	6 Earthen	40	8	0	5	0*
	2	9	0	5	3*		41	9	0	5	5*
	3	9	0	5	3*		42	9	0	5	4*
	4	8	0	4	6*		43	3	0	10	1‡
	5	8	3	5	0		44	3	0	10	0‡
2 Earthen	6	7	10	4	6		45	6	0	3	6
	7	3	0	10	2†		46	8	0	4	7*
3 Stone	8	3	0	10	2†		47	6	5	4	0§
	9	3	1	10	2†		48	6	0	4	3*
	10	3	1	10	2†		49	6	0	3	6
4 Wooden	11	3	0	4	3†		50	5	10	3	8
	12	3	0	10	1†		51	5	6	3	6
	13	3	0	10	0†		52	4	5	3	9*
	14	3	0	10	0†		53	4	5	3	9*
	15	3	0	10	1†		54	6	0	4	0
	16	7	0	4	1		55	6	0	4	0
	17	7	0	4	1		56	6	0	3	4

No. of Guns & descriptions of Battery		Length.		Diameter.		No. of Guns & descriptions of Battery		Length.		Diameter.	
		ft.	in.	in.	ths.			ft.	in.	in.	ths.
4 Wooden	18	7	10	5	0	6 Earthen	57	5	10	3	3
	19	7	10	4	5		58	5	6	3	5
	20	3	0	10	0		59	6	0	3	6
	21	3	0	10	1	8 Circular Fort	60	6	3	3	5
	22	2	9	5	4		61	5	10	3	2
	23	3	0	10	0		62	5	10	3	3
	24	3	0	10	0	‡9 Connette	63	6	8	4	0±
	25	3	0	10	0		64	6	8	4	0±
	26	2	6	7	1		65	6	8	4	0±
	27	3	0	10	1		66	6	8	4	1±
	28	2	9	6	1		67	6	8	4	0±
	29	7	10	5	0		68	6	0	3	9±
	30	10	0	5	5		69	6	10	4	0±
	31	10	0	5	6		70	7	0	4	0±
5 Connette	32	8	0	4	4		71	7	0	4	0±
	33	8	6	4	6		72	6	10	4	0±
	34	8	0	4	6		73	6	0	3	9±
	35	3	10	10	0‡	10 Earthen	74	4	11	3	2
6 Earthern	36	3	0	10	0		75	6	1	4	2*
	37	3	0	10	0		76	6	0	4	3*
	38	7	10	4	8*		77	6	0	4	
	39	8	0	5	1*						

European. † Dismounted. ‡ Uncovered. § Muzzle broken. ± Outer Islands.
‡9 Connette Battery constructed for 21 guns on the second island.

H.M.S. "Wellesley," 31st August, 1841.

(Signed) *John V. Fletcher, Commander.*

Outer Island.—West Fort, 5; and a small round fort, no guns; S. W. Fort, 7; S. S. W. Fort, 5; South Fort, 5; East Fort, 4. Inner Island—South Fort, 8; West Fort, 6; East Fort, 12. All quite new, but no guns.

(True Copies) *T. H. Maddock, Secretary to the Government of India.*

Re-published by order of the Right Honourable the Governor in Council.

Robert Clerk, Secretary to Government.

XIV. PROCLAMATION.

REPORT OF THE FOKIEN MANDARINS RESPECTING THE CAPTURE AND RECAPTURE OF AMOY.

The English barbarians on the seventh moon and ninth day (25th August, 1841) proceeded to attack Hea-mun (Amoy), and on the 10th they ascended the hills from the River She-keang, and seized the fortifications of the city.

Their Excellencies, Yen, the Governor, and Lew, the Taou-tae, withdrew into Fung-an, and on the 16th summoned forward Tseun-chow troops, 4000; from Chan-chow, 2000; village braves, 6000; and from the various villages of Chan-chow, 4000 brave militia. There were military Heu graduates and military Lew graduates, who became the patriotic leaders of the people. From Kin-mun there were also 1200 troops, and 4000 brave seamen from Yung-an, while 7000 outlaws of Hea-mun banded themselves together for opposition. The troops and the militia of Chang-chow and Kin-mun proceeded without delay, having combustibles and arms, in small boats, each of which had seventy or eighty oars, and carrying powder, sulphur, muskets, and shields. From the road of Pih-shih-tow and Koo-lang-yu they made their entrance. When the Admiral heard this, he took more than ten war ships, with which he had been searching for pirates, and straightway entered Tae-tan, and from the Tsing-le gate he advanced to the attack. His Excellency Yu-poo-wun, commander of the land forces, leading his troops, and forming a junction with the governor, crossed over the Woo-tung lake, and fixed his quarters at Kin-ke.

The commander of the Yungan encampments, receiving the summons of the governor, led, in person, the troops and militia over Woo-tung to Kaou-ke, and directly entered the mouth of the river, and both divisions, forming a junction, advanced. The sea and land forces from every quarter assembled together. On the night of the 17th, and during the first watch, the governor fired off his line of signal guns, and taking his flag on horseback with him, he, in person, directed the ranks to make an immediate attack upon the barbarians. On the night, the north-east wind blew exceedingly strong, and there was a vast abundance of small rain. On a sudden, in front of the ranks, a company of troops was perceived, which was headed by a single individual, whose head was adorned with a blue button, and his hand grasped a long lance. This was understood to be the soul of the venerable Chang-yew, who came to fight at the head of the ranks. On that night, the barbarians were sound asleep; but suddenly, hearing of the gathering together of our land and naval forces, the barbarian military chief issued orders to fire their cannon, and summoned his troops to Hew-shay-poo, and there, with our troops, they joined in mutual conflict. Then was to be seen the soul of the venerable Chang-yew aiding us, and all the barbarians, falling down with dizziness, found it difficult to serve their guns, and we put to death and arrested them without number. Our admiral, perceiving the barbarian ships at anchor in the bay at the end of Shapo, ordered the guns to be made to bear upon them. The barbarians also wished to return the fire, when suddenly was seen one of the gods, with dishevelled hair and bare feet, holding a sword in his hand, and descending from heaven, leading a numerous host of brave soldiery. At this, the souls of the barbarian troops were affrighted out of their bodies, and being set upon by the celestial corps, were unable to work their guns. Our troops, without intermission, played upon them with several tens of great guns. We destroyed eight three-masted ships, six two-masted vessels, four fire-wheel ships, and upwards of twenty ships' boats. Of the barbarian troops that were slain it would be impossible to state the number. Of camp-followers there fell more than 200, while upwards of 700 white devils and more than 900 black devils (Sipahis) were slain.

The Commander-in-Chief, with the chief officer of Kin-mun, fought up to the third watch, and then ascended the hill with the governor, and in a body entered the city. The barbarian troops, having not yet fled, our soldiers proceeded to arrest them all, after having put to death between 300 and 400. There were seven military chiefs who were taken alive. The transports which escaped destruction, perceiving the victory to be lost, forthwith proceeded out to sea.

That Amoy was recaptured on the 17th, was owing, first, to the aid of the gods; second, to the assistance afforded by the soul of the venerable Chang-yen; and, third, to the love which the governor cherished for his country and the people.

At present the various seaports are "guarded by our troops, and are in a state of preparedness should the barbarians again return, and within the river the. fort of Sha-po is mounted with more than a thousand cannon. When the barbarians captured the forts they did not injure a single gun, and now we have all back again without loss.

XV. NOTIFICATION

Fort St. George, December 30, 1841.

His Lordship in Council has great satisfaction in republishing the following notification of the government of India; and directs that a royal salute be fired in honour of the brilliant achievements of the combined naval and military forces of her Britannic Majesty, and the honourable Company, on the coast of China, in which the troops of the Madras Presidency, under the immediate direction of their Commander-in-Chief, his Excellency Lieutenant-General Sir Hugh Gough, G. C. B., have borne so conspicuous apart.

By order of the Right Honourable the Governor in Council,

H. Chamier, Chief Secretary.

NOTIFICATION.

Political Department, Monday morning, Dec. 20th, 1841.

The Right Honourable the Governor-General of India in Council has the highest satisfaction in publishing, for general information, the subjoined despatches from his Excellency Rear-Admiral Sir W. Parker, K.C.B., Naval Commander-in-Chief on the East India Station, and his Excellency Lieutenant General Sir H. Gough, G.C.B., commanding the military branch of the expedition, detailing the brilliant successes, on the coast of China, of the combined naval and military forces of her Britannic Majesty and the honourable Company, the results of which have been the total defeat and dispersion of Chinese armies of far superior numbers; the destruction of extensive fortifications of the enemy; the capture of a large quantity of ordnance, of other munitions of war. and of stores; the surrender of numerous prisoners; and the occupation, with very trifling loss, on the part of the British troops, of the important and populous cities of Tinghae, Chinhae, and Ningpo.

A royal salute will be fired in honour of these achievements.

By order of the Right Honourable the Governor-General in Council.

T. H. Maddock, Secretary to Government.

*

To the Right Honourable the Earl of Auckland, G.C.B., &c. &c. &c. "Wellesley," at Chusan, 4th October, 1841.

My Lord,—I have much pleasure in reporting to your lordship that the island of Chusan was reoccupied by the combined forces of her Majesty on the 1st instant.

My last communication from Amoy, on the 31st of August, will have informed your lordship of our hopes of immediately quitting that anchorage; but a continuance of bad weather prevented the expedition from putting to sea before the 5th of September. We were, however, favoured in our progress to the northward with fair, but light breezes, until the 13th, when the north-east monsoon set in strong against us, with thick weather, causing the unavoidable separation of many of the transports, and it was only by considerable perseverance, and taking advantage of the tides in shore, which we were enabled, by the regularity of the soundings, to approach with confidence, that we succeeded, on the 21st instant, in reaching the Chusan group of islands, where I had the satisfaction of collecting several of the missing ships and steam vessels, and gained the anchorage off the little isle of Just-in-the-way, on the 24th, with the preconcerted intention of making our first attack on Ching-hae, and pressing forward by the Tahae River, to take possession of Ningpo.

The transport in which Sir Hugh Gough and his staff were era-barked having fallen far to leeward before we got sight of Chusan, the "Cruiser" was despatched to convey him to the fleet, and rejoined with his Excellency on the evening of the 25th.

The weather was now too boisterous to approach the exposed position of Ching-hae, we therefore, on the following day, made a very satisfactory reconnoissance of the defences of Ting-hae and Chusan harbour, in the "Phlegethon" and "Nemesis" steam vessels, and determined on immediate preparations for re-occupying the island.

The Chinese have been indefatigable in erecting batteries since the British forces were withdrawn in February last; and it is almost inconceivable that so much has been done by them. From the western extremity, outside Guard Island, to the eastern termination of their works, which extend half a mile beyond the commanding position of the Joss-house, or Temple-hill, (now greatly strengthened,) there is a continued line of strong battery on the sea-face, principally constructed of mud, comprising 267 embrasures for guns, and ninety-five of various calibre, actually mounted on different points, independently of forty-one planted on the ramparts of the city, and numerous ginjalls in every direction.

The rapidity of the tides in the different channels to Chusan harbour is so great as to render large ships frequently quite unmanageable, even with the assistance of steam vessels; and the chance of placing them in any precise position for action so uncertain, that it was at once seen our object would be best effected by landing the troops, seamen, and marines, to the westward of the sea defences, and take them in reverse. We found a stone-work with eight embrasures, constructed near Guard Island, to defend the point on which we proposed to disembark the troops, but no guns yet placed in it. About 1200 yards above it, on a steep hill, was also a strongly fortified encampment, in which a large body of Chinese were posted; Captain Eyres was therefore detached with the "Modeste," "Columbine," and "Nemesis," to anchor close to the battery, and prevent its occupation, or any movement of the Chinese to strengthen their position. This duty was, with the usual zeal of himself, Commander Clark, and Mr. Hall, most effectually performed, and a considerable breach made by the Nemesis guns in the wall of the fortified encampment.

A continuance of north-east gales, with incessant rain, rendered it impracticable to move the fleet from the anchorage off Just-in-the-way, before the 29th, when we reached the outer harbour of Chusan, with part of the transports.

The "Blonde," "Modeste," and "Jupiter," with the "Queen" steam vessel, immediately proceeded to take up a position on the south side of the Macclesfield and Trumball Islands, to cover and assist a party of the Royal Artillery under Captain Knowles, in erecting a battery of one 68, and two 24-pounder howitzers, against the Joss-house Hill, and the adjoining works, which kept up a frequent, but ineffectual fire, and this service was, with infinite labour, accomplished with a celerity that reflects much credit on all the officers and men employed on it.

The "Wellesley" was moved as close as possible to the intended point of landing; the "Cruiser" and "Columbine" were advanced within 200 yards of the beach; and by occasional well-directed shot from those vessels, and shells from the "Sesostris," the Chinese were completely kept in check.

The remainder of the transports having joined in the course of the 30th, and the preparations being completed, the disembarkation was ordered on the morning of the 1st instant, in two columns; the first, about 1500 strong, to take possession of the heights, and then to move on to the city; the second, (to which the Royal Marines and a party of seamen were attached,) altogether 1100 strong, to carry the sea line of battery, by pushing round on their right, and proceeding to make a lodgment in the suburbs to attack the Joss-house Hill.

Our resources in boats did not admit of more than one column being landed at a time, including a portion placed in the "Phlegethon" and "Nemesis," and finding these small vessels had scarcely power to tow the boats with the troops against the tide, I was compelled to keep the "Sesostris" to facilitate their disembarkation. With this additional assistance, it was nearly half-past ten o'clock before the first column, under their gallant Commander-in-Chief, reached the shore, when they were assailed by a heavy discharge of ginjalls and matchlocks from-the heights, but immediately formed and supported by the fire of the ships, the advance quickly ascended the hill, and gallantly carried everything before them, although a more resolute stand was made by the Chinese than had been previously experienced in any encounter with them.

The howitzers on the island were opened simultaneously with the advance of the troops to the shore, when the "Queen" endeavoured to tow the "Blonde" into a favourable position against the Joss house and Eastern batteries; the strength of the spring tide, however, unfortunately baffled every effort to place her satisfactorily, but the exertions of Captain Bourchier throughout entitles him to my best thanks. The lighter draught of water of the "Modeste" and "Queen" enabled them to get into good situations; and by the excellence of their fire, in conjunction with that from the Mortar Battery on Trumball Island, the Joss-house Battery was silenced, and the Chinese troops driven from that post and the batteries to the eastward of it.

The Marines and part of the seamen were landed as fast as the boats could return for them, but before the second column got on shore, the Chinese abandoned the western end of their sea defences, which were entered by part of the troops of the first column, who completely cleared the line of batteries, and took possession of the Joss-house Hill.

The steam vessels moved into the inner harbour as soon as the troops were landed, to assist in the reduction of Tinghae, on which the main body was rapidly advanced; the walls were escaladed without opposition, and by two p.m. the British colours were flying in every direction.

Thirty-six new and well-cast brass guns are mounted in the batteries, and will be shipped in one of the transports. I-believe a considerable store of government rice has been found in the city.

I fear the troops has suffered a loss of one ensign and one private killed, and about twenty-four men wounded. The casualties in the squadron are confined to one seaman, in the "Cruiser," severely wounded, (since dead,) another slightly wounded, and one man, of the "Phlegethon," slightly wounded. The "Blonde" had one of her quarter-deck guns disabled, but no further mischief was sustained.

The unremitting exertions of every officer and man of her Majesty's squadron, Royal Marines, and Indian Navy, throughout the operations, merits my warmest commendation. I subjoin a statement of the ships present.

Captain Herbert, of the "Blenheim," whose zeal is always conspicuous, handsomely volunteered to head the landing party of seamen and marines; and I gladly acknowledge the valuable assistance I have derived from the local knowledge and skill of Captain Maitland, of this ship, who has conducted her with much ability in the intricate and difficult navigation amongst these islands.

Command Giffard, of the "Cruiser," has been indefatigable in the duty assigned him of superintending the disembarkation, which he has performed to the entire satisfaction of the General and myself.

The fire from the ships and steam vessels covering the landing party did much execution; it was indeed directed with such precision, that two or three individuals fell by a single cannon-shot at a distance of 700 yards, one of them while in the act of waving the Chinese banners.

It is out of my province to observe on the movements of the land forces, but I may be permitted to express my admiration of the gallantry which was throughout displayed by our companions of the army and their distinguished chief, and I can but express my regret that circumstances did not admit of the officers, seamen, and Royal Marines of her Majesty's squadron, as well as of the Indian Navy, participating to a greater extent in the operations of the day.

Sir Henry Pottinger has witnessed all the proceedings of the expedition, and, considering the lateness of the season, it is a subject of congratulation to his Excellency, as well as to Sir Hugh Gough and myself, that the reoccupation of this island has been secured.

Your lordship may be assured that not a moment will be lost in making the contemplated movement on Chinghae and Ningpo, whenever the state of the weather renders it practicable.

I have the honour to be, my lord, your lordship's most obedient servant,

W. Parker, Rear-Admiral.

*

A List of her Majesty's Ships and Vessels, and of the Steam Vessels of the Indian Navy, present at the reduction of Chusan, the 1st October, 1841.

- Wellesley, 72 guns, Rear-Admiral Sir Wm. Parker, K.C.B., Captain Thomas Maitland
- Blenheim, 72 guns, Captain Thomas Herbert.
- Blonde, 42 guns, CaptainThomas Bourchier.
- Modeste, 18 guns, Captain Harry Eyres
- Cruiser, 16 guns, Commander H.W. Giffard
- Columbine, 16 guns, Commander T.J. Clarke
- Bentinck, 10 guns, Lieutenant R. Collinson
- Jupiter (troop ship), Master Commanding, Robert Fulton
- Rattlesnake, Troop Ship, Master Commanding, James Sprent
- Steam Vessels:
- Sesostris, 4 guns, Acting Com. Ormsby
- Phlegethon, 2 guns, Lieut. McCleverly, R.N.
- Nemesis, 2 guns, Master W.H. Hall, Master, R.N.
- Queen, 6 guns, Mr. Wm. Warden, Acting Master, R.N.

W. Parker, Rear-Admiral.

*

To the Right Honourable the Earl of Auckland, G. C.B., &c. &c. "Modeste," at Ningpo, 11th October, 1841.

My Lord,—My despatch of the 4th instant, in which I had the honour of communicating to your lordship the reoccupation of Chusan by her Majesty's forces, would apprize you of the anxiety of Sir Hugh Gough and myself to commence operations against Chinghae, as soon as a change of weather should enable the ships of the expedition, with common prudence, to approach that exposed position.

On the 7th, the wind veered to the desired point, and every preliminary arrangement having been made, not a moment was lost in embarking the troops intended for the expedition. The following day most of the transports were moved to the anchorage off Just-in-the-way, four leagues in advance; and the general and myself, accompanied by Sir Henry Pottinger, proceeded, at the same time, in the "Phlegethon" and "Nemesis" to reconnoitre the points of our intended attack, where we were fully informed, and found that every preparation for resistance had been made.

The city of Chinghae, which is enclosed by a wall thirty-seven feet in thickness, and twenty-two feet high, with an embrasured parapet of four feet high, and nearly two miles in circumference, is situated at the foot of a very commanding peninsular height, which forms the entrance of the Tahee River, on its left or north bank. On the summit is the citadel, which, from its strong position, is considered the key to Chinghae, and the large and opulent city of Ningpo, about fifteen miles up the river; and it is so important as a military post, that I trust I may be excused for attempting to describe it.

It stands about 250 feet above the sea, and is encircled also by a strong wall, with very substantial iron plated gates at the east and west ends. The north and south sides of the height are exceedingly steep; the former, accessible only from the sea by a narrow winding path from the rocks at its base, the south side and eastern end being nearly precipitous. At the east end of the citadel, outside its wall, twenty-one guns were mounted in three batteries of masonry and sand bags, to defend the entrance of the river.

The only communication between the citadel and city is on the west side, by a steep, but regular causeway, to a barrier gate at the bottom of the hill, where a wooden bridge over a wet ditch connects it with the isthmus and the gates of the city, the whole of which are covered with iron plates, and strongly secured. The space on the isthmus between the citadel hill and the city wall is filled up towards the sea with a battery of five guns, having a row of strong piles driven in a little beach in front of it, to prevent a descent in that quarter; and on the river side of the isthmus are two batteries adjoining the suburbs, and mounting twenty-two and nineteen guns, for flanking the entrance; twenty-eight guns, of different sizes, and numberless ginjalls, were also planted on the city walls, principally towards the sea.

The main body of the Chinese forces were posted on the right bank of the river, in fortified encampments, on very commanding and steep hills; field works and entrenchments being thrown up in every advantageous position, with twenty-three guns and innumerable ginjalls mounted in them to impede the advance of the troops. The principal landing place on this side is within a considerable creek, close to the south entrance of the river, and across this creek we found a row of piles driven. Four batteries, mounting thirty-one guns, were also newly-constructed on this side of the river, to flank the entrance, and about half a mile above its mouth a similar obstruction of larger piles was carried completely across, space only being left for one junk to pass at a time. In short, the Chinese had exercised their ingenuity to the utmost, to make their defences secure; and a great amount of treasure and labour must have been expended in the execution of these works, fully evincing the importance which they attached to this position.

The plan of attack agreed upon by the General and myself, was to land the troops in two columns on the right bank of the river, inside the small islands called the Triangles, the main body under his immediate command (about 1040 strong) to disembark a short distance beyond the creek above referred to, the other (about 500 strong), immediately at its entrance, where it appeared to us practicable to put them securely on shore outside the piles, under the cover of one of the brigs, good anchorage being found within a few yards of the spot.

The attack of the citadel and city on the left bank of the river, was assigned to the naval branch of the force, strengthened by about twenty-three of the Royal, and twelve of the Madras Artillery, under Lieutenants the Hon. F. Spencer and Molesworth, and fifty Sappers, under Captain Cotton and Lieutenant Johnston, of the Madras Engineers. It was calculated that the advance of the two columns of troops by different routes, would not only secure every point on the right bank, but cut off the retreat of many of the Chinese; and by a simultaneous bombardment of the citadel and city by the squadron, we entertained confident hopes of complete success, which has been happily realized in every respect.

On the evening of the 9th, the whole of the squadron, as per subjoined list, and the transports, were anchored off Chinghae, in convenient situations for the intended operations; and at an early hour on the following morning, the troops proceeded in the "Queen," "Nemesis," and "Phlegethon" steamers, and the boats of the transports, to the points of debarkation, where the "Cruizer," "Columbine," and "Bentinck" most judiciously took up their positions, under the direction of Commander Giffard. A few shot from them cleared the shore of about 300 of the Chinese, who had assembled to oppose the landing, and by half-past nine o'clock, under his excellent arrangements, every man was safe on shore.

The "Wellesley," "Blenheim," "Blonde," and "Modeste," were appointed to cannonade the citadel and eastern part of the city walls, and the "Sesostris," "Queen," and "Phlegethon," after landing the troops, and towing up the ships to their stations, to shell the citadel in flank, and enfilade any of the batteries in the harbour which their guns could bear upon; the "Nemesis" to join in the attack on the north side, in readiness to cover the landing of the seamen and marines, as soon as it became practicable.

The citadel hill cannot be approached for an attack by large ships, except on the north side, and the water in that direction is so shallow, that it is only in the calmest weather that they can be carried with safety sufficiently near to fire with effect. The day was, fortunately, everything we could desire, and the "Wellesley," as soon as the tide served, was towed by the "Sesostris" into an excellent position, where the anchor was dropped about a quarter before nine o'clock, in four fathoms, about 1300 yards from the citadel and town walls. As the water ebbed, she settled imperceptibly into a bottom of soft mud, and was as steady as a land battery, Commander Ormsby, (with very commendable activity,) immediately afterwards brought in the "Blenheim." The "Blonde" and "Modeste," favoured by a light breeze, took their stations under sail; and every ship was placed, to my entire satisfaction, as close as possible; the "Blenheim" and "Modeste" touching the bottom at low water. The precision of the fire, both of shots and shells, from all, exceeded my most sanguine expectations; and the destruction of the works from the commencement of the attack was never doubtful.

As the troops on the right bank of the river moved forward, Commander Giffard advanced the sloops towards the entrance of the harbour, and the steamers all took up very good positions, and performed excellent service with their guns; they were for a considerable time under a heavy fire from the river batteries, but fortunately sustained no damage.

About 11 o'clock we had the gratification of seeing the British colours planted by the troops in one of the batteries on the opposite shore; and, within a few minutes, the others on that side were all carried, and the Chinese observed flying in every direction before our gallant soldiers on the heights.

At a quarter past 11, the wall of the citadel was breached by the fire from the ships; and the defences being reduced to a ruinous state, the Chinese abandoned their guns, which they had hitherto worked with considerable firmness, and a large portion of the garrison retreated precipitately towards the city. Not a moment was lost in making the signal for landing the battalion of Seamen and Marines, with the detachments of Artillery and Sappers, (the whole under the command of Captain Herbert, of the "Blenheim.") Before noon the boats were all on shore; every impediment presented by the difficulty of landing on rugged rocks was overcome; and the force gallantly advanced to the assault, with a celerity that excited my warmest admiration. An explosion at this time took place in a battery near the citadel gate, and the remnant of the garrison fled without waiting to close it. The citadel was therefore rapidly entered, and the union-jack displayed on the walls. Our people had scarcely passed within them, when another explosion occurred, happily without mischief, but whether by accident or design is uncertain.

Captain Herbert, having secured this post, quickly re-formed his men, and advanced towards the city, the Chinese still occupying, in considerable force, the walls of it, as well as the two batteries beneath the hill on the river side, against which our troops had already turned some of the guns taken on the right bank. A few volleys of musketry speedily dislodged them from both positions, and the battalion of Seamen and Marines pushed on in steady and excellent order to attack the city. The wall (twenty-six feet high) was escaladed in two places, and in a short time complete possession was taken of Chinghae, the Chinese troops having made their escape through the western gates.

While in the act of scaling the city wall, a third and formidable explosion took place at one of the river batteries, within a short distance, by which, I regret, one man of the "Blenheim" was killed. There is strong suspicion that it was caused by a mine intentionally sprung, and, considering the number of our men which were assembled at the time, it is most providential that the consequences were not more disastrous.

The seamen immediately returned on board, for the security of the ships, which, with the rising tide, were moved into secure berths, Captain Herbert remaining with the Marines in charge of the town until the evening, when Sir Hugh Gough arrived, and a considerable portion of troops were conveyed across the river, in the "Phlegethon," to garrison it.

I have sincere pleasure in again bringing before your lordship's notice the gallantry and excellent conduct of every officer and man of her Majesty's ships and the Indian navy under my command.

To Captain Herbert my best acknowledgments are due, for his zeal for the public service, and animating example on all occasions; and he speaks in strong terms of commendation of the gallant support he received from Captain Bourchier of the "Blonde," Major Ellis, of the Royal Marines, and the officers and men of every description attached to the force placed under his command, of which, and of those employed in the boats, I transmit a list, and cordially join in every praise that can be bestowed on them. I must also state, that although Captains Maitland and Eyres were not directly attached to the battalion of Seamen and Marines which disembarked, they landed at the same time, and accompanied them in their operations.

To Captain Maitland, of my flag ship, I feel much indebted for the able and zealous assistance which he at all times affords me and my obligations are equally due to Captain Eyres, for the invaluable services of the "Modeste."

The activity and ardour of Commanders Giffard, Clarke, Fletcher and Watson, and of Lieutenant Collinson in command of the "Bentinck," has been eminently displayed on this and every other opportunity, and I have no less pleasure in bearing testimony to your lordship, that the same spirit of enterprise and zeal has been conspicuously evinced by Commander Ormsby, Lieutenant McCleverty, Mr. Hall, and Mr. Warden; and, indeed, of every officer and man in the steam vessels attached to the expedition.

I may be permitted, also, to notice that my flag lieutenant, Charles Tennant, has attended me in every operation since I took command of the squadron, and his zeal and attention is deserving of my highest approbation.

By official Chinese documents found in Chinghae, we have good reason to believe that the regular Tartar troops quartered, on the 10th, in the city, and batteries on the left, bank of the river, amounted to upwards of 3,000; of which about 700 composed the garrison of the citadel or Joss-house Hill; their loss on these points is calculated at 150 men.

The troops opposed to Sir Hugh Gough were estimated at 10,000, and they have sustained a heavy loss, but no amount of force as yet met with in this country can withstand the gallant band under his command, into which his active and energetic example infuses unbounded confidence.

The total number of guns which have fallen into our hands amounts to ninety iron and sixty-seven brass; the latter will be embarked without delay in one of the transports, with a large quantity of metal, which has been found in a cannon-foundry at Chinghae.

I have the honour to be, my lord, your lordship's most obedient servant,

W. Parker, Rear Admiral.

*

A List of Her Majesty's Ships and Vessels, and of the Steam Vessels of the Indian Navy, present at the reduction of Chinghae, the 10th of October, 1841.

- Wellesley, 72 guns, Rear-Admiral Sir Wm. Parker, K.C.B., Captain Thomas Maitland
- Blenheim, 72 guns, Captain Thomas Herbert.
- Blonde, 42 guns, CaptainThomas Bourchier.
- Modeste, 18 guns, Captain Harry Eyres
- Cruiser, 16 guns, Commander H.W. Giffard
- Columbine, 16 guns, Commander T.J. Clarke
- Bentinck, 10 guns, Lieutenant R. Collinson
- Jupiter (troop ship), Master Commanding, Robert Fulton
- Rattlesnake, Troop Ship, Master Commanding, James Sprent
- Steam Vessels:
- Sesostris, 4 guns, Acting Com. Ormsby
- Phlegethon, 2 guns, Lieut. McCleverly, R.N.
- Nemesis, 2 guns, Master W.H. Hall, Master, R.N.
- Queen, 6 guns, Mr. Wm. Warden, Acting Master, R.N.

W. Parker, Rear-Admiral.

*

Artillery.

- Lieutenant Honourable F. Spencer, 23 Guns, Royal Artillery, and two 5-1/2 inch mortars, and nine and twelve pounder rockets.
- Lieutenant Molesworth, 12 Guns, Madras Artillery.
- Captain Cotton and Lieutenant Johnston, with thirty Madras Sappers.

Officers in charge of Boats.

Wellesley:

- Lieut. Lord Compton and Lord A. Beauclerk, Mate, in the Launch.
- Mr. Crofton, Mate, in the Pinnace.
- Mr. Kennedy, Mate, in the Barge.
- Mr. Niblett, 2nd Master, in the Cutter.

Blenheim:

- Mr. Kevern, Mate, in the Launch.
- Mr. Denny, Mate, in the Barge.
- Mr. Konnielar, Greek, Mate, in the Pinnace.
- Mr. Pascoe, 2nd Master, in the Gun-boat.
- Mr. Swinburn, Midshipman, in the 1st Cutter.
- Mr. Gell, Midshipman, in the 2nd Cutter
- Mr. Beneraft, Vol. 1st Class., Midshipman, in the Jolly-boat.

Blonde:

- Lieut. Dally Midshipman, in the Launch.
- Mr. Hamilton, Midshipman, in the Pinnace.
- Mr. Anderson, Mate, in the Gun-boat.

Modeste:

- Mr. H. Crofton, Mate, in the Pinnace.

(Signed) *J. Herbert, Captain.*

W. Parker, Rear Admiral.

*

Return of Officers who landed with the Right Column under the Command of Captain Herbert, at Chinghae, 10th October, 1841. Captain Bourchier, Commanding the Battalion of Seamen.

Wellesley.

- All landed with 1st, 2nd and 3rd Companies, Seamen battalion.
- Lieut. Symons; Lieut. Maitland; Lieut. Carmichael; Mr. King, Mate; Mr. Halsted Mate; Mr. Birthwhistle, Midshipman; Mr. Butler, Midshipman; Mr. Jackson, Midshipman; Mr. Smith, Asst. Surgeon

Blenheim.

- Landed with 4th, 5th, and 6th Companies, Seamen Battalion.
- Lieut. Hawkins; Lieut. Matthews; Mr. St. Leger, Mate; Mr. Norman, Mate; Mr. Dowell, Midshipman; Mr. Adair, Vol. 1st Class; Mr. Scott, Vol. 1st Class, A.D.C; Mr. Thomas, Asst. Surgeon

Blonde.

- Landed with 7th Company, Seamen Battalion.
- Lieut. Sir F. Nicholson; Mr. Walker, Mate; Mr. Rolland, Mate; Mr. Lambert, Midshipman; Messrs. Lyon and Coke, Mids., A.D.C

Modeste.

- Landed with Subdivision of 8th Company
- Lieut. Birch; Mr. Pearce, Mate

Major Ellis, Commanding Battalion of Royal Marines.

- Landed 276 Royal Marines.
- Capt. Whitcomb; Lieut. White; Lieut. Usher; Lieut. Whiting; Lieut. Hewett; Lieut. Farmer; Lieut. Polkinghorne; Mr. Tweeddale, Asst. Surgeon, Blenheim; Mr. Stanley, Assistant Surgeon, Blonde

*

The Right Honourable the Earl of Auckland, G.C.B., &c. &c.&c. "Modeste," off Ningpo, 14th October, 1841.

My Lord,—It is with feelings of the greatest satisfaction that I have now the honour of addressing your lordship from the anchorage off the walls of Ningpo, on which the British colours are flying.

The progress of the expedition has been greatly favoured by the fine weather, which enabled it to complete the reduction of Chinghae, on the 10th instant, and to place the large ships and transports on the following day at a safe anchorage, after landing the requisite supplies for the army, for the wind changed to the north-east on the 12th, and blew strong. The ships, however, were all in security; the Blonde, with the sloops and steamers, and part of the transports, having found sufficient water and excellent shelter within the Tahea river, a few of the piles being taken up for their admission.

I removed on the 11th to the Modeste; and that no time might be lost in prosecuting our further operations, I directed Captains Maitland and Herbert, when the Wellesley and Blenheim were anchored off "Just-in-the-way," to return by one of the steam vessels, with the boats and 150 seamen from each ship, in readiness to advance on "Ningpo," and on the 12th, I proceeded in the Nemesis to ascertain the practicability of taking the large steamers and sloops up the river. We found it wide, free from shoals, and carried not less than fourteen feet at low water to the walls of the city, which appeared not only unprepared for resistance, but a general panic pervading the inhabitants, who were evacuating the town in every direction, with their goods and families. Sir Henry Pottinger, Sir Hugh Gough, and myself, therefore deemed it expedient to move on it without delay, to check as much as possible the departure of the respectable portion of the population, and the ravages which are invariably committed by the lower orders of the Chinese on all property which is left unprotected.

The whole of the troops (with the exception of a garrison for Chinghae and the citadel,) were consequently embarked on the following morning in the Sesostris, Queen, Phlegethon, and Nemesis, and the supernumerary seamen and marines were distributed in the Modeste, Cruiser, Columbine, and Bentinck, the Blonde being ordered to remain at Chinghae, for the support of the garrison.

Sir Henry Pottinger and the general accompanied me in the Modeste, and the expedition proceeded up the river soon after 9 a. m.; but, owing to some unavoidable delays, did not reach Ningpo until 2 p. m., when the Nemesis and Phlegethon, which contained a large portion of the troops, anchored within a few feet of a floating bridge, which connects the city at its east gate with the suburbs across the river. The men were disembarked with the greatest facility by stages from the bows of these vessels. The battalion of seamen and marines, under Captain Herbert, landing at the same time in the suburbs on the city side, a short distance below them.

The gates of the city were all found secured and barricaded inside, but an entrance was soon forced, when her Majesty's forces marched in, and took possession without a symptom of resistance being indicated in any quarter. The mandarins and troops had all left the city; the latter having, since their defeat at Chinghae, refused to fight.

Her Majesty's sloops and the steam vessels are anchored under the walls of the city, and his Excellency the General is actively exerting himself in securing all the government property on shore, and endeavouring to establish order, and prevent the pillage of this populous and opulent place, where, I am happy to say, such of the respectable inhabitants as have remained, evince much less apprehension at the presence of the English than was exhibited either at Amoy or Chusan. From the number of large junks found in the river, the trade with Ningpo, by sea, must be extensive, but an embargo will be laid on all vessels until measures can be concerted for our further proceedings.

A few war-junks, and a trifling amount of naval stores, have fallen into our hands.

I beg to offer my congratulations to your lordship, on the result of our operations, and I have the honour to be, my lord, your lordship's most obedient servant,

W. Parker, Rear Admiral.

*

To the Right Honourable the Earl of Auckland, G.C.B., Governor General, &c. &c. &c.
Head Quarters, Tinghae, Island of Chusan, October 3, 1841.

My Lord,—I, feel much satisfaction in acquainting your lordship that Chusan is in our possession, notwithstanding the extraordinary exertions made by the Chinese to strengthen the defences since our departure in February last, and rather a gallant defence on their part, particularly on the heights west of the city, generally denominated the forty-nine hills, and along the shore, where, as a defence to the inner harbour, (which was our former part of attack,) a new line of battery has been constructed, presenting so formidable a front, that, with due regard to the peculiarity of the tides, it would not have been advisable to bring in the ships of war.

2. The fleet had passed Chusan, and assembled at an anchorage off Silver Island, half way between Chusan and Chinhae, when, after waiting three days, the continuance of contrary winds, together with the lateness of the season, induced his Excellency the Naval Commander-in-Chief to propose a change in the plan of operations, which I mentioned to your lordship in my last report. I fully concurred with Sir William Parker in the expediency of attacking Chusan first, under these circumstances, instead of proceeding to Chinhae and Ningpo, particularly as in a reconnoissance which we made in the "Phlegethon" steamer, with his Excellency Sir Henry Pottinger, we ascertained that two forts, in progress of construction upon the base of the heights already named, were, although nearly completed, not yet armed. This reconnoissance confirmed me in the opinion which I had previously formed, from the reports of officers acquainted with the ground, that this would be the most eligible point of attack. I must add, that the fire opened on the "Phlegethon," as she skirted the harbour, also established that the sea line of battery was efficiently armed.

3. I shall leave it to the Admiral to detail the movements of the fleet, but I cannot deny myself the gratification of expressing how greatly I am indebted to him for his judicious arrangements, and the cordial assistance which I have experienced throughout, anticipating my wishes, at the same time that the arm over which he so ably presided has been brought prominently forward whenever practicable; and I must be allowed to remark that the precision of the fire from the ships surpassed my most sanguine expectations, and did great execution wherever it could be brought to bear.

4. The greater part of the fleet assembled in the outer roadstead on the 29th ultimo, and during that night and the following day a battery was thrown up on Trumball Island by a detachment of the Royal and Madras Artillery, under Captain Knowles, of the former corps, aided by Lieutenant Birdwood, of the Madras Engineers, for the purpose of shelling the Joss-house Hill, which the enemy had strongly fortified, following out the unfinished plan of our own engineers. The remaining ships having arrived in the meanwhile, it was determined to make the attack on the 1st instant.

5. I beg to refer your lordship to the annexed disposition of attack, which will shew what were my intentions. Early on the morning of the 1st, the first division, consisting of the Madras Artillery, with eight guns, the Sappers, her Majesty's 18th and 55th regiments, and the rifle company of the 36th Madras Native Infantry, were placed in steamers and boats in tow of them, and under the zealous superintendence of Captain Giffard, of H.M.S. "Cruiser," who conducted the disembarkation, were landed as soon as practicable, though

not without some delay, from the extraordinary strength of the tides at this point. Finding that the enemy, whose occasional shots from the ships had hitherto kept under cover, now crowned the heights, and opened a galling fire of ginjals and matchlocks, and that some of my men were falling, I deemed it advisable to push on at once the two flank and a third company of the 55th, that were first on shore, directing the remainder, who closely followed, to move up in support. This duty was gallantly performed under the directions of Lieutenant-Colonel Craigie, commanding the column, and Major Fawcett, in the temporary command of the regiment; and, notwithstanding the steepness and ruggedness of the ascent, and a heavy and well-sustained fire from an infinitely superior force, this gallant corps carried the whole extent of the ridge of hills, terminating in a fortified camp, and drove everything before them. Lieutenant-Colonel Craigie has brought to my notice the prominent conduct of Lieutenant and Adjutant Butter, who was with the advance at this point, and seized the first of the enemy's colours; as also of Captain Campbell and Lieutenant Cuddy, who led the two flank companies.

6. This movement completely turned the right of the enemy's position, and gave us the command of a bridge which led direct on the flank of the whole line of sea defence. The 18th and Artillery being landed, and the light guns placed so as to enfilade this line of batteries, I felt it best to change my first intention of attacking the sea defences by the right column, and ordered the 18th at once to push forward to the attack on this point. This was executed with equal gallantry by Lieutenant-Colonel Adams, in the face of a very large force, which contested the whole line with more than ordinary spirit, apparently led by one of the principal Mandarins, who, with several of inferior rank, was killed on the spot, when the Chinese fled, and the 18th pushed on and occupied the Joss-house Hill, which the well-directed fire of the guns on Trumball Island, under the Honourable Lieutenant Spencer, of the Royal Artillery, and of the detached squadron under Captain Bourchier, had compelled the enemy to evacuate. Lieutenant-Colonel Adams speaks warmly of the spirited manner in which Captain Wigston led the Grenadier Company of the Royal Irish in this attack.

7. Considering it advisable to support the 18th, I had pushed forward across the valley, the Light and another company of the 55th, with Lieutenant-Colonel Mountain, who is well acquainted with the country, and most judiciously placed them in a position close to the west gate of the city, so as to prevent any support being given from the town, and intercept the enemy in falling back on it. The Rifle Company of the 35th having joined me, I moved on with the remainder of the 55th, covered by the Rifles, for the heights overlooking the city to the north-west, which we occupied. During

these operations, by the praiseworthy efforts of the Madras Artillery, under Captain Anstruther, the light field guns had been brought to the summit of the heights, and opened their fire on the walls and town. The enemy was now in full retreat through the north and east gates, although a few guns and ginjals, with some matchlocks, continued to be fired from the walls; and I directed the 55th to proceed to the escalade, whilst Captain Simpson, with the Rifles, rapidly passed down a deep wooded ravine, to cut off the retreat to the north. The scaling ladders had been brought up on most difficult and rugged heights by the great exertions of the Madras Sappers, and were now gallantly flanked, under the directions of Captain Pears, who was the first to ascend, and I had soon the satisfaction of seeing the colours of the 55th regiment waving on the walls of Ting-hae, while those of the Royal Irish were planted on the Joss-house Hill above the suburb. Captain Anstruther reports that Captain Balfour and Lieutenant Fowlis had the opportunity of distinguishing themselves, in bringing up the guns and directing their fire.

8. Although the 49th regiment and Royal Marines whom I first ordered, together with a body of seamen, to form the right column, under Lieutenant-Colonel Morris, and attack the sea defences, could not be landed in time for that purpose. I was much pleased with the promptitude with which those two corps moved on to the support of the 18th; the 49th proceeding to occupy the south gate of the city.

9. The loss of the enemy has been very considerable, both on the sea line and upon the heights; several of their principal mandarins, it would appear, were killed, and the Chinese fled in all directions, throwing away their arms and clothing. The loss on our side, I am happy to say, has been wonderfully small. I have the honour to enclose your lordship the return, together with a list of the ordnance captured.

10. On the 2nd, I directed Lieutenant-Colonel Adams to move westward with the 18th and Rifle Company on Tsing-kong, to which point the Admiral has despatched two of the ships of war, and from whence the Lieutenant-Colonel is to proceed to-day to Sahoo. This morning I have moved 300 men, under Major Blyth, 49th regiment, eastward to Sinkea-Mun, where he will also meet a ship of war; also three companies of the 55th, under Captain Campbell, over the northern hills to Pishoon, from whence they will march to Kanlon and Mowah, returning by a different pass to head quarters. By these movements, I hope that every one of the fugitives will be driven off the island or captured.

11. It is difficult to mete out praise, where every man did his duty well, but I feel it.right to express my sense of obligation to the following commanding officers of columns and corps:—Lieut.-Colonel Craigie, commanding left column; Lieutenant-Colonel Morris, commanding the right column;

Lieutenant-Colonel Adams, commanding 18th; Major Fawcett, commanding 55th; Major Stephens, commanding 49th; Major Ellis, commanding Royal Marines; Captain Simpson, commanding Rifle Company 36th M. N. Infantry; Captain Knowles, Royal Artillery, senior officer of Artillery; Captain Pears, senior officer of Engineers; Captain Anstruther, commanding Madras Artillery; and Captain Cotton, Assistant Field-Engineer.

From Lieutenant-Colonel Mountain, Deputy Adjutant-General, and Captain Gough, Acting Deputy Quarter-Master-General, I have received, throughout the whole operations, the most valuable assistance. I must also mention the active services of Lieutenant Gubbith, my A. D. C.

I have to repeat my thanks to Captain Giffard, of the Royal Navy, who, after ably conducting the disembarkation, rejoined me, and accompanied me during the rest of the day, as did Major Malcolm, the Secretary of Legation.
I have the honour to be, my lord,

Your lordship's most obedient humble servant,

H. Gough, Major-General, Commanding the Expeditionary Force.

*

General Orders to the Expeditionary Force.
Head-quarters, Tinghae City, October 3, 1841.

Major General Sir Hugh Gough has again the pleasure to congratulate the troops under his command upon their success in the recapture of the island of Chusan, and city of Tinghae, on the 1st instant.

2nd. The conduct of the 55th, whose good fortune it was to land first, and who gallantly gained and cleared the heights, under a brisk and sustained fire from the enemy, was most creditable to the corps, and gave it the further advantage of being the first to scale the city walls.

3rd. That of the 18th Royal Irish, who landed next, was equally praiseworthy in driving the enemy before them, despite of his resistance, from the long line of sea batteries until the regiment gained and reoccupied its old station on the Pagoda Hill.

4th. The well-directed fire of the detachment of Royal and Madras Artillery, from Trumball Island, and the exertions of the Madras Artillery, on Chusan, in getting their guns over almost impracticable ground, and their fire from successive points were alike distinguished.

5th. The Major-General was also gratified by observing the spirited manner in which the Madras Rifle Company advanced in extended order over the hills to the city, and the active zeal of the Madras Sappers and Miners in carrying the scaling ladders over these steep and difficult heights and planting them against the walls.

6th. Circumstances, which it was impossible to foresee, having hastened the moment of attack, the 49th regiment and Royal Marines were not landed in time to perform all that had been allotted to them, but the Major-General noticed with much satisfaction the rapidity with which they moved off to support the advance.

7th. Sir Hugh Gough addresses himself, therefore, to all, in expressing his thanks to commanding officers of columns and corps, and to the general and personal staff, and directing that his sentiments be made known to all of every rank under their respective command.

By order.

(Signed) *Armine S. H. Mountain, Lieutenant-Colonel, Deputy Adjutant-General.*

(True copy.) *Armine S. H. Mountain, Lieutenant-Colonel, Deputy Adjutant-General.*

*

Disposition for Landing at Chusan, September 30th, 1841.

Left Column.—Lieut.-Col. Craigie.			
Ordnance.		**Officers**	**Other ranks**
4 4-2/5 Mountain Howitzers. 2 5-1/2 inch Brass Mortars.	Madras Artillery, Captain Anstruther	8	204
	Do. Sappers, Captain Pears	6	117
	H.M. 55th Regiment, Major Fawcett	25	720
	H.M. 18th Regt. Lieutenant-Col. Adams	14	286
	Rifle Company, Captain Simpson	4	110
	Total	**57**	**1437**

Right Column.—Lieut.-Col. Morris			
Ordnance.		**Officers**	**Other ranks**
2 9-Pounders.	Madras Artillery, Captain Moore	2	50
	Do. Sappers, Captain Cotton	2	50
	H.M. 49th Regt., Major Stephens	34	435
	Royal Marines, Major Ellis	7	201
	Royal Seamen Battalion	15	250
	Total	**60**	**986**

On Trumball Island— Captain Knowles			
Ordnance.		**Officers**	**Other ranks**
1 8-in. Howitzer, 2 Brass 24 Pounders	Royal Artillery	2	31
	Madras Artillery	1	12
	Do. Sappers	1	20

By Order. (Signed) *Armine S. H. Mountain, Lieut. Colonel, D. A. G.*

(True Copy.) *Armine S. H. Mountain, Lieut.-Col. Deputy Adjutant-General.*

*

Return of Officers and Men Killed and Wounded of the Force under the Command of Major General Sir Hugh Gough, K.C.B.,at the re-capture of the Island of Chusan, on the 1st instant.

Tinghae City, Oct. 1841.

Killed.	Officers.	Sergeants.	Rank & File.
Sappers and Miners	0	0	1
18th Royal Irish	0	0	1
55th Regiment	1	0	0
Total	**1**	**0**	**1**

Wounded		Officers.	Sergeants.	Rank & File.
Sappers and Miners	Dangerously	0	0	0
	Severely	0	1	0
	Slightly	0	0	0
18th Royal Irish	Dangerously	0	0	1
	Severely	0	1	1
	Slightly	0	0	4
55th Regiment	Dangerously	0	0	3
	Severely	0	0	5
	Slightly	0	0	11
Total		**0**	**2**	**25**

55th Regiment, Ensign R. Duel, killed. Total, 2 killed; 27 wounded.

Armine S. H. Mountain, Lieut.-Col., Deputy Adjutant-General.

*

Return of Ordnance captured in Chusan, and mounted on the Defences, in the Action of the 1st October, 1841.

	Iron			Brass.				
	From 1 to 3 Pounders	From 3 to 5 Pounders	From 5 to 9 Pounders	9 Pounders	10 Pounders	12 Pounders	20 Pounders	32 Pounders
On Temple Hill Redoubt		1	1	10				
Battery to the East of Temple Hill Redoubt			10		5	5		
Battery to the West of Temple Hill Redoubt		8						
On the Western Line			40				15	
On the Ramparts of the City	19	15	6					1
Total	**19**	**24**	**57**	**10**	**5**	**5**	**15**	**1**

Grand Total,—Iron: 100, Brass:36

- Ginjals (carrying balls from 1/2 lb. to 1 lb.): 540
- Matchlocks in considerable numbers lying on the Works, but all destroyed.

- Gunpowder Tubs: 584
- Rockets, Bamboo: 30
- Rocket, Arrow Cases: 20
- Balls (Leaden), Boxes, and Tubs: 100

N.B.—The brass guns are remarkably well bored, and although of great thickness of metal, yet evidently shew considerable advance on the part of the Chinese in casting.

Some of the gun carriages are superior to those hitherto in use with the Chinese, particularly one on which a brass gun is mounted, and the models of gun carriages and sweeps which have been found, prove that the Chinese are quite ready to introduce improvements.

J. Knowles, Captain Commanding Artillery Brigade.

Chusan, 3rd October, 1841.

*

To the Right Honourable the Earl of Auckland, G.C.B., Governor-General of India, &c. &c. &c.

Head Quarters, October, 18, 1841.

My Lord,—With feelings of the deepest thankfulness I have the honour to acquaint your lordship, that, under the protection of a gracious and all-wise Providence, perfect success has attended her Majesty's combined forces in all our projected operations. Considering the extent of the enemy's preparations, the strength of his different positions, and his overwhelming numbers, the loss on our side has been surprisingly small, while that on the part of the Chinese has been almost appalling.

2. My last dispatch will have informed your lordship of our proposed movement on Chinghae and Ningpo. On the 8th instant, I accompanied their Excellencies Sir Henry Pottinger and the Admiral in a steamer, for the purpose of reconnoitring the former place. For the period of the monsoon, upon a lee shore, the weather was singularly favourable. Both on this and the following days, the enemy allowed us to come within short range without firing a shot, and the Admiral and I were thus at once enabled to make our dispositions.

3. The fortified city of Chinghae, the great military depot of this province, is situated on the left bank of the Tahia, or Ningpo river, occupying, with its suburb, the whole space be tween the river and the sea. The walls are nearly three miles in circumference, and their sea face runs for about a mile along a massive stone embankment, that extends for three or four miles further up the coast. At the south-eastern extremity, separated only from the walls by a narrow gorge, a precipitous rock rises abruptly from the sea, throwing out a steep and rugged spur, at the point of which is the entrance to the river. Upon the summit of this rock, there is a large joss-house, extending along the

coast of the ridge, and forming a sort of citadel, the several buildings being loop-holed, and connected by castellated walls ; and in front of the outer gate, commanding the spur before men tioned, a battery armed with some pieces of heavy ordnance, has been recently constructed. From information I obtained, it would appear that the joss-house was occupied by 400 men, while 3000 held the city, and various small encampments without the walls.

4. The same information led me to believe, and the reconnoissances confirmed the statement, that the great body of the troops were strongly posted on the right bank of the river, upon a range of steep hills overlooking the city and joss-house, with heavy batteries armed, for the most part, with new brass guns, commanding the entrance to the river, which was staked across. All these heights were fortified, and presented both a sea defence and military position of great strength, consisting of a chain of en trenched camps, on all the prominent points difficult of approach, from the natural steepness of the hills, which had been further scarped in several places; field redoubts crowned the summits, and hill and ravine bristled with ginjals, A low swampy flat reaching to the shore, and only to be crossed by narrow winding causeways, lay in front of the left of this position, which was also protected by a deep canal, that, after skirting the hills, runs through the flat into the sea; but I ascertained that there were two bridges over this canal.

5. We returned to Chusan the same evening, and the troops which I had ordered for this service having been previously embarked, as thick as they could store, on board the transports selected by the Admiral as fittest in regard to the extraordinary currents on this coast, the squadron arrived the following evening off the mouth of the Tahea river.

6. I beg herewith to enclose, for your lordship's information, the disposition for landing. It appeared to me advisable, in which Sir William Parker concurred, that we should make a conjoint attack on both banks of the river, first drawing the attention of the enemy to the right bank; and the dispositions were accordingly made for attacking in three columns, while the two line-of-battle ships, with the "Blonde" and "Modeste," were to cannonade the Joss-house Hill and sea line of the city defences; the smaller vessels of war and the steamers to cover the landing, and to support, when practicable, the advancing columns by their fire. Sir William Parker will detail to your lordship the truly spirited manner in which the several ships of war and steamers took up their positions and fulfilled his orders. It only remains for me to say that the cordial co-operation and powerful support which I have received upon the present—indeed, upon every occasion, from the ships of war under the direction of their gallant chief, is matter of the warmest thankfulness.

7. At daylight on the morning of the 10th, the left column, consisting of

a wing of the 18th, five companies of the 55th, the Rifle company of the 36th Madras N.I., a company of Madras Artillery, and one of Sappers—in all, 1040 men—with four light howitzers and two 51-inch mortars, was embarked in the steamers. This column I placed under Lieutenant-Colonel Craigie, but accompanied myself; and at eight o'clock the steamers having run in close to the shore, the troops were promptly landed, without any opposition, under the judicious superintendence of Captain Giffard, ably aided by Lieutenant Somerville, of the Royal Navy, at a rocky point, having the low flat and the canal already mentioned to their right.

8. The centre column was soon after landed about a mile to my right, under a detached rocky hill, near the mouth of the canal, but on the opposite bank, having in its front a part of the low flat between it and the enemy's position, my object being to threaten a front attack, and deter the enemy from weakening his centre to support his right, which the left column under my own superintendence was destined to turn. The centre column consisted of the 49th regiment, detachments of the Royal and Madras Artillery, under Captain Knowles, of the former corps, and 50 men of the Sappers, amounting altogether to 440 men, with two 12-pounder howitzers and two 9-pounder field-guns, under Lieut.-Colonel Morris.

9. Immediately after landing, the left column moved rapidly over a succession of steep hills that skirted the intervening flat in front of the enemy's position, until it reached a point, from whence I had a full view of the whole position and of the two bridges over the canal. That to my front, I ordered the Rifle Company to protect by occupying a few houses on our side, supported by the 18th, and I directed Lieutenant-Colonel Craigie, with the 55th, accompanied by Captain Pears, commanding engineer, to move quickly on the second bridge, which was about a mile further up the flat, cross it, and push on for the hills beyond, thus turning the extreme right of the enemy's position, and threatening to cut off his retreat. By this time, the centre column had formed, and shewed its head at the opposite side of the flat, just out of ginjal range, threatening a front attack. Captain Simpson very promptly performed the duty entrusted to him, and I ascertained that the bridge was uninjured, but had been barricaded by a solid wall of masonry, with merely an aperture so narrow, that (soon after the gate was with some difficulty removed) a single soldier could not pass through without unstrapping his great coat. Having assembled the 18th at the foot of the bridge, to cover the Rifles, that company passed over in Indian file, in face of a large body of the enemy, assembled in an advanced redoubt upon the summit of an eminence within 150 yards of us, who cheered our advance, but most unaccountably preserved their fire. Having placed the Rifles behind a hill just beyond the bridge, I directed the 18th to cross and form, and,

finding the 55th had arrived at its point of attack, sent orders for the 49th to advance, which they did with a spirit worthy of that gallant corps.

10. From the rapidity of these movements and the difficulties of the ground, the guns could not be brought forward enough to act, but Captain Anstruther, of the Madras Artillery, with the usual alacrity of that corps, brought up the rockets, which now began to play. The moment the advance of the 49th got into action, the 18th and Rifles rapidly moved forward, and the 55th having crossed the upper bridge, pressed the enemy's right. I have seldom witnessed a more animated combined attack: the Chinese, cheering until we got close to them, now poured in a very heavy but ill-directed fire, and displayed in various instances acts of individual bravery that merited a better fate—but nothing could withstand the steady but rapid advance of the gallant little force that assailed them, field-work after field-work was cleared, and the colours of the 49th were displayed on the principal redoubt above the sea and river batteries, while the 18th, who had charged up a deep gorge to the left, broke through the central encampment, carrying everything before them. From 1200 to 1500 of the enemy, that had stood longest, were driven down the heights into the river, their retreat being cut off by the flank movement of the 55th. Many were drowned in attempting to swim across to the city, others sought concealment on a rock in the stream, and were afterwards picked up by the boats of the "Queen," and nearly 500 surrendered as prisoners.

11. I feel a difficulty in naming any individual where all so well merit my warmest meed of praise, but I cannot avoid bringing to your lordship's special notice, as having fallen under my own personal observation, the conduct of Captain Reignolds, of the 49th, and Lieutenant and Adjutant Browne, of the same corps, whose bold advance up the first hill—the one with his company, the other with a covering party of his regiment—was most conspicuous. Lieutenant-Colonel Morris reports most favourably of the spirited manner in which Captain Tabor, with his light company, covered his right flank.

12. The operations on the right bank having thus terminated I had a full view of the effect of the fire from the ships of war and steamers on the Joss-house Hill, and of the landing of the right column. This column, which consisted of the Seamen battalion, Royal Marines, a detachment of Royal Artillery, and fifty Sappers, in all about 700 men, with two five and a half inch mortars, I had entrusted to Captain Herbert, of H.M.S. "Blenheim," whom Sir William Parker placed at my disposal, sending with him Captain Cotton, of the Madras Engineers. Captain Herbert was instructed to land at the extremity of the spur, under the Joss-house, and to storm and take it by the sea-front whenever the fire from the ships should make it practicable; and it was left to his discretion to push on and take the city, if the effect of a

plunging fire from the hill, aided by a powerful cannonade from the ships of war, should justify the advance

13. I had it only in my power, as the flying enemy had carried off every boat from the right bank of the river, to aid the operations on the left bank, by turning such of the captured guns as our artillery could at the moment bring to bear upon the city, and by a well-directed fire of rockets; but it appeared to me evident that more aid was necessary, as the admirable fire of the ships of war and steamers occasioned fearful devastation on the Joss-house Hill. The right column landed a little after eleven o'clock, and the seamen, with characteristic spirit, dashed up the face of the nearly precipitous rock, supported by the steady advance of the Royal Marines. A magazine in the new battery, before the outer gate, exploded. The way was thus cleared, and the column entered, the garrison escaping into the town, and the union-jack was displayed on the Joss-house walls. Captain Herbert, with his usual sound judgment, instantly determined upon taking advantage of the general panic, quickly followed up the retreating enemy, and cleared the city rampart in his front by a sharp fire of musketry. At this moment a tremendous explosion took place in a battery below the hill, by which the Chinese suffered severely, and a drummer of the Marines received so severe a wound that he soon after died. The column escaladed at the south-eastern angle, where the city wall is about twenty feet high, the enemy flying before it, as it rapidly pushed along the ramparts, and escaping through the western gates. I cannot omit to mention here that Sir William Parker accompanied this column, and, with the true spirit of a British sailor, was among the first to scale the walls. Thus the fortified city of Chinhae, with the several shore batteries, as well as the enemy's works and fortified encampments on the right bank of the river, all of which he had been for the last year busily employed in strengthening at an immense expense, fell into our possession. Of the principal mandarins, some are reported to have been killed, others to have destroyed themselves, and the Chinese army dispersed, the fugitive soldiers throwing away their arms and military clothing.

14. Captain Herbert speaks in high terms of the zealous and spirited conduct of every individual under his command, and particularly calls my attention to the able assistance he received from Captain Bourchier, of the "Blonde," commanding the battalion of Seamen; Major Ellis, commanding Royal Marines; and Captain Whitcomb, of that corps, an old and zealous officer; and Captain Cotton, of the Madras Engineers. I beg, therefore, to bring these officers to your lordship's favourable notice.

15. The obstructions at the river's mouth having been removed, by the boats from the ships of war and the steamers, the latter came in, and I passed over in the afternoon, leaving a sufficient force on the right bank to collect

the arms, protect the brass, and destroy the iron guns.

16. I have not been able to ascertain the actual strength of the Chinese army, but from the heavy masses collected at different points upon the right bank, from the numbers I saw upon the walls of Chinhae, as well as from the multiplicity of arms found over the whole face of the hills, and on the ramparts and in the streets of the city, I am led to conclude that my information before stated, as to the force on the left bank, was correct, and that from 8000 to 9000 men occupied the works and position on the right, where the bodies of several mandarins were found amongst the killed, while others, supposed to be mandarins, were seen to drown themselves when their retreat was intercepted.

17. We found Chinhae to be, I may almost say, one great arsenal, with a cannon foundry and gun-carriage manufactory, in active operation on improved works, together with warlike stores of various descriptions. In a battery upon the river, one of the carronades of the "Kite" was found, with an excellent imitation alongside it, and many of the new Chinese brass guns are very efficient.

18. It having been determined to push on with the least possible delay to Ning-po, Sir William Parker proceeded on the 12th, in the "Nemesis" steamer, to ascertain the practicability of the river, and actually reached, without the slightest attempt at opposition, the bridge of boats, which connects this city with the opposite suburb. Upon his return in the evening, arrangements were made for the attack on the following morning, lest the enemy, by his apparent submission, should intend to entrap us. Having left the 55th, with the exception of the Light Company, 100 of the Royal Marines, with detachments of Artillery and Sappers, in Chinhae, the rest of the force, about 750 bayonets, exclusive of the Artillery and Sappers, in steamers, by eight a.m., on the 13th, and we reached Ningpo at three o'clock. No enemy appeared, and it was evident that no ambuscade was intended, as the inhabitants densely thronged the bridge of boats, and collected in clusters along both banks. The troops landed on and near the bridge, and advanced to the city gate, which we found barricaded, but the walls were soon escaladed, and the Chinese assisted in removing the obstructions and opening the gate. This little force of soldiers, seamen, and marines drew up on the ramparts, the band of the 18th playing "God save the Queen." The second city of the province of Che-keang, the walls of which are nearly five miles in circumference, with a population of 300,000 souls, has thus fallen into our hands. The people all appear desirous to throw themselves under British protection, saying publicly that their mandarins have deserted them, and their own soldiers are unable to protect them. I have assembled some of the most respectable and influential of the mercantile class that have remained, and have assured them of my

anxiety to afford them all protection, consistent with our instructions to press the Chinese government. Proclamations have been issued, calling upon the people to open their shops, which I have engaged shall not be molested. This they have done to some extent, and confidence appears to be increasing. It affords me very great gratification to be enabled to report to your lordship that the orderly conduct of the troops calls for my warmest commendations, evincing the constant attention of the officers, and the true British feeling which exists in this little force.

19. I have placed the troops in two large public buildings; as comfortable quarters as I could find, consistent with security. The duties to guard against any sudden attack, and to protect the Chinese against, gangs of robbers of their own countrymen, are necessarily very severe. Cholera has appeared, I regret to say, both in Chinhae and in this city; in the former, six of the Marines have died—here, all the cases have recovered, and I trust that, by the unremitting attention and judicious arrangements of Dr. French, the superintending surgeon, the progress of the disease has been arrested.

20. I have spoken of the forbearance of the troops towards the inhabitants under temptations of no ordinary nature, and it is with equal pride that I feel myself called upon to bring to your lordship's notice their excellent conduct in the field throughout the operations I have detailed. Every officer and soldier has merited my approbation. I will, therefore, only further beg leave to name the commanding officers of columns and corps:—Captain Herbert, R.N., commanding right column; Lieutenant-Colonel Craigie, 55th, commanding left column: Lieutenant-Colonel Morris, 49th, commanding centre column; Captain Bourchier, H.N., commanding Seamen battalion; Lieutenant-Colonel Adams, commanding 18th Royal Irish; Major Blyth, commanding 49th regiment; Major Faucet, commanding 55th; Major Ellis, commanding Royal Marines; Captain Simpson, commanding Rifles, 36th M.N.I.; Captain Knowles, commanding Royal Artillery, (senior officer, of that arm); and Captain Anstruther, commanding Madras Artillery. From Captain Pears, the commanding engineer, I have received every assistance.

Lieutenant-Colonel Mountain, Deputy Adjutant-General, and Captain Gough, Acting Deputy-Quarter-Master-General, have continued their able and active services with unabated zeal.

This despatch, together with plans of Amoy, Chusan, and Chinhae, will be delivered by Lieutenant Gabbith, of the Madras Artillery, my aide-de-camp, whom I beg to recommend to your lordship, and who will be able to afford any further information you may require.

I have the honour to be, my lord, your lordship's most obedient humble servant,

H. Gough, Lieutenant-General, Commanding Expeditionary Land Force.

*

GENERAL ORDERS.

Head Quarters, H.M. Ship "Wellesley," 9th October, 1841.

The following is the proposed Order for landing for the attack of the Citadel and fortified heights of Chinhae:—

The Troops, with the Seamen Battalion and Royal Marines, to land in three Columns.

Left column, under Lieutenant Colonel Craigie, with which Major-General Sir Hugh Gough will land.

	Officers.	Other Ranks.
Madras Artillery and Gun Lascars	7	114
Royal Artillery	0	4
Sappers	4	100
55th Regiment	18	417
18th Regiment	12	280
Rifles	4	110
Total	**45**	**1025**

Ordnance.

- 4 x 4-2/5 Mountain Howitzers, 2 x 5-1/2-inch Mortars
- Doolie Bearers and Natives to carry shot: 112

Centre Column, under Lieutenant-Colonel Morris.

	Officers.	Other Ranks.
Royal Artillery	0	4
Madras Ditto	1	50
Madras Sappers	1	40
H.M. 49th Regiment	23	346
Total	**25**	**440**

Ordnance.

- 2 x 12-pounder Howitzers, 2 x 9-pounder Field-Guns
- Doolie Bearers, and Natives to carry shot:40

Right Column, under Captain Herbert, Royal Navy.

	Officers.	Other Ranks.
Royal Artillery	1	23
Seamen Battalion	15	255
Royal Marines	8	230
Madras Sappers	1	30
Total	**25**	**538**

Ordnance.

- 2 x 5-1/2 inch Mortars
- Doolie Bearers, and Natives to carry shot: 30

By Order. (Signed) *A. S. H. Mountain, Lieut. Col.*

Deputy Adjutant-General Expeditionary Force.
(True Copy.) *Armine S. H. Mountain, Lieut. Col.*
Deputy Adjutant-General Expeditionary Force.

*

Return of Killed and Wounded of the Force under the command of Lieutenant General Sir Hugh Gough,K.C.B., at the storming of the fortified Heights and Citadel of Chinhae, on the 10th October, 1841.

Head Quarters, Ningpo, 16th October 1841.

- Royal Artillery—One private severely wounded.
- 18th Royal Irish Regiment—One rank and file killed, two rank and file severely, and one slightly wounded.
- 49th Regiment—One rank and file dangerously, one officer, one sergeant, three rank and file severely, and four rank and file slightly wounded.
- Royal Marines—One drummer killed.
- 55th Regiment—One camp follower severely wounded.
- Rifle Company 36th M.N.I.—One private killed.

Recapitulation.

Three rank and file killed; two rank and file dangerously wounded; one officer, one sergeant, and six rank and file, severely wounded; five slightly wounded. One camp follower severely wounded.—Total, 3 killed; 16 wounded.

Name of Officer Wounded: Lieutenant J. M. Montgomery, 49th Regiment.

Armine S. H. Mountain, Lieut. Col., Deputy Adjutant-General Expeditionary Force.

*

Return of Ordnance and Military Stores found in Ningpo, when occupied by the Force under the command of his Excellency Lieutenant-General Sir Hugh Gough, K.C.B., Commander-in-Chief, on the 13th October, 1841.

Guns, Iron.

Mounted on the Walls of the City:

- 1 x 9 pounders, 15 x 6 pounders, 2 x 3 pounders

In the Magazines (not mounted):

- 1 x 9 pounders, 4 x 6 pounders, 2 x 3 pounders
  Total: 2 x 9 pounders, 19 x 6 pounders, 4 x 3 pounders
  Grand Total: 25 Guns.
- Gunpowder Tubs: 1017—about 100,000 lbs.
- Sulphur Tubs: 7
- Saltpetre Tubs and Jars: 9
- Bamboo Canister, filled with leaden balls, No. 1080.
- Rockets, Bamboo: Considerable quantities

- Rockets, Arrow Cases: Considerable quantities
- Gun-carriages with wheels: No. 12
- Shot: about 50 Tons
- Shells, Chinese: 9 Boxes
- Leaden Balls, 405 boxes, and a number of packages; the average weight of the boxes about 150 lbs.

A large collection of ginjals, matchlocks, swords, and spears, were found in the different magazines, which, with the gunpowder and gun-carriages, have all been destroyed.

J. Knowles, Captain, Commanding Royal Artillery.

*

Return of Ordnance found on the Batteries on the banks of the Ningpo River, 10th October, 1841.

On the Right Bank	Brass						Iron						
	9 Pounders	12 Pounders	16 Pounders	18 Pounders	24 Pounders	30 Pounders	6 Pounders	7 Pounders	8 Pounders	9 Pounders	12 Pounders	18 Pounders Carronades	30 Pounders Guns
1. (Ay. Battery) facing Battery on the left Bank	4	1		1			6						
2. Sapper's Battery			1	2		2					2		
3. Lower Battery, facing the North, and commanding entrance to the River		2			4								2
4. Upper Battery firing over No. 3					2								2
5. In the gorge of the Hill to the right							1						
6. Firing down a Pass, facing N.E.		1					2						
7. Gorge of Hill, between two Camps, facing E. by S.		1						1					
8. Encampment on Hill, facing S.S.E.		7					1	1	1	5			
Total	**4**	**12**	**1**	**3**	**6**	**2**	**10**	**2**	**1**	**5**	**2**	**2**	**4**

On the Left Bank	Brass					Iron						
	9 Pounders	12 Pounders	12 Pounder Carronades	18 Prs. Guns	24 Prs. Guns	4 Pounders	9 Pounders	12 Pounders	12 Pounder Carronades	24 Prs. Guns	24 Pounder Carronades	68 Prs. Guns
1. N.E. Battery, left bank of River		1	4	1	12			3	1			
2. Flank Battery, facing entrance to River		4	3	3	1	3		4	1		2	
3. Between Joss-house Hill and City Wall							5					
4. Upper Battery of Joss-house Hill	2					6						
5. Second Battery of Joss-house Hill						3	1				1	
6. Third Battery of Joss-house Hill								7				1
7. City Walls, Sea Face		3			3	6	15			1		
8. In Foundry, fit for service		2								3	3	
Total	**2**	**10**	**7**	**4**	**16**	**18**	**21**	**14**	**2**	**4**	**4**	**1**

Grand Total: Brass Ordnance 67, Iron 90

N.B.—All the defences on the left bank of the river, as well as the entrenched heights on the right bank were covered with ginjalls, matchlocks, spears, &c.

The Ordnance, both brass and iron, are nearly all of a very superior description, and although having great thickness of metal, yet the arrangements in the foundry and gun-carriage manufactory shew great improvements to be in progress, our carriages and guns being taken as models.

J. Knowles, Captain, Commanding Royal Artillery.

Lieutenant-General Sir Hugh Gough, K.C.B., Commander-in-Chief, &c. &c. &c.

*

To the Right Hon. the Earl of Auckland, G.C.B., Governor-General, &c. &c. &c.

"Wellesley," at the Anchorage of Just-in the-way, Sept. 25, 1841.

My Lord,—I have the honour to transmit for your lordship's information, the copies of two letters from Mr. Hall, commanding the Honourable Company's steam-vessel, "Nemesis," reporting the destruction of a Chinese battery, on the island of Quemoy, on the 31st of August, and of three, together with three war junks, within the harbour of Shei-po, on the 17th instant; and I have much pleasure in adding my commendation of the spirit of enterprise and activity which is exhibited by Mr. Hall, his officers and crew, upon every opportunity.

I have the honour to be, my lord,

Your lordship's most obedient servant,

W. Parker, Rear Admiral.

*

To Rear-Admiral Sir Wm. Parker, K. C.B., &c. &c. &c.

H. C. S. "Nemesis," Amoy, 31st August, 1841.

Sir,—I have the honour to inform you, in compliance with your orders, conveyed to me through Captain Fletcher, that, after having towed the boats to the respective forts on the northern shore to be destroyed, I proceeded to reconnoitre the island of Quemoy. On my way across, I observed three forts on different islands to the south-westward of us, without any guns in them. After closing the island of Quemoy, at 10 a.m., saw a small round tower fort on the larboard bow, bearing S. E., which I steered for. As we approached, observing the Chinese soldiers deserting the fort, I sent away the first cutter and first gig, under the command of Mr. Freese, my chief officer, to destroy the fort. At 10-25, the boats returned, having destroyed three guns, one ginjall, and about thirty-five stand of matchlocks, thirty-five cutlasses, and a quantity of spears and gunpowder; at the same time, observed a sandbank fort, mounting thirteen guns, with a number of large junks, and an encampment, with banners displayed in every direction, at the entrance of a river, distant about two miles to the eastward and close to a tower, apparently of some note, from the appearance of the buildings and mandarin houses, &c.

Having fulfilled my orders, I rejoined Captain Fletcher, and embarked him and his party on board.

I have the honour, &c.

(Signed) *W. H. Hall, Commander.*

*

To Rear-Admiral Sir William Parker, K.C.D., &c. &c. &c.
H. C. Steamer "Nemesis," Buffalo's Nose, 19th Sept. 1841.

Sir,—I have the honour to inform you that the Honourable Company's steamer "Nemesis," under my command, was obliged to part company with the fleet, (being light, and consequently very leewardly,) and tide it up in-shore in smooth water.

On the morning of the 17th instant, being off Shei-poo, the wind being strong against us, and the weather looking very threatening, and having only one day's fuel left, I deemed it necessary to proceed to the nearest port to procure wood. Having procured a fisherman to act as pilot, I entered the harbour of Shei-poo, and just inside passed an island on which were two forts, but which allowed us to pass without firing; I then had hopes of getting wood without being obliged to proceed to extremities; I hauled in to an anchor close off the town, (off which were anchored upwards of a hundred merchant junks;) as we neared the anchorage, a fort, situated at the southern end of the town, opened fire on us, which I immediately returned, my crew being at quarters. I then anchored by the stern in good position, within pistol-shot of the fort. We soon silenced them, and I then landed with my crew, the enemy retreating as we advanced. After setting fire to the barracks, and destroying four guns (two of them brass, nine feet six inches long, and four inches bore,) in the fort, I returned on board, immediately despatched boats, manned and armed, to search for wood, and succeeded in obtaining seven boat loads, (about twenty-five tons,) sufficient to fill the bunkers and holds. After completing our wood, I sent the boats to destroy three large war junks, which they accomplished by setting fire to them after having towed them to the opposite side of the harbour, clear of the town and merchant junks; one of these junks mounted fourteen guns, which, as well as a quantity of matchlocks, cutlasses, and gunpowder, we effectually destroyed. A large body of troops having collected to the southward of the town, I weighed and steamed close in and dispersed them with grape and canister. I then proceeded to the upper end of the harbour, firing at the two forts on the island in passing, and came to an anchor to allow the men to get their dinner. After which I weighed and proceeded to attack the two forts on the island; when within good range, opened fire with round shot and rockets. The enemy not returning the fire, I anchored, and landed with three boats manned and armed; on entering the forts, found the enemy had deserted them. Having destroyed in one fort five guns, and the other four guns, I burnt the carriages and tents of the encampment, and returned on board, weighed, and proceeded out of the harbour.

During the whole time we were engaged, thousands of the in habitants, and nearly all the crews of the merchant junks, were unconcerned spectators of the scene, quietly looking on, and ap peared perfectly to understand that we were at war only with the government. Even a fleet of merchant junks thus arrived during the day, passing close to us in beating up the harbour. I cannot speak too highly of Mr. Auchmuty Fylden Freese (Mate R. N.), my first officer, and the rest of my officers and crew. I am happy to say this was achieved without any casualty on our side, although the loss on the side of the enemy must have been very great.

I have the honour to be, &c. &c. &c.

(Signed) *Wm. H. Hall, Commander.*

*

To the Right Hon. the Earl of Auckland, G.C.B., Governor-General, &c. &c. &c.

"Wellesley," at the Anchorage of Just-in-the-Way, September 25th, 1841.

My Lord,—The accompanying copies of letters from Lieutenant M'Cleverty, R.N., commanding the Hon. Company's steam vessel, "Phlegethon," will detail to your lordship the treacherous conduct of some of the inhabitants of the town of Ko-kew-so, or Ko-gi-sau, in decoying part of the crew of the "Lyra," an English trading vessel, under the promise of selling them stock and vegetables into an ambuscade of Chinese troops; by which one of the seamen was killed, and Mr. Wainwright, the chief mate, after being desperately wounded, fell into their hands. Another seaman was also wounded, but escaped on board.

As this base proceeding occurred within a very short distance of the village where Mr. Stead, the late master of the "Pestonjee Bomanjee" transport, was murdered, in March last, Lieutenant M'Cleverty promptly determined on landing and attacking the mandarin military post, and, supported by the masters and crews of the merchant vessels, "Lyra" and "Anne;" after gallantly putting to flight a very superior force, he caused their barracks, as well as the small town adjoining the village, where Mr. Stead was assassinated, to be destroyed.

Intimation has been given of the motives which induced this measure of retribution, and I sincerely hope that it may have the effect of checking similar acts of atrocity on the part of the Chinese.

Lieutenant M'Cleverty, who is on all occasions most zealous and active, speaks highly of the conduct of Acting-Lieutenant Ryves, and all the party that accompanied him. The latter officer has served long, with an excellent character, as mate, in her Majesty's service; he is the orphan son of a most estimable naval officer, and, I understand, he was amongst the foremost of the party from the "Phlegethon," who entered the first battery, which was taken possession of, outside the barrier wall in the late attack on Amoy. I have the honour to be, my lord,

Your lordship's most obedient servant,

W. Parker, Rear Admiral.

*

To Rear Admiral Sir William Parker, K.C.B., &c. &c. &c. Commander-in-Chief.

H. C. Steam Vessel, "Phlegethon," Kie-tow Point, Sept. 17th, 1841.

Sir,—I beg leave to enclose, for your information, a letter received from Mr. Hubertson, Master of the brig "Lyra," on my arrival at this place, detailing an act of treachery by the Chinese, killing his first mate and one of his sea-cunnies.

On the receipt of this letter, consulting with the Masters of the "Lyra," "Anne," and "Ariel," who gallantly offered their services, I determined to attack the mandarin station, and proceeded for that purpose, at daylight on the 16th instant. When we arrived, I found that it was the village in which Mr. Stead, the Master of the transport "Pestonjee Bomanjee," had been murdered. I destroyed the village, and took three prisoners, from whom I learnt that the principal station of the soldiers was in the town where the "Lyra's" people had been murdered, that they mustered five hundred, and expected to be attacked.

At eleven, a.m., I proceeded to the town, having forty British and eighty Lascars. At twelve, they opened a heavy fire of ginjals and matchlocks, which, failing to do any execution, and finding we were rapidly closing on them, they retreated up the mountain. We found their barracks and magazines, blew them up, set fire to the whole town, and totally destroyed it.

Having now accomplished" the object of our expedition, we returned on board, and I am happy to say without any loss.

In performing this service, I beg leave to express my thanks to Messrs. Hubertson, Denham, and Woodman, Masters of the "Lyra," "Anne," and "Ariel," for their efficient support.

It would be invidious in me to praise anywhere—all behaved well; but I beg leave to recommend to your notice the First Lieutenant, Mr. Herbert Ryves, and Lieutenant R. B. Crawford, R. M., a passenger belonging to the transport service, who gallantly volunteered to lead, and was of the greatest possible assistance to me.

I have the honour to be, &c.

(Signed) *James J. M'Cleverty, Lieutenant commanding.*

P.S. The Chinese sustained a loss of six men killed; but it was impossible to ascertain their wounded, as they carried them with them.

*

To Captain M'Cleverly, R.M., Steamer "Phlegethon."
Brig "Lyra," off Singlosau, September 15, 1841.

Sir,—I have the painful duty to report to you, as the only officer present, belonging to Her Majesty's fleet, a case of the most unparalleled treachery and murder, on part of the Chinese, at the village of Kogisau, abreast of where we are lying, and beg you will report the same to his Excellency the Commander in Chief.

I arrived here, in company with the "Ariel" and "Anne," on the 10th instant, and anchored off Kogisau. The following day we all armed our boats, and went on shore to look for fresh water, and endeavour to procure some stock. The natives at first appeared frightened, but shortly came down to us, and entered on the most friendly terms, promising to supply us with fresh stock on fair terms; and on Sunday morning, the 12th, I went on shore with my launch and cutter, and the same friendly communications subsisted, and the principal man of the place gave my linguist a written paper, stating the time he would have what things they could supply us with, ready; in consequence of which, I again sent my launch at noon, in charge of my chief officer, Mr. Wain-wright, and who, on proceeding to the village, and finding no person, was returning to the boat, when his party was surrounded by 200 or 300 soldiers, and fired at with ginjals and matchlocks, and I regret to say, Mr. Wainwright was twice wounded, and either killed or taken prisoner, and one of my sea-cunnies was shot through the head, and killed on the spot, and one man wounded in his side, but escaped on board; on hearing which, I immediately consulted with the Masters of the "Ariel" and "Anne ;" the result was, that we immediately seized several boats, and by their crews sent chops on shore, offering sp. drs. 1000, for the bodies dead or alive, if not mutilated; but to which I have received no answer.

I now beg you will be kind enough to use such measures as you may deem most necessary to procure the release of my officer, if alive.

I have the honour to be, &c.

(Signed) *George J. Hubertson, Master of the "Lyra."*

www.ingramcontent.com/pod-product-compliance
Lightning Source LLC
LaVergne TN
LVHW091129080826
845145LV00008B/2094

* 9 7 8 1 7 8 1 5 8 3 6 0 9 *